CONTEMPORARY CRIMINOLOGY IN PRACTICE IN SOUTH AFRICA

CONTEMPORARY CRIMINOLOGY IN PRACTICE

IN SOUTH AFRICA

EDITOR **FRIEDO J.W. HERBIG**

Henri Fouche | Benjamin Häefele | Anni Hesselink

Anthony Minnaar | Marelize Schoeman

OXFORD
UNIVERSITY PRESS
SOUTHERN AFRICA

OXFORD
UNIVERSITY PRESS

Oxford University Press is a department of the University of Oxford. It furthers the University's objective of excellence in research, scholarship, and education by publishing worldwide. Oxford is a registered trade mark of Oxford University Press in the UK and in certain other countries.

Published in South Africa by
Oxford University Press Southern Africa (Pty) Limited

Vasco Boulevard, Goodwood, N1 City, Cape Town, South Africa, 7460
P O Box 12119, N1 City, Cape Town, South Africa, 7463

First published 2014

Contemporary Criminology in Practice in South Africa

ISBN 978 0 1990 7873 8

Typeset in Utopia std 9.5 pt on 12 pt
Printed on 70 gsm woodfree paper

Acknowledgements
Publishing manager: Alida Terblanche
Publisher: Penny Lane/Lydia Reid
Project manager: Marguerite Lithgow/Tanya Paulse
Editor: Patricia Myers Smith
Indexer: Tanya Paulse
Permissions investigator: Patricia Rademeyer
Typesetter: The Purple Turtle Publishing CC
Designer: Shaun Andrews
Cover designer: Gisela Strydom
Cover image: Studio
Printed and bound by ABC Press, Cape Town
122353

The authors and publisher gratefully acknowledge permission to reproduce copyright material in this book. Every effort has been made to trace copyright holders, but if any copyright infringements have been made, the publisher would be grateful for information that would enable any omissions or errors to be corrected in subsequent impressions.

Contents

About the authors

Content editor

Friedo J. W. Herbig (National Diploma: Nature Conservation; BA (Police Science) (Unisa); BA Honours (Criminology) (Unisa); MA (Criminology) (Unisa); DLitt et Phil (Criminology) (Unisa)) is a full professor and Chair of the Department of Criminology & Security Science at the University of South Africa (Unisa). He is actively engaged in research relating to conservation crime, forensic psychophysiology and incarcerated offender dynamics. Professor Herbig has published several articles relating to the synthesis of conservation crime with criminology and is endeavouring to promote the phronesis of the conservation crime dialectic. He is also is the author of various book chapters and articles dealing with this and allied phenomena.

Authors

Henri Fouche is an Associate Professor at the Department of Criminology and Security Science at the University of South Africa (Unisa) (August 2011 to date). Henri lectures on contemporary crime issues to post graduate students, and is also the coordinator of the Masters and Doctorate program of the Department. His specialities are the policing of maritime piracy, and law enforcement in the maritime domain; and also experience in law enforcement in government and private sectors; as well as in police training. Henri was previously an independent contractor for both Unisa and TUT, where he handled the supervision of masters and doctorate students, as well as lecturing crime investigation and forensic investigation to students. Prior to that Henri was a senior lecturer at Tshwane University of Technology, where he handled the supervising of masters students in Policing; as well as conducting workshops and reading papers on law enforcement aspects relating to maritime crime and terrorism at national and regional conferences. Henri has authored and co-authored many titles on maritime crime, maritime piracy and other related topics.

Benjamin White Häefele (D Litt et Phil) (UFH) is a senior lecturer in the Department of Criminology and Security Science, College of Law at the University of South Africa (Unisa) and the Manager at the Centre for Criminological Science at the College of Law. Dr Häefele has published various articles in local and international journals in the field of criminology. He was formerly a senior researcher at the Centre for Military Science, Military Academy in Saldanha, South Africa, and a researcher in the Safety and Security Committee at Parliament.

Anni Hesselink holds a D Litt et Phil in Criminology. She is a NRF C3 rated researcher. Anni has to date contributed 9 chapters to books on crime, criminological assessment and offending behaviour and she has published same on national and international forums. She is a full Professor at the Department of Criminology and Security Science at the University of South Africa.

Anthony Minnaar (D Litt et Phil (History) (Unisa)) was appointed a full professor in July 2003, and has since January 2009 been the Programme Head: Security Management for the merged Department of Criminology & Security Science in the School of Criminal Justice of the College of Law at the University of South Africa (Unisa). In January 2013 he was appointed as a research professor at Unisa. In 1990 he received the Human Sciences Research Council (HSRC) President's Medal for Creative Research for the project Historical Perspectives on the Present-Day Violence in African Areas of Natal/Kwazulu with Specific Reference to So-Called Faction Fights, and in 1994 the HSRC Council Award for multi-disciplinary research. He was project team leader for the project The Dynamics of Hostels in South Africa with Specific Reference to the Present-Day Violence. In 1995 he received the HSRC Council Award for Multidisciplinary Research for the sub-project contribution The Political Mobilisation Of Youth in South Africa since 1970 to the National Co-operative Project on Youth in South Africa. From 2003 to 2012 he was a National Research Foundation (NRF) Rated Researcher (C3), and in 2013 was re-rated as a National Research Foundation (NRF) Researcher (C1). In 2006 he received the University of South Africa (UNISA) Chancellor's Prize for Research: School of Criminal of Justice. From 2005 to 2010 he served as president of the Criminological & Victimological Society of Southern Africa (CRIMSA) and was an honorary member of CRIMSA (2010). In 2011 he became editor-in-chief of *Acta Criminologica: Southern African Journal of Criminology*. He has published widely and presented at numerous international conferences on a wide variety of topics and issues in criminal justice. His current research interests are private security industry issues (specifically crime prevention and private policing, community policing, and community safety initiatives); regulation and monitoring of the private security industry in South Africa; security at ports of entry; information security and cybercrime; and the use of CCTV surveillance systems for security and neighbourhood safety/crime prevention.

Marelize Schoeman qualified as social worker (1993) at the University of Pretoria, South Africa. She was employed for 10 years as a social worker at the Department of Correctional Services. During this period she specialised in Criminal Justice Social Work and obtained a Masters degree in 1998 and her DPhil degree in 2004. She conducted research part-time until 2005 when she started a research and training consultancy. Since then she has been involved in various research projects for, amongst others, the Department of Correctional Services, CSIR Crime Prevention Centre, Khulisa Social Solutions, Restorative Justice Centre and NICRO. She is currently an Associate Professor in the Department of Criminology and Security Science at the University of South Africa. Marelize has been a speaker at national and international conferences and published widely in scientific journals and subject specialist books.

Acknowledgements

Chapter 1

pp. 4–5 Herbig & Hesselink quotation followed by footnote 1: Herbig, F. J. W., & Hesselink, A. E. (2009). The role and function of criminologists in the criminal justice and private sector. *Journal of Psychology in Africa, 19*(3), 441–448. Reprinted by permission of Taylor & Francis Copyright © Routledge. http://www.informaworld.com; **p. 5** Hesselink & Herbig quotation followed by footnote 2: Hesselink, A. E., & Herbig, F. J. W. (2009). The scientific basis of criminology. *Journal of Psychology in Africa, 19*(2), 275–279. Reprinted by permission of Taylor & Francis Copyright © Routledge. http://www.informaworld.com

Chapter 2

p. 7 Bruce quotation followed by footnote 1: Bruce, D. (2010b). Anger, hatred, or just heartlessness? Defining gratuitous violence. *SA Crime Quarterly, 34,* 13–20. Reprinted by permission of the Editor: *South African Crime Quarterly*; **p. 7** Silber & Geffen quotation followed by footnote 2: Silber, G., & Geffen, N. (2009). Race, class and violent crime in South Africa. *SA Crime Quarterly, 30,* 35–42. Reprinted by permission of the Editor: *South African Crime Quarterly*; **p. 9** Bruce quotation followed by footnote 3: Bruce, D. (2006). Racism, self-esteem and violence in SA: gaps in the NCPS' explanation? *SA Crime Quarterly,* 17, 31–37. Reprinted by permission of the Editor: *South African Crime Quarterly*; **p. 9** Bruce quotation followed by footnote 4: Bruce, D. (2010b). Anger, hatred, or just heartlessness? Defining gratuitous violence. *SA Crime Quarterly, 34,* 13–20. Reprinted by permission of the Editor: *South African Crime Quarterly*; **p. 16** Holtmann quotation followed by footnote 5: Holtmann, B. (2008). Why law enforcement is not enough: lessons from the Central Karoo on breaking the cycle of crime and violence. *SA Crime Quarterly, 13,* 13–20. Reprinted by permission of the Editor: *South African Crime Quarterly*;

Chapter 3

p. 34 IMO quotation followed by footnote 2: Resolution A.1025(26) Adopted on 2 December 2009 CODE OF PRACTICE FOR THE INVESTIGATION OF CRIMES OF PIRACY AND ARMED ROBBERY AGAINST SHIPS, http://www.imo.org/OurWork/Security/PiracyArmedRobbery/Guidance/Documents/A.1025.pdf; **p. 49** IMO quotation followed by footnote 4: International Maritime Organisation (IMO). (2005). Consolidated text of the *Convention for the Suppression of Unlawful Acts against the Safety of Maritime Navigation and of the Protocol of 2005 to the Convention.* ARTICLE 3.

Chapter 4

pp. 59–60 Lynch & Stretsky quotation followed by footnote 1: Lynch, M. J., & Stretsky, P. B. (2003). The meaning of green: contrasting criminological perspectives. *Theoretical Criminology*, *7*(2), 217–238. Copyright © 2003 by SAGE. Reprinted by permission of SAGE; **p. 60** Gibbs, Gore McGarrell, and Rivers III quotation followed by footnote 2: Gibbs, C., Gore, M. L., McGarrell, E. F., & Rivers III, L. (2009). Introducing conservation criminology. *British Journal of Criminology*, *1*, 1–21. Copyright © 2009 Centre for Crime & Justice Studies. Reprinted by permission of Oxford University Press; **pp. 62–63** South quotation followed by footnote 3: South, N. (1998). A green field for criminology? A proposal for a perspective. *Theoretical Criminology*, *2*(2), 211–233. Copyright © 1998, SAGE Publications. Reprinted by permission of SAGE; **p. 76** Eliason quotation followed by footnote 4: Eliason, S. L. (2003). Illegal hunting and angling: the neutralization of wildlife law violations. *Society & Animals*, *11*(3), 225–243. Copyright © 2003, Brill. Reprinted by permission of Brill; **p. 77** Milner-Gulland & Williams quotation followed by footnote 5: Milner-Gulland, E. J., & Williams, N. L. (1992). A model of incentives for the illegal exploitation of black rhinos and elephants: poaching pays in Luangwa Valley, Zambia. *Journal of Applied Ecology*, *29*(2), 388–401. Copyright © BRITISH ECOLOGICAL SOCIETY. Reproduced with permission of BLACKWELL PUBLISHING LTD.

Chapter 5

p. 88 Hübschle quotation followed by footnote 1: Hübschle, A. (2011). *Organised crime in Southern Africa: first annual review*. Pretoria: Institute for Security Studies. Reprinted by permission of the ISS; **p. 91** Jasper quotation followed by footnote 2: Jasper, K. (2011). *Sociological theory of drug abuse*. Retrieved June 8, 2011, from http://www.ehow.com/about_5393359_sociological-theory-drug-abuse.html.; **p. 91** Leggett quotation followed by footnote 3: Leggett, T. (2004). Still marginal: crime in the coloured community. *SA Crime Quarterly*, *7*, 21–26. Reprinted by permission of the Editor, *SA Crime Quarterly*; **p. 93** Hübschle quotation followed by footnote 4: Hübschle, A. (2011). *Organised crime in Southern Africa: first annual review*. Pretoria: Institute for Security Studies. Reprinted by permission of the ISS; **p. 93** Kapp quotation followed by footnote 5: Reprinted from *The Lancet*, Vol. 371(9608) Kapp, C. Crystal meth boom adds to South African health challenges. *The Lancet*, 371(9608), 193-194. Copyright C 2008, with permission from Elsevier. Retrieved April 11, 2011, from http://www.thelancet.com/journals/lancet/article/PIIS0140-6736%2808%2960120-8/fulltext; **p. 94** Michael quotation followed by footnote 6: Michael, J. (2006). Growing up with meth. *Children's voice: Child Welfare League of America*, *15*(1), 22–28. Retrieved March 4, 2012, from http://www.cwla.org/voice/0602meth.htm © Child Welfare League of America Inc.; **p. 94** Kapp quotation followed by footnote 5: Reprinted from *The Lancet*, Vol. 371(9608) Kapp, C. Crystal meth boom adds to South African health challenges. *The Lancet*, 371(9608), 193-194. Copyright C 2008, with permission from Elsevier. Retrieved April 11, 2011, from http://www.thelancet.com/journals/lancet/article/PIIS0140-6736%2808%2960120-8/fulltext; **p. 96** Hübschle quotation followed by footnote 8: Hübschle, A. (2011). *Organised crime in Southern Africa: first annual review*. Pretoria: Institute for Security Studies. Reprinted by permission of the ISS.

Chapter 6

p. 133 Choo quotations followed by footnotes 6, 7, 8: Choo, K-K. R. (2007). Zombies and botnets. *Trends & issues in crime and criminal justice.* No. 333, March. Canberra: Australian Institute for Criminology (AIC) © Copyright AIC. Reprinted by permission of AIC.

Chapter 7

p. 156 Gavrielides quotation followed by footnote 1: Gavrielides, T. (2005) Some meta-theoretical questions for restorative justice. *Ratio Juris, 18*(1), 84–106. Copyright © 2005 John Wiley and Sons; **p. 156** Gavrielides quotation followed by footnote 2: Gavrielides, T. (2005) Some meta-theoretical questions for restorative justice. *Ratio Juris, 18*(1), 84–106. Copyright © 2005 John Wiley and Sons; **p. 167** Table 7.1 heading followed by footnote 3: McCold, P., & Wachtel, T. (2003, August). *In Pursuit of paradigm: a theory of restorative justice.* Paper presented at the 13th World Congress of Criminology, Rio de Janeiro, Brazil.

Chapter 8

p. 188 Brezina & Topalli quotation followed by footnote 1: Brezina, T., & Topalli, V. (2012). Criminal self-efficacy: exploring the correlates and consequences of a 'successful criminal' identity. *Criminal Justice and Behavior, 39*(8), 1042–1062, copyright © 2012 SAGE Publications. Reprinted by permission of SAGE Publications; **p. 189** Table heading followed by footnote 2: Van der Laan, A. M., Blom, M., & Kleemans, E. R. (2009). Exploring long-term and short-term risk factors for serious delinquency. *European Journal of Criminology, 6*(5),428-435, copyright © 2009 by SAGE Publications. Reprinted by permission of SAGE; **p. 201** "Ex-wife of 'Modimolle Monster' tells of torture" quotation followed by footnote 3: Ex-wife of 'Modimolle Monster' tells of torture. (SAPA 2012, November 20). SowetanLIVE. Retrieved July 27, 2013, from http://www.sowetanlive.co.za/news/2012/11/20/ex-wife-of-modimolle-monster-tells-of-torture, but originally from SAPA. Reprinted by permission of SAPA; **p. 202** Labuschagne quotation followed by footnote 4: Labuschagne, I.(2009). The nature of the beast: a critical discussion of profiling. *SA Crime Quarterly*, 27, 31–34. Reprinted by permission of the Editor: *South African Crime Quarterly*; **p. 202** Devery quotation followed by footnote 5: Devery, C. (2010) . Criminal profiling and criminal investigation. *Journal of Contemporary Criminal Justice*, 26(4), 393–409, copyright © 2010 by SAGE Publications. Reprinted by Permission of SAGE Publications.

Chapter 1

Orientation

FJW Herbig

1.1 Introduction

This book, unlike its antecedents, focuses on the utilitarian and egalitarian nature of the criminological discipline and its philosophy, so as to provide a conceptual framework for understanding the dimensions of and approaches to applied criminology. Furthermore, the book percolates and explores the boundaries of criminology and its adjuncts, and probes practitioner significance and didactics in order to introduce students and functionaries equally to criminological constructs and criminology (criminological theory) in practice in a South African context. In addition, the book introduces the reader to some topical criminological issues that have emerged somewhat peripherally to mainstream awareness, but are steadily evolving in South African society. Although it is not possible to address all surfacing crime types or phenomena, the crimes considered in this book are deemed representative of those whose profiles are worthy of further investigation.

In essence, this work provides a phenomenological snapshot (a detailed description of conscious experience) of criminological functionality, moving away somewhat from the metaphysical and spiritual dimension in which criminology is frequently cosseted – avoiding the all too common diachronic narrative and homilies rooted in the criminological diaspora. An attempt will be made to answer an ever-elusive question: how does criminology work in practice? This question underpins the very essence of discipline relevance, erudition and authenticity, and is a testament to criminology's diversity. It should be noted, however, that the customary means of addressing crime have not entirely vanished with the modernist transfer to application, though they may these days be afforded a different standing in the hierarchy of credibility. The verve of moral, religious and commonsensical ways of explaining, and indeed addressing, crime is cogently acknowledged.

This volume will unpack and evaluate the harmonisation of applied criminology for crime causation and modulation, and will provide case studies that distil certain high-profile nascent types of crime in Africa. The primary purpose of the book, therefore, is to act as a feedstock for criminological scholars (students and practitioners alike) who can contribute to the development of knowledge at a transitional and advanced level by applying their assimilated knowledge to addressing some of society's more residual crime risks. The book is by no means presented as a panacea to the crime challenges in South Africa, but it should broadcast some valuable empirical food for thought regarding the itinerary of practice-oriented criminology.

A further purpose of this book is for students and practitioners alike to secure the competencies needed to:

- deal with complex issues both systematically and creatively and transition into practice
- make sound judgements using data and information at their disposal
- communicate their conclusions clearly to specialist and non-specialist audiences
- demonstrate self-direction and inventiveness in confronting and solving problems

- act autonomously in planning and implementing tasks at a professional or equivalent level
- continue to advance their knowledge, understanding and skills in the field of criminology.

Pure or basic research spawns knowledge for the sake of knowledge (Kraska & Lawrence Neuman, 2012) – generating knowledge is regarded as an end in itself and has no utility beyond making us more knowledgeable; to wit, knowledge is not pursued for any instrumental purpose. Although criminal studies is essentially an applied discipline, rudimentary research still plays a critical role. Foundational knowledge refuting or supporting theories that explain crime ponders major historical and contemporary shifts in our reaction to crime and examines how both fit into our social structure and culture. Applied research (as distinguished from pure or basic research), is essentially a genre of research in which a study is conducted to address a specific concern or to offer solutions to a problem (Kraska & Lawrence Neuman, 2012); it is central to studies of crime and justice. Our collective mission, as part of the knowledge-generation process, includes the mitigation of crime and its related harms, the endorsement of justice, and the augmentation of government responsiveness. Applied criminology is the sphere of criminology in which studies are directed at addressing or interrogating a specific concern or at offering solutions to a problem. These advances are made not only by answering questions, but also by questioning answers – only when we do this can we make discoveries.

Over the past decade, criminology in South Africa has evolved from a conformist discipline to a contemporary practical field, in which criminologists as intellectuals have contributed significantly. Fundamental contributions made by South African criminologists within the criminological field will be underscored in each of the crime phenomena addressed in this book. In each case, research contributions and outputs regarding the specific crime phenomena, as well case studies, will be presented.

1.2 Conventional criminology: towards practice-based remedies

Ever since the investiture of criminology as a science, criminologists have busied themselves as researchers studying crime and criminal behaviour to establish disciplined methods to assess, evaluate and explain the nature, extent, cause, and control of criminal behaviour. Atypical views have been espoused about the practice of criminology. Firstly, it was perceived as a science that develops knowledge and methods to reduce crime, secondly, to pursue theoretically based endeavours in practice, and thirdly, to guide policymakers (Fichtelberg & Kupchik, 2011).

Criminologists have customarily analysed and applied their skills to promote a better understanding of crime control, prevention and reduction, as well as criminality in total. Criminology achieved repute as an academic area of study because of the inveterate threat of crime worldwide and the social problems underpinning it. A great deal of scepticism and censure, however, still resonates among professionals within social and human sciences regarding the role, application, value and contributions of criminologists. Criminology intrinsically tenders theory and empirical research – at heart, the core focus of crime as a social phenomenon (Herbig & Hesselink, 2009; Hesselink-Louw, 2004; Shearing, 2007).

Internationally, some scholars, practitioners and professionals believe that criminology is defeasible and, as a discipline, lacks relevance to the reality of criminal justice, policymaking, and private and corporate sectors. This archaic view lashes criminology and criminologists to a paper-bound and a tractate-condensed bibliometric science. That is to say, criminologists are judged to have little influence on and to make little contribution to contemporary practical society; criminology is reduced to pure academe that comprises teaching, research, professional advice, and community service. Such notions ostracise criminologists and question the integrity of the profession, intensifying their difficulty of being allocated a position of simply being the vessels and historiographers of ongoing professional and social exclusion (Petersilia, 1993; Robinson, 2004).

1.3 Contemporary criminology: redefining the traditional notion

Currie (1999) acknowledges that criminologists have for far too long been accustomed to standing in a one-dimensional position; in other words, they have been engaged in a mere recounting science to which politicians and their ilk pay little attention.

Owing to current shortages of specialists (that is, psychologists and social workers) and other human resources, criminologists have been in increasing demand as professional practitioners within both the criminal justice sector and private and corporate environments (Herbig & Hesselink, 2009; Hesselink-Louw, 2004). South African criminologists have – through innovation and a desire to resist marginalisation – redefined their directive by shifting emphasis from the accumulation of research findings within a chronicling profession to the dissemination of known facts applicable in practice (Robinson, 2004). They have campaigned and marketed their unique expertise, skills, knowledge and contributions to practical and well-needed multidisciplinary outputs (that is, criminological assessments of offending behaviour). This action was facilitated through the establishment of important alliances, such as that with the Department of Correctional Services (DCS), in which criminological support includes the scientific and professional identification, assessment, analysis, examination and explanation of crime and criminal behaviour in all its spheres pertaining to inmates. Hence, criminologists have pledged themselves as important sources of knowledge and active role players in the comprehension of offending behaviour in practice (Herbig & Hesselink, 2009; Hesselink-Louw, 2004; Robinson 2004).

Currently, the South African contemporary criminological focus is rapidly evolving in response to societal and other needs; that is, needs for a more practicable and civic participatory criminology and practice. In this regard, criminologists provide a practically oriented role that enhances interrelated service delivery within the criminal justice, corporate and private sectors (Herbig & Hesselink, 2009; Hesselink-Louw, 2004).

1.4 South African criminology: onwards and upwards

Opinions and debates on crime and related matters are dissimilar to those on ecological, biological or chemical matters. Discussions about crime sometimes evoke expert-proletarian opinions and theories, seeing that public opinion is vocal about what to do about crime and offenders. Consequently, the relationship between criminological research and criminal justice and public value systems is a complex one. Here, criminology – with its scientific discourse and development of complex theories of crime and careful theoretical scrutiny – makes a unique and important contribution to thinking patterns and debates about crime and criminal justice (Fichtelberg & Kupchik, 2011).

1.5 What contributions should criminologists be making in practice?

In a democratic society, criminologists are not philosopher monarchs who dictate policy or instruct the population from above. Rather, they make their professional contributions as offerings, albeit highly skilled ones; their work must be heard by and assimilated through the public, private, corporate and criminal justice sectors. For this reason, criminologists – with their specialised focus and methods – are placed in a complex yet awkward position in relation to the government, public, academic, private, corporate and criminal justice sectors. These sectors should appreciate criminologists as experts who can make unique and skilled contributions. This, in essence, directs democratic criminology (Fichtelberg & Kupchik, 2011).

In this regard, criminology in South Africa is not just a paper-based, technical discipline based on theories and theoretical issues. It is, rather, an integrated, multidisciplinary field that amalgamates academic criminology with contemporary social concerns about crime; this has a more practical application, such as victim empowerment (that is, victim-impact statements), pre-sentence evaluation reports and assessments, criminological offender assessment, and profiling practices (Herbig & Hesselink, 2009; Hesselink-Louw, 2004).

In South Africa, the Criminological Society of South Africa (CRIMSA), a professional and ethical body, regulates the academic and professional standards for academic and practising criminologists. This body ensures that criminologists adhere to specified standards and appropriately apply their skills, knowledge and expertise within academia and practice (Herbig & Hesselink, 2009).

1.6 South African research interests and outputs

The South African accredited criminological journal, *Acta Criminologica*, serves as testimony to the various crime-related research outputs delivered by academic and practising criminologists in South Africa. Research topics vary from academic or theoretical debates and development of indigenous crime-related theories to research outputs concerned with aspects such as, but not limited to, the following:

> **The practical role, benefit and application of criminology; victimology; criminologists' role and contribution in pre-sentencing evaluation reports in courts; criminological profiling; rape in prison; hate crimes; bullying at school; domestic violence and rape in marriage; rape myths; drug abuse among learners; bank robberies; hi-jackings; child and adult prostitution; conservation crime, specifically rhino poaching and related matters; [cyber crime;] polygraphy and criminology; white-collar crimes and offender profiles; sex offender profiles and assessment [i.e., paedophiles]; serial offenders (rape and murder); farm attacks and killings; child abuse (sexual, physical, emotional and neglect); muti-murders (i.e., murder of individuals for indigenous practices and beliefs); prison gang involvement; [incest;] recidivism among the South African offender population; abuse of women and the elderly; murder of police officials; contract killings; [sea piracy; mothers and children behind bars; gangsterism; police**

brutality; and women who kill their intimate partners/spouses] (Herbig & Hesselink, 2009, p. 441).[1]

The aforementioned examples demonstrate South African criminologists' dedication to the development of the science of criminology, as well as the diversity and potential application of practitioners within various spheres related to crime and criminal behaviour.

Conclusion

Criminologists are multifaceted behavioural specialists who are schooled professionals in crime and criminality in its entirety; they are pundits who analyse, explain and understand the conditions and influences that contribute to crime, behavioural background, triggers to criminal actions, the causes of crime, and the various motives for crime. In South Africa, the role and function of criminologists have extended to professional practitioners - 'contemporary criminologists' (Hesselink & Herbig, 2009, p. 277)[2] - with major contributions to make within society, practice, and the criminal justice system.

At its core, contemporary South African criminology assesses the needs and risks of offenders, and it offers significant direction to corrections and to other professionals regarding understanding of, and involvement with, offenders and criminal behaviour. In practice, an ultimate crime-assessment scenario would include an in-depth holistic, empirical criminological assessment that unpacks the crime phenomenon and dissects it into its constituent parts.

Crime risks should be identified for intervention purposes, and this identification should be interspersed with relevant theory clearly demonstrating how the discipline in its pragmatic persona permeates the criminal justice and allied domains. The practical criminological field possesses tremendous potential to shed much-needed empirical light on the topics and issues addressed in this book. Note, however, that credible knowledge generation is possible only through the most rigorous social scientific methods, independent - to the extent that this is possible - of governing interests.

References

Currie, E. (1999). Reflections on Crime and Criminology at the Millennium. *Western Criminology Review*, *2*(1). Retrieved from http://wcr.sonoma.edu/v2n1/currie.html.

Fichtelberg, A., & Kupchik, A. (2011). Democratic criminology: the place of criminological expertise in the public sphere. *Journal of Theoretical and Philosophical Criminology*, *3*(1), 57–88.

Herbig, F. J. W., & Hesselink, A. E. (2009). The role and function of criminologists in the criminal justice and private sector. *Journal of Psychology in Africa*, *19*(3), 441–448.

Hesselink, A. E., & Herbig, F. J. W. (2009). The scientific basis of criminology. *Journal of Psychology in Africa*, *19*(2), 275–279.

Hesselink-Louw, A. E. (2004). *Criminological assessment of prison inmates: a constructive mechanism towards offender rehabilitation* (Unpublished doctoral thesis). University of South Africa (Unisa), Pretoria.

1 Reprinted by permission of Taylor & Francis Copyright © Routledge. http://www.informaworld.com.

2 Reprinted by permission of Taylor & Francis Copyright © Routledge. http://www.informaworld.com.

Kraska, P. B., & Lawrence Neuman, W. (2012). *Criminal justice and criminology research methods* (2nd ed.). Boston: Pearson.

Petersilia, J. (1993). Defending the practical value of criminological research. *Journal of Research in Crime and Delinquency*, *30*(4), 497.

Robinson, M. (2004). *Why crime? An integrated systems theory of antisocial behavior*. Upper Saddle River, NJ: Prentice-Hall.

Shearing, C. (2007). National Research Foundation (NRF) status quo roundtable: Criminology and Criminal Justice, 29–30 March 2007, The Farm Inn, Pretoria.

Violent crime and criminology in South Africa

A Hesselink

2.1 Introduction

Everyone in South Africa is affected by crime, the fear of being victimised, and/or a sense of insecurity. Some people are direct victims, while others experience crime through the victimisation of friends and family. Almost all South Africans experience trauma via the news media that characteristically portray profuse and gratuitous violence that is characteristic of this country (Silber & Geffen, 2009).

South Africa has one of the highest rates of violence in the world. Ever since the 1990s, South Africa has acquired a reputation for being the so-called 'crime capital of the world'. This international stereotypification status is not without foundation (Altbeker, 2005; Davies & MacPherson, 2011). Statements and crime stories that link South Africa to 'being one of the most violent countries in the world'[1] often feature a high level of cruelty, a 'culture of violence',[2] and appalling and inexplicable gratuitous forms of violence (Bruce, 2010b, pp. 13–14; Silber & Geffen, 2009, p. 36).

The violent nature of South Africa is clearly indicated by the Global Peace Indexes (GPIs) of 2010 and 2013, which listed South Africa as number 121 out of 149 (2010), and 121 out of 162 (2013) disordered countries in the world – taking into consideration factors such as the likelihood of violent demonstrations and the levels of organised internal conflict (Global Peace Index (GPI), 2013; Ratele, 2010). Crime and violence are, debatably, the prime barriers to a flourishing and peaceful South Africa in which citizens and visitors can live without fear (Holtmann, 2008).

Even the Office of the Presidency acknowledged in 2010 that the rate of violent crime – especially murder, rape, aggravated assault, robbery, and vehicle hijackings – is higher in South Africa than in other countries. Consequently, violent crime poses a major challenge to the safety and security of all South Africans (Office of the Presidency, 2010).

This chapter evaluates violence and violent crime in South Africa and presents a well-known media profile of a serious violent offender. A criminological assessment is also provided to determine possible personality traits and tendencies of the offender.

2.2 Definitions/key concepts

It is necessary to clarify the terms 'violence', 'violent crime' and 'gratuitous violence' as utilised, understood, and experienced within a South African context. Violent crime in South Africa consists of many elements representative of unique types of crimes.

---

1 Reprinted by permission of the Editor: *South African Crime Quarterly.*

2 Reprinted by permission of the Editor: *South African Crime Quarterly.*

2.2.1 Violence

Davies and MacPherson (2011) summarise a definition of violence comprising five elements that reflect South Africa's unique circumstances. These researchers maintain that violence within a South African context refers to:

- use of intentional threats
- infliction or causation of physical, sexual, and psychological harm
- application of force
- that may result in criminal or civil liability (such as serious physical pain, injury or death)
- whether or not serious and inclusive of a weapon.

2.2.2 Violent crime

In broad terms, violent crimes entail elements of threats or actual actions or attempts of:

- physical injury
- death
- force
- violence
- damage to another person
- the use of a weapon (Hesselink-Louw, 2004; Hesselink et al., 2009).

The South African Police Service (SAPS) Crime Statistics Overview for South Africa for 2011/2012 distinguishes between 'contact crimes' and 'contact-related crimes' (SAPS, 2012, p. 6). Contact crimes encompass actual acts and attempts of murder, sexual offences, assault with grievous bodily harm, robbery aggravating and common assault. Contact-related crimes include crimes associated with arson and malicious damage to property.

According to Bezuidenhout (2011), South African crimes of a violent nature include major crimes such as assault, murder, rape, and robbery. Prominent and typical South African sub-categories of murder involve:

- serial murder
- mass murder
- spree murder
- contract or hired killings
- muti murder
- murders on farms/farm killings
- murder of police officials.

Sub-types of assault in the South African context are:

- school violence
- hate crime (based on grounds of race, gender, religion, sexual orientation, ethnic origin or disability)
- xenophobia
- homophobia (Bezuidenhout, 2011).

Major categories of robbery include:

- home robbery
- business robbery
- vehicle hijackings
- automated teller machine (ATM) bombings

- cash-in-transit heists
- bank robberies (Bezuidenhout, 2011).

Another illustrative definition of violent crime within a South African context is provided by Bruce (2006). This researcher unravels the term 'violent crime' as:
- assaults related to domestic violence and arguments
- robbery (including armed robbery)
- rape and sexual assault
- conflict between groups over territory (taxi wars, gang warfare and political violence)
- violence against state and economic institutions (violent protests)
- violence to resist law enforcement interventions
- excessive force by public and private policing agencies and vigilantism
- violent child abuse
- culpable homicide linked to negligent fatal violence (mostly involving motor vehicles)
- other forms of violence inclusive of serial killings, muti murders and other premeditated murders not covered such as violence related to kidnappings (Bruce, 2006, pp. 32–33).[3]

2.2.3 Gratuitous violence

The term 'gratuitous violence' encapsulates many forms and aspects associated with unusual or excessive violence. Bruce (2010b, pp. 13–19) describes this type of violence as violence 'for nothing'[4] (not a strong motivation for money or property) – meaning violence associated with the following concepts or attributes:
- sadistic pleasure
- disproportionate
- purposeless
- often unprovoked
- an 'overkill'
- enjoyment from engaging in violence
- acting out rage
- anger
- hatred
- brutality
- cruelty
- control and domination of others
- callousness (unemotional)
- lacking victim empathy (empathy deficits)
- no inhibitions against violence
- cold-blooded.

For example, a man's ears are cut off by robbers, seemingly to punish him for not having a cellphone, money or other valuable items for them to take (Bruce, 2010b). Another South African example is that of an adult Limpopo man who raped a seven-year-old girl numerous times within a few hours – the child was a stranger to the offender, and he apparently lured her to a dilapidated house in a veld, where he raped her (Louw-Caarstens, 2013).

3 Reprinted by permission of the Editor: *South African Crime Quarterly*.
4 Reprinted by permission of the Editor: *South African Crime Quarterly*.

2.3 The media and violence

Lancaster (2013) alludes to the fact that President Jacob Zuma declared before parliament on 7 March 2013 that

> **we should not lose sight of the fact that the overwhelming majority of the 52 million South Africans are peaceful, caring, law abiding citizens.**
>
> **They love their country. They do their best each day to make South Africa a better place. Therefore, when expressing outrage, we should be careful not to then paint all South Africans as violent and brutal. We should be careful not to rubbish our country.**
>
> **We should not and cannot lose faith in our own humanity and our collective ability to correct the wrongs that we see in our country.**
>
> **We also dare not portray our beautiful country as an inherently violent place to live in. South Africa is a stable, peaceful country. Like all countries, there are elements that conduct themselves in a shocking and unacceptable manner (Zuma, 2013).**

Global media has, contrary to the president's statement, depicted South Africa as an intrinsically violent country. Lancaster (2013) mentions the example of Alex Perry's report in the 11 March edition of *Time* titled 'Oscar Pistorius and South Africa's culture of violence and questions whether such cases are indeed isolated or whether South Africa is a violent country.

Crime sells - this is evident in national and international media reports on mainly hideous and gratuitous forms of violence. The more sensational, the better the publicity is received, the more interest and outcry there seems to be. A case in point is the Oscar Pistorius incident - Pistorius, the so-called 'Blade Runner', shot his girlfriend Riva Steenkamp on Valentine's day 2013. This case was covered all over the world. However, the media may portray an image that the criminal justice system and authorities cannot control and address the crime problem in South Africa. Such impressions may instil even more fear among citizens and within the international arena (Bezuidenhout, 2011). For this reason, one needs to have an informed approach (based on research and statistics) to crime and violence - not one based just on media reports.

2.4 A culture and history of violence

In 2008/2009 just under 50 people per day were murdered in South Africa. The murder rate decreased in 2011/2012 to 30.9 per 100 000 people in South Africa (Institute for Security Studies (ISS) Fact Sheet, 2011/12; Silber & Geffen, 2009). It is not surprising, therefore, that the majority of South African offenders are incarcerated for violent and aggressive crimes. During 2011, over 70 per cent of all offenders were incarcerated for violent crimes (Loots & Louw, 2011).

Experts and crime analysts mostly rely on the SAPS annual crime statistics to relate to and evaluate violent crime in South Africa. In this regard, SAPS has recorded in a 10-year period approximately 2 million serious crimes (on an annual basis), of which a third was ascribed to crimes such as murder, vehicle hijackings, armed robbery, and rape (Holtmann, 2008).

Victimisation surveys analysed in conjunction with the SAPS annual crime statistics would perhaps provide a more balanced view, and fill the gap between crimes that are not reported or recorded by the SAPS and crimes that are (Altbeker, 2005; Redpath, 2010). However, Bruce (2010a) points out that there have been persistent media reports on the manipulation of SAPS crime statistics, which outlined the existence of incentives within the SAPS not to record violent crime. It is precisely due to this peculiarity that current violent crime statistics cannot be relied on as an indicator of representative trends of violent crime in South Africa.

Although South African residents from an array of economic and racial backgrounds are unduly affected by serious violent crime, black people and poor people are disproportionately affected (Silber & Geffen, 2009).

A longitudinal breakdown of overall national crime rates documented yearly confirms that the general crime levels peaked in 2002/03, after which there was a slow decline until 2007/08, when crime started to increase again. More recently, SAPS statistics indicate that violent crime reduced overall for the period 2009/10 to 2011/12, except for organised violent crime (gang warfare), which is still at a high level (Burger, Gould, & Newham, 2010; SAPS, 2012).

CRITICAL REFLECTION

Access the internet and research incidents of violence during strikes and unrest between the public and the South African Police Service (SAPS). Find out about the following, for example: the 2013/14 incidents at Relala (outside Tzaneen), where thousands of strikers stormed a satellite police station and injured several police officers; violent unrest at the Tshwane-metro offices; and the Marikana shooting.

In your search, relate your findings to the gratuitous violence used by the public and members of SAPS, the culture of violence in South Africa, and the role of the media.

2.5 Rationale for violence and violent crime in South Africa

Rapid Evidence Assessment (REA) conducted research as to why South Africa is so violent. In sum, REA proclaims the reasons to be manifold and interrelated. Single factors related to violent crime in South Africa were found to be unsound, while the most profound factors seemed to be a combination of political-historical, environmental, and individual factors (Davies & MacPherson, 2011).

2.5.1 Contextual factors of violence and violent crime

Not all poor people in South Africa deficient of income and employment engage in crime or violence, yet these socio-economic drawbacks are associated with criminality and violent crime. Noteworthy factors that contribute to violent crime are categorised by Davies and MacPherson (2011) as:

- cultural attitudes to crime and violence
- the presence of aiding contributors (that is, firearms, alcohol and drugs)
- adverse socio-economic conditions (that is, illegal immigration)
- inadequate regulatory systems (that is, the police, courts, and corrections).

These risk factors explain crime worldwide, even though some are more distinct in South Africa. The high rate of crime in South Africa is related to these risk factors because they predominantly reign in South Africa, while other countries are predisposed by only a few (Davies & MacPherson, 2011).

High levels of gender inequity, income inequality and low economic development are strongly connected to, and serve as strong predictors of, rates of violence, especially for murder and major assaults. South Africa exhibits great inequality of income as well as the high rate for murder (as already specified in section 2.4). Inequality and poverty are the main drivers of crime. Other factors that contribute to violent crime are:

- substance use and abuse
- the increase of firearms
- the intergenerational cycle of violence
- the prevailing patriarchal edifice of masculinity (Davies & MacPherson, 2011).

2.5.2 Political–historical factors

South Africa's colonial and apartheid legacy generated circumstances in which violence was normalised, perceived and utilised as a mechanism for solving problems and conflict. During the twentieth century, black people in South Africa were subjected to institutionalised and informal racialised violence that incorporated dispossession and social dislocation. Thus, violence was previously an element of the state's reaction to civil society, and some South Africans learned that violence is an instrument in the conflict resolution, justice, and the acquisition of power. The freedom struggle in South Africa produced a generation that grew up with endemic violence, subsequent feelings of anger and resentment, and normalised pro-violent patterns of thinking (Dastile, 2010; Davies & MacPherson, 2011).

During the apartheid era the inadequacies of the police and judiciary resulted in disdain for the law and the justice system – resulting in a lingering mistrust of authorities and the rule of law. Ambivalence to the law drew upon the oppressive role of the criminal justice system and the law of the time. Weaknesses within the police and the criminal justice system led to unnoticed and unpunished violent acts that facilitated vigilantism and summary justice (Dastile, 2010; Davies & MacPherson, 2011).

2.5.3 Environmental factors

It is important to understand the connection between violent behaviour, individual factors and environmental factors. Here, social and gender attitudes and roles, substance abuse, availability of firearms, existence of gangs, and family and child socialisation play significant roles in explaining environmental factors and violence in South Africa.

Often, fractured families and child socialisation in South Africa are characterised by missing or absent parents, harsh and inconsistent discipline, physical and emotional abuse, and inadequate limit-setting. This can lead to poor self-worth, lack of self-confidence, and violent behaviour (Davies & MacPherson, 2011; DeLisi & Conis, 2012).

Antisocial groups and gangs provide children, adolescents, and adults with a sense of identity and self-worth and the opportunity to use violence to acquire goods. The increase in violence within, and between, South African gangs created a 'winner-takes-all' scenario to resolve competition for economic and social status (Davies & MacPherson, 2011, p. 13).

The ready availability and use of firearms in South Africa increase offenders' coercive power and dangerousness, and hence their confidence about being able to dominate others through the use of threat or violence. Extensive access to unlicensed or stolen firearms, increased acquisition of guns by citizens for self-defence against escalating crime and violence, and the regular loss of SAPS firearms have aggravated this problem. Firearms in the hands of those who are criminally inclined radically amplify their coercive power, dangerousness, and confidence about dominating others through the use or threat of violence (Davies & MacPherson, 2011).

Substance abuse is prevalent in South Africa and a major factor contributing to violence. It is responsible for disinhibited behaviour and aggravated violence linked to the need to pay for drugs (for example cocaine and tik) and subsequent gang battles for dominance of the supply. Substance abuse (especially alcohol abuse) contributes to many deaths in South Africa that are associated with the use of firearms, other types of weapons, and fighting between men during socialisation. Such violence commonly occurs in public spaces and climaxes over leisure periods, including weekends and celebratory periods (Davies & MacPherson, 2011; Prinsloo, 2012). It is also common for robbers (in some robberies) to be under the influence of a substance that, in effect, suppresses emotional responsiveness, intensifies aggression, reduces inhibitions and self-control, and impedes judgment. There is also a relationship between drugs such as methamphetamines and violent sexual behaviour. It has been noted that such drugs are utilised 'to get a woman high so that several men could rape her without resistance' (Davies & MacPherson, 2011, p. 14; DeLisi & Conis, 2012).

Gender (social) attitudes and roles are also interrelated with violence against women in South Africa, where cultural values and norms serve to foster disregard for women, and strengthen abusive behaviour and practices against women. In specific cultural environments within which violence occurs in South Africa attitudes such as the following are pervasive (Dastile, 2010; Davies & MacPherson, 2011, pp. 15–16):

- 'A man who beats his wife often is regarded with approval because he knows how to discipline his wife.'
- 'Women get beaten because they do not listen' and/or 'when they stand for their rights.'
- 'A man proves his love to his women if he beats her – some women feel neglected and not loved if they are not beaten at home.'
- 'Even your mother will not support you if your man is unfaithful – in the case of adultery – your own mother will not go against your man.'
- 'Unless it breaks certain cultural norms, the use of coercion, force and violence by males are tolerated, except where the victim has a higher social stand than the perpetrator.'

Children are also frequently victimised under socially accepted norms according to which they are treated as 'adult possessions' in terms of sexual violence at the hands of adults who are accountable for them. An example of this is the 'virgin cleansing' myth whereby some adult men believe that they will be cured from HIV/Aids if they have sex with a virgin (Davies & MacPherson, 2011, pp. 15–16; DeLisi & Conis, 2012).

Protective factors can stop children and individuals from committing violent crime. Such protective factors comprise the following (Davies & MacPherson, 2011):

- Environmental processes: such as non-criminal and non-violent neighbourhoods, schools, peer groups, community groups, and community institutions.
- Familial processes: including sound family resources, parental characteristics, parental behaviour and parenting skills.
- Self-system processes: such as connectedness, social responsibility, competence, and nurturing.
- Individual characteristics: including cognition, health, self-belief, and development.

Absence of these protective factors creates vulnerable individuals who might be prone to violent and aggressive behaviour.

2.5.4 Individual factors

Individual factors in South Africa are regulated by age, gender, education, and profiles (economic, psychiatric, and psychological). Age is not a cause of violence, but it is strongly associated with violent crime. Violent crime is more widespread amongst younger people, with violent young people being more likely to reoffend. A youthful age is, therefore, related to a risk of future violence. Davies and MacPherson (2011) state that an early age of onset of violent behaviour and prominent levels of aggression are factors that distinguish violent young offenders from non-violent young offenders.

Regarding gender, in South Africa, as it is on an international level, violent behaviour is overpoweringly the domain of men. Violent women choose family members as targets, and women are more inclined to act violently at home, rather than in public. Circumstantial factors that drive violent offences by men include substance abuse and prescribed psychotropic medication (Davies & MacPherson, 2011; Prinsloo, 2012).

Violent risk factors that relate to education are low maternal education, low caregiver education, low personal school performance and motivation, and school dropout – each of these factors exists in parts of South Africa. Recurring failure at school, truancy, and suspension or expulsion from school are associated with dangerous behaviour in later life (Davies & MacPherson, 2011).

The psychological profile of a violent person consists of a broad range of psychological conditions. Characteristics such as the following are believed to be present when an individual has been exposed to a disrupted family life and fractured socialisation:

- emotional difficulties
- impulsivity
- early onset behaviour problems (aggressive, oppositional, disruptive, and destructive behaviours)
- low self-worth
- deficits in inhibitory control
- rage
- lack of self-control
- lack of self-confidence
- hostility
- hyperactivity
- risk-taking
- attention-deficits (Davies & MacPherson, 2011; Prinsloo, 2012).

The psychiatric profile of a violent person relates to the occurrence of violent behaviour in psychopathic individuals. Active psychotic symptoms are imperative violence predictors. A moderate to strong connection exists between violence and psychopathy, while other personality disorders (such as the paranoid and passive–aggressive disorders) are also linked to violent behaviour, especially with male offenders (Davies & MacPherson, 2011; Prinsloo, 2012).

Davies and MacPherson (2011) further state that the economic profile associated with a violent person consists of poverty and inequality factors that are crucial elements that contribute to South Africa's burden of violent crime. These factors are linked to stress, anger, and frustration, and violence might be used to expand resources, power, and influence that others have, or are perceived to have.

CHECK POINT

- Certain socio-economic, political, environmental, and individual factors play a role in violent crime.
- During the apartheid years violence was used to solve political problems and to eliminate possible opposition. This created a culture of violence in South Africa.
- Proviolent and discriminatory attitudes contribute to violence in South Africa. Other antecedents to violent crime are access to legal and illegal firearms, the abuse of alcohol and drugs, and the existence of gangs.
- Young age, male gender, lack of education, unstable emotional well-being, and mental illness are precursors to violent crime in South Africa.

2.6 Other important factors related to violent crime

Various factors contribute to violent crime in South Africa. These factors can broadly be divided into social factors and intrapersonal factors.

2.6.1 South African research on violent crime

Research proves that social factors related to violent crime include the following:

- poverty-related variables (for example unemployment)
- availability of illegal (and legal) firearms
- levels of (gender) inequality
- substance abuse and use (alcohol and drugs)
- arguments and conflict (over money, family, sexual relationships, and work situations)
- urbanisation
- the influx of illegal immigrants
- a lack of policing
- economic inequality (Bruce, 2006; Burger et al., 2010, Holtmann, 2008; Loots & Louw, 2011; SAPS, 2012).

Other South African research, conducted by Hesselink-Louw (2004), cites the following as reasons for the high rate of violent crime rate in South Africa:

- poor economic circumstances
- political transition
- cultural perspectives
- school maladjustment
- the reopening of South African borders to trade
- low educational levels.

Burger et al. (2010) refer to the global economic downturn of 2007 to 2010 as the reason for increases in some types of crime (that is, robbery, assault, and property crimes) in South Africa. These authors claim that almost 16 per cent of all murders in South Africa occur as a result of robbery (and subsequent assaults), indicating a correlation between assault and robbery and murder (Burger et al., 2010).

During a media discussion regarding why South African offenders so readily apply gratuitous violence, Hesselink linked unjustified violence or violent behaviour with the following:

- daily exposure to (and witnessing of) violence and aggression
- a lack of respect for self and others
- criminal role models
- violent unrest
- school violence
- normlessness
- negative or criminal peer group pressure
- population density
- rapid urbanisation
- a culture of violence
- a violent past (apartheid)
- unemployment
- poverty (Hesselink, 2013).

Hesselink (2013) further noted that individuals who commit unwarranted types of violence are often emotionally numb, and they display a total disregard for life.

Bruce (2006) states that South Africa's culture of violence is related to violence used as an instrument of political rivalry, and violence used as a vehicle for competing claims over economic resources. According to Bruce (2006) and Ratele (2010), masculine domination and a preoccupation with machismo displayed by South African men play a vital role in interpersonal conflict and subsequent violent acts and homicidal victimisation.

Holtmann mapped the context of crime and violence in the Central Karoo and found that 'the victim is the same person as the offender – just at a different point in the life cycle' (2008, p. 16).[5] This life cycle often commences with the following:

- dysfunctional families (mostly as a result of unwanted pregnancies)
- absent father figures
- poverty
- child abuse and neglect
- normalised violence (at an early age) – exposure to violence and aggression
- parental substance abuse
- a lack of parental and adult supervision
- ignored fundamental needs of children (that is, love, protection, physical contact related to love and supervision).

It is then precisely these children (current victims) who become the perpetrators of the future.

Research by Loots and Louw (2011) and Hesselink and Prinsloo (2011) shows a strong link between violent crime and intrapersonal factors linked to antisocial personalities, psychopathy, antisocial personality disorder (ASPD), and dissocial personality disorder (DPD). It is also a common denominator that offenders diagnosed with these personalities or disorders commit more violent crimes and reoffend more than offenders not so diagnosed. Other intrapersonal factors related to violent crime are:

- a low self-esteem or a so-called 'fragile self-concept'

5 Reprinted by permission of the Editor: *South African Crime Quarterly*.

- anger
- aggression
- rage
- depression
- rejection
- skills deficits
- victim empathy deficits
- feelings of inferiority and insecurity
- revenge
- status competition (violence linked to insecurity about status)
- a lack of insight and understanding (Bruce, 2006; Hesselink-Louw, 2004).

2.6.2 Children and violent crime

Even children in South Africa are not safeguarded against violence (as victims and/or perpetrators). The SAPS annual crime statistics for April 2011 to March 2012 indicate that 50 688 children were victims of reported contact crimes, such as murder, attempted murder, sexual offences, assault, and assault with grievous bodily harm (SAPS, 2012). Frank (2005) reports (in a Cape Town case study of children involved in violent organised gangs) that violent child perpetrators of crime in South Africa are involved in organised armed violence. The children formed these violent organised groups to protect the neighbourhood(s) and to develop the immediate community (that is, they were financially supporting families). The children described their involvement in daily vigilantism and/or the carrying out of executions. The following are contributory factors linked to the forming of these gangs:

- impoverished surroundings
- single-parent families
- subjection to domestic violence
- overcrowded living
- school dropout
- access to girls, guns and consumer goods
- lack of alternatives
- status
- a preference for spending time on the street with other armed groups
- revenge
- access to surrogate families and friends (Frank, 2005).

Furthermore, Frank (2005) found that the children routinely witnessed armed violence and death, and reported being shot at or being hit by gunfire. Most of the children also said that they were involved in, or aided in, the shooting or murder of other people.

A more recent case that astonished South Africans is that of a 14-year-old South African boy from Daveyton (East Rand, Gauteng), who hacked his family (his mother, 3-month-old sister and 7-year-old brother) to death with an axe. According to Zwecker (2013), involvement in satanism may have played a role in the killings. This is also linked to the juvenile's modus operandi (a satanistic ritual) associated with the crime.

School violence in South Africa also seems to be an increasing phenomenon. Vos (2013) reports that since 2008, sexual assault at schools (by fellow learners) increased by 6.3 per cent. The Centre for Justice and Crime Prevention (CJCP) researched violence at high schools in South Africa and found that 22.2 per cent of the school learners were exposed to physical and sexual violence or threats of violence, and 85 per cent of school principals acknowledged that physical assault occurred at their schools (Vos, 2013).

Extensive international research conducted by Hawkins et al. (2000) on youth violence indicates the risk factors shown in Table 2.1 to be associated with youth violence.

Table 2.1 Risk factors associated with violent crime

Individual factors	Family factors	School factors	Peer-related factors	Community and neighbourhood factors
Pregnancy and delivery complications (prenatal and delivery trauma)	Parental criminality	Academic failure	Delinquent siblings	Poverty
Low resting heart rate	Child maltreatment	Low bonding to school		Community disorganisation
Internalising disorders (nervousness/withdrawal, worrying, and anxiety)	Poor family management practices		Delinquent peers	Availability of drugs and firearms
Hyperactivity, concentration problems	Low levels of parental involvement	Truancy and dropping out of school	Gang membership	Neighbourhood adults involved in crime
Restlessness and risk-taking behaviour	Poor family bonding	Frequent school transitions		Exposure to violence and racial prejudice
Aggressiveness (early initiation of violent behaviour)	Family conflict			
Early initiation of violent behaviour	Parental attitudes favourable to substance use and violence			
Involvement in other forms of antisocial behaviour (stealing and destruction of property, smoking and early sexual intercourse)	Parent–child separation			
Beliefs and attitudes favourable to deviant or antisocial behaviour (dishonesty, attitudes favourable to violence, and hostility toward police)				

According to Muňos and Frick (2012), there is a definite link between absence in empathy and guilt in violent youth offenders and callousness, provocation to threat, and failure to consider consequences of actions and alternative responses (to aggression or violence). These researchers found that violent youth offenders are more prone to non-verbal angry behaviour (throwing of items), and are less emotionally responsive to sad emotional expressions of persons or animals in distress. Violent youth offenders, furthermore, lack behavioural inhibitions, and they display low fearfulness (Muňos & Frick, 2012).

CRITICAL REFLECTION Access the web sites of the Institute for Security Studies (ISS) and the Centre for Violence and Reconciliation (CVR). Familiarise yourself with these prominent South African research institutions' findings on violent crime in South Africa.

2.7 Criminological analysis and explanation of violent crime in South Africa

DeLisi and Conis (2012) and Hesselink-Louw (2005) assert that violent offenders are significant to criminologists in order to analyse their behaviour (causes, motives, triggers, high-risk situation) and to sharpen theoretical ideas. These foci afford criminology as a science and discipline greater credibility and authenticity within academia and in society. Violent offending behaviour (and offenders) affects the morality rate in South Africa and is responsible for a lower quality of life (for ordinary citizens). Offenders in this category victimise and injure members of the society; instil fear; contribute to lost and reduced productivity in South Africa; and cost the criminal justice system a great deal of money in terms of offender management and supervision endeavours. Therefore, the general public expects the police and courts to apprehend, prosecute, and detain violent offenders.

Various commonalities exist in the lives of serious and violent offenders; however, one needs to recognise that there are also significant distinctions between them. Criminology can with poise claim that individual-level factors (for example empathy and self-control deficits) are dominant within violent offenders, and this science identifies that the pathology in some serious violent offenders is characteristic-related to biological factors - thus, a multifarious interaction between nature and nurture (DeLisi & Conis, 2012). The discussion, furthermore, necessitates an understanding that violent behaviour is entwined with social, medical, and behavioural sciences, but still many profiles of violent offenders emerge from criminological literature, as 'criminologists have copiously documented the individual-level characteristics of violent offenders and core personality traits that appear repeatedly in the literature' (DeLisi & Conis, 2012, pp. 11, 13).

For decades, violent offending behaviour was explained from a variety of perspectives - including those of criminological theories. For most of the twentieth century, the focus was on normal processes and situations which linked violent offending behaviour to an association with antisocial peers, poverty, living in a poor and disorganised neighbourhood, strain, stress, discrimination, and anomie. During the 1960s and 1970s, the criminal justice system (police, courts, and the correctional system) were blamed for crime causation. The 1980s and 1990s infused crime causation with ideas from psychology, criminology, biology, and economics - including the idea that crime is a rational choice intertwined with factors such as family background, social class, environmental influences, low self-control, prior experience, education, and the development of life-course persistent offending behaviour (associated with biological factors) (DeLisi & Conis, 2012).

Contemporary foci of explanations of violent crime rely on individual-level factors (criminogenic traits) inclusive of the following – a process known as reductionism:

- self-control
- childhood abuse
- trauma and neglect
- procriminal and proviolent attitudes
- long-term violence problems
- attachments
- a sense of entitlement
- alienation
- psychopathy
- empathy
- childhood abuse and trauma
- power and control issues
- self-centredness
- rigid and inflexible thinking patterns
- poor impulse control
- irrational behaviour
- limited levels of reflectivity
- problematic interpersonal relationships
- intimacy problems
- impulsiveness
- poor problem-solving skills
- inability to cope with stress
- poor coping mechanisms
- irresponsibility
- moral reasoning
- weak socialisation
- temperament
- inner rage
- self-indulgence
- temper
- personality (DeLisi & Conis, 2012; Hesselink-Louw, 2004; Hesselink-Louw, 2005; Hesselink & Prinsloo, 2011).

It is therefore important to understand the specific characteristics that appear to typify violent offenders, of course in conjunction with correlates such as:

- an early onset of violent and aggressive behaviour
- low school and academic achievements
- employment status
- peer pressure and susceptibility of negative, violent and criminal peer pressure or influences
- substance use and abuse
- a history of violent and aggressive behaviour
- ethnicity

- neighbourhood and type of residency
- poverty
- individual emotions
- an adverse home environment (DeLisi & Conis, 2012; Hesselink-Louw, 2005; Hesselink & Prinsloo, 2011).

The box below presents a case study to demonstrate a criminological assessment in order to determine possible personality traits and tendency anomalies for offender needs and risk rehabilitation and management purposes.

CASE STUDY: The Modimolle Monster

The so-called 'Modimolle Monster' is a prominent media example of a gratuitous violent offender and serves to illustrate multifaceted factors that played a role in this offender's rationale, offending behaviour, and personality traits.

The Modimolle Monster

On 3 January, 2012, Johan Kotzé kidnapped, attacked, tortured (repeatedly raping), and attempted to murder his estranged wife, Ina Bonnette, in his rented Modimolle home. Ina's son from a previous marriage was shot and killed in the house on the same day by Kotzé. Johan Kotzé, labelled as the 'Modimolle Monster' by the media, sexually mutilated, kidnapped, assaulted, and orchestrated the gang-rape of Ina Bonnette, and murdered his stepson Conrad, 19. At the time Bonnette was still married to Kotzé, but lived in her own flat. Kotzé's three co-accused (Andries Sithole, Pieta Mohlake, and Sello Mphaka) pleaded not guilty to the charges. They claimed Kotzé forced them to take part in the attack on Bonnette and said they had only pretended to rape her. Sithole, Mohlake, and Mphaka claimed Kotzé threatened to shoot them if they did not cooperate. They insisted they merely pretended to rape Bonnette because they could not get erections. Bonnette testified the three men looked on while Kotzé sexually tortured her and mutilated her breasts before they took turns to rape her. She was still tied to a bed with tape over her mouth when she heard her son repeatedly say, 'Please uncle, don't shoot', followed by three shots. He died at the scene after being shot in the face, chest, and knee. Bonnette testified that Kotzé tortured her with various objects before instructing the other three to rape her. She told the court that she listened to her son pleading for his life before he was shot in the head and heart.

Kotzé denied guilt, claiming he could not be held accountable for his actions that day. The so-called 'Modimolle Monster' argued non-pathological incapacity in his defence, despite three psychiatrists finding him fit to stand trial. A defence psychologist testified that Kotzé had a narcissistic personality disorder and suffered from an acute stress disorder and major depression, which resulted in a state of dissociation during the incident. A State psychologist, however, testified that Kotzé did not suffer from any mental disorders and could be held accountable for his actions.

Events prior and up to 3 January 2012

Johan Kotzé blamed his wife for his deeds. His friend Dirk van der Merwe testified that Kotzé phoned him on 3 January 2012 after allegedly torturing his wife, orchestrating her rape, and killing her son. He was crying and said he no longer wanted to live. He said Van der Merwe would never see him again and should not search for him. Kotzé phoned him again the night after the crime. When Van der Merwe asked him 'what the hell he had done', Kotzé said it was all (his wife) Ina's fault. He said he had tried twice to commit suicide, but could not get it right. Van der Merwe urged Kotzé to hand himself over to the police and even offered to go with him, but Kotzé said he first had a few tasks to perform and would then go to the police. About a week later, a tired and worn-looking Kotzé arrived at his workplace and 'just stood there'. 'I just said "oh Johan, oh Johan" and told him to sit down. He said he wanted to talk to me but I said there was no time. I phoned the police and he was arrested,' Van der Merwe said.

Van der Merwe testified that he and Kotzé had coffee at Kotzé's house the morning of 3 January. Kotzé told him he was tired, and he had watched Ina and did not like what he saw. He said he had business in Hammanskraal that day and also had to go and fetch his daughter in Pretoria. Shortly after 11 a.m., Kotzé phoned and said he and Ina had an appointment for later that afternoon and were going to talk things through. He repeatedly warned Van der Merwe not to come to his house, because he said he needed 'alone time' with Ina. Kotzé phoned him again a while later to make arrangements for the removal of palm trees in front of his house and told Van der Merwe he had stopped three men in the street to help him. Two of the men went with Van der Merwe to re-plant the palms, but Kotzé insisted that one called Andries should stay with him and repeatedly told Van der Merwe to bring the other two back to his house.

They did not talk when Van der Merwe dropped the two off at Kotzé's house, but Kotzé phoned him at about 1.45 p.m. and again told him not to come to the house. He did not sound different, but was crying when he phoned Van der Merwe again a few hours later and told him he no longer wanted to live. Van der Merwe told the court about an incident over the preceding Christmas period when Kotzé took another woman called Lizette on a holiday trip with him. The woman's relationship with Kotzé soured after he hit her with an oar while they were river rafting. The woman told Kotzé it was the last time he would hit her and thereafter distanced herself from him.

Kotzé's 18-year-old daughter from a previous marriage, Jo-Marie Kotzé, testified that she had spent the Christmas period with her father and had an arrangement to visit him again on 3 January this year. He phoned her a few times to make sure she was okay and then phoned her again at about 4 p.m. He told her he had caught Aunt Ina with another man. He loved her very much, was very disappointed and could not believe she (Ina) could do something like that to him. She remembered telling her father to leave Ina so that they could get on with their lives. He sounded quite normal and arranged with her to wait for him at his friend's house. She was not worried about her father and never suspected anything was wrong at that stage. She only spoke to him again on the day of his arrest, when he told her to enjoy her matric year and to come and fetch her furniture and motorbike at his house. She said Kotzé had always tried to protect her and never really showed her what he was really feeling, although he told her things were not going well with Ina. He always appeared to be happy and was always smiling when he saw her. Kotzé's daughter started crying while giving evidence, and sobbed when she hugged her father after testifying against him. The court orderly at first refused to allow her to go near her father, but later allowed her to talk to him for a few minutes. The two stood talking quietly and Kotzé consoled his daughter as she stood sobbing in his arms.

Experts' opinions

Dr Louis Pienaar told the court that Kotzé was 'tired and dejected but well oriented' when he examined Kotzé. Dr Pienaar said Kotzé 'knew who I was. I summed him up as well oriented.' Police asked him to examine Kotzé after his arrest on 11 January 2012. He said he had treated Kotzé twice before. Based on his appearance, Kotzé did not suffer from anxiety or disassociation, he said. 'I think it was a matter that he had reached the end of his week on the run.'

Clinical psychologist Tertia Spangenberg said during cross-examination it would be difficult for a narcissist, which she believed Kotzé was. She said Kotzé's narcissism crumbled when he lost face in public after being accused of murder and assault. Van As asked whether this meant Kotzé was no longer a narcissist. Spangenberg answered: 'No that is not what I meant. He still is one.' Spangenberg, who was called by Kotzé's defence, found he was not accountable for his actions. She found Kotzé had a narcissistic personality disorder, major depression, and untreated and unresolved acute stress disorder, which resulted in a state of psychological dissociation during the attack. She said individuals with his narcissistic disorder were noted for their egotistic self-involvement. According to her findings, Kotzé was obsessed with Bonnette. When he saw her with another man on New Year's Eve 2011 it caused trauma, which led to stress disorder. 'I am of the opinion that Mr Kotzé was not accountable for the alleged actions of which he stands accused,' she said last week.

In contrast, clinical psychologist Dirk Coetzee, who assessed Kotzé at Weskoppies psychiatric hospital in Pretoria, found he could be held criminally responsible for his actions. 'At the time of the commission of the offence the accused was criminally responsible for the offence charged, and was capable of appreciating the wrongfulness of his act and could act in accordance with an appreciation of the wrongfulness of his act,' Coetzee's report read. Coetzee spent seven-and-a-half hours doing his assessment on Kotzé at Weskoppies. This was spread over five visits. He described Kotzé as cooperative and attentive during interviews. 'At the time of the incident he did not suffer from any clinical psychiatric disorder.' Coetzee said Kotzé showed traits of a compulsive personality. Some depressive symptoms were also noted.

Sentencing

Acting Judge Bert Bam rejected Kotzé's plea that he did not know what he was doing at the time and could not be held accountable for his actions. The Judge said Kotzé had carefully planned the revenge attack on Bonnette and her 19-year-old son Conrad. He ruled that Kotzé's co-accused Andries Sithole was also guilty of murdering Conrad Bonnette because he knew Kotzé wanted to hurt Bonnette's son and had foreseen that Conrad would be killed. Kotzé, Sithole, Pieta Mohlake and Sello Mphaka were all convicted on four counts of raping Bonnette, kidnapping her and assaulting her with the intent to seriously injure her. The judge rejected the three's claims that Kotzé had forced them to participate and that they had only pretended to rape Bonnette. The court found that all four were equally responsible for the actions of the others when they sexually assaulted and raped Bonnette.

The State argued the Kotzé hoped his wife would contract HIV, after being raped, and submitted that he and his co-accused should be jailed for murder. The defence team said that Kotzé may have used the men 'as tools to hurt his wife'. Bonnette's ex husband at the time, Rex, said that on the day he heard his son was killed, 3 January, his sister phoned him around 6 p.m. and said: 'Kotzé shot a child.' He assumed it was one of Kotzé's children. 'I was later phoned by Ina, who said there was an incident and Conrad didn't make it,' he told the court. The next day he met Bonnette at the Modimolle police station. Rex said Bonnette told him Kotzé held three men at gunpoint and forced them to rape her. 'If they didn't rape her he would shoot them,' he told the court.

Judge Bam accepted Bonnette's evidence as honest and reliable. He said although she was not a 'perfect' witness, her evidence on how she was sexually tortured, mutilated and raped was reliable. The court also accepted Bonnette's evidence that she had heard her son begging for his life before Kotzé shot him three times. The court rejected the evidence of a defence psychologist that Kotzé had a narcissistic personality and acute stress disorder and suffered from major depression, which contributed to a state of non-pathological incapacity. Judge Bam said it was clear that Kotzé had lied to his psychologist about what had really happened at the scene that day and that her findings were based on his inaccurate version. He accepted the evidence of a state psychologist that Kotzé had no mental illness and was accountable for his actions.

Bam said it appeared Kotzé was excessively jealous over Ina Bonnette. He said she was badly injured and raped by a man she trusted, accompanied by three masked men. 'A more shocking and traumatic experience is unfathomable.' The trauma and humiliation she underwent would be difficult to describe, Judge Bam said. 'The injuries were serious and also left her psychologically scarred,' Bam said. 'It wouldn't have been strange if she was at times unsure of events,' acting Judge Bert Bam said in his judgment. Sithole, Mohlake, and Mphaka claimed Kotzé threatened to shoot them if they did not cooperate. Bam said Bonnette was cross-examined by three experienced attorneys. He said this must have been traumatic and painful for her. 'She is just a human being. Any person makes mistakes,' Bam said. He said it was not uncommon for a witness, who was as emotional as Bonnette, to be unsure at times. He said she was not a perfect witness, and that it was not realistic to think such a person existed. 'There was a sound of truth [to her testimony].' One of many examples of this was her testifying that, after the rape, she pleaded with her eyes for Kotzé's three co-accused to help her. 'It is unlikely that any witness would think of something like that,' said Bam.

'Conrad's murder was planned. It was a pre-planned murder.' Judge Bert Bam said the 'Modimolle Monster' seemed inherently evil. Kotzé and his three co-accused were handed life sentences, and each of the four was convicted of kidnapping, and of four charges relating to the rape of Ina Bonnette. Mohlake and Mphaka received 10 years for kidnapping. All four men were each given a life sentence on the rape charges. For assault with intent to do grievous bodily harm, Kotzé received 15 years, and the other three eight years each. 'It was a senseless act,' Bam said. 'However, in this case there was no sign of remorse from any of the accused.'

(*Sources:* 'Modimolle monster's' accountability to be disputed. (2013, April 16); 'Modimolle monster' blamed wife, says friend. (2012, November 27); The so-called 'Modimolle Monster' Johan Kotzé and all co-accused have been found guilty of kidnapping and the gang rape of Ina Bonnette in the North Gauteng High Court in Pretoria on Monday. (2013, July 15); Modimolle co-accused HIV+, court hears. (2013, July 11); Bonnette a believable witness – judge. (2013, July 15); Kotzé 'inherently evil'. (2013, July 17); MODIMOLLE Monster Johan Kotze was today convicted on charges of murdering his stepson as well as kidnapping, raping and severely assaulting his former wife Ina Bonette. (2013, July 15); 'Modimolle monster' testimony perhaps altered: court told. (2013, April 24).)

The Modimolle Monster case is not an isolated example of gratuitous violent behaviour. The following examples are also reminiscent of gratuitous violence in South Africa:

- An elderly man (87 years) was hacked to death on a smallholding with an axe. His wife (68 years) is in a stable condition in hospital after she was attacked with a spade by five attackers (Van Rooyen, 2014).
- Two men were shot and injured in a tavern at Freedom Park (Rustenburg). A vigilante mob accosted one of the perpetrators believed to be a citizen from Lesotho. They took him back to the tavern where they burned him alive (Smith, 2014).
- A taxi boss and father of three children was assassinated in his taxi while playing games on his phone; he had four gunshots wounds (Matipa, 2014).

- A distressed father shot a social worker, his ex-wife and her husband in the presence of his daughter. It is alleged that the man (the gunman) was suffering from depression (Cilliers, 2014).
- A minor girl was raped and killed by an adult man and it is alleged that more than one perpetrator was involved in this hideous rape and killing (Pauw, 2014).
- Residents of Khutsong (west of Johannesburg) hunted down youth gangsters alleged to have been terrorising the community. Six people had been killed, four had been beaten and burned alive and two were stoned to death (Dixon, 2013).
- An elderly couple (aged 76 and 73) was tortured by intruders when they poured boiling water on them and burned the woman's breasts with a steam iron. The perpetrators broke the safe out of the wall and fled with the couple's bakkie/truck (GunSite South Africa, 2014).

2.7.1 A criminological assessment of the so-called 'Modimolle Monster'

For the purpose of this chapter, a criminological assessment is conducted from the aforementioned media snippets (without consultation with Mr Kotzé and/or access to any police or court documentation). This means that the author of this chapter will deduce necessary and relevant assessment criteria from the case study. This endeavour at criminological assessment is based on years of practical experience in correctional centres and in working with offenders within the Department of Correctional Services. The following personality traits and tendencies are representative of a very serious violent offender and *may* be present in this case:

- unresolved disturbed emotional feelings and/or personal turmoil, and emotional distrust
- problematic interpersonal relationships
- callousness and a display of gratuitous violence
- victim empathy deficits
- proviolent attitude and thinking patterns
- social isolation and social incompetence
- no remorse and guilt, denial, no sense of personal responsibility, shifting blame, and justification of own behaviour (rationalisation, neutralisation, and minimalisation)
- possible cognitive distortions and thinking errors
- sadism, brutality, destructive notions, and stalking behaviour
- deceitful, cunning behaviour and a sense of entitlement
- a history of violent and aggressive behaviour/tendencies
- power and control issues
- revenge driven
- fantasies (violent, sadistic, and sexually deviant)
- obsessive-compulsive behaviour, jealousy, anger, rage, and loss of control
- a fluctuating grandiose self-esteem versus a low self-esteem, low self-worth, and a lack of respect for self and others
- exposure or personal victimisation of childhood trauma, abuse (inclusive of physical abuse) and/or neglect, and poor parental-child bonds/attachments
- personal maladjustment and interpersonal conflict
- violent calculated goal-directed actions
- a lack of sexual boundaries
- acceptance of abusive behaviour as a means of improving personal control
- low emotional intelligence

- manipulation
- fear of rejection and an inability to cope with this
- poor copying mechanisms, and poor insight and understanding into own behaviour.

The author of this chapter did not interview the so-called 'Modimolle Monster' in person and, for this reason, cannot determine the unique and individual causes; contributory factors; motives; triggers; high-risk situations; and personal, familial and environmental background factors that shaped the offender's behaviour. Therefore, no criminological explanation (theoretical explanation) can at this stage be provided for his behaviour.

However, research on male-on-female intimate partner violence demonstrates general factors or themes associated with this type of violent crime (Harris, Hilton, & Rice, 2011; Piquerro, Theobald & Farrington, 2014; Swogger, Kosson, Cashman-Brown, & Caine, 2012). These themes can be divided into childhood factors, parental factors, and personality factors:

- Childhood factors include:
  - juvenile aggression
  - prior arrests for violence
  - school problems
  - nervous/withdrawn as a boy
  - troublesomeness
  - physical abuse (creating a cycle of violence perpetrating during adulthood)
  - rejection.
- Parental/family factors include:
  - poor child rearing
  - parental conflict
  - a criminal father
  - a disrupted family
  - family adversity
  - poor supervision
  - relationship problems with parents
  - harsh attitude/discipline of parents
  - criminal record of a parent
  - large family size
  - parental disharmony
  - neurotic/depressed parents
  - separated parents
  - violent and aggressive parents.
- Individual/personality factors include:
  - mental illnesses
  - neuropsychological deficits (low verbal IQ)
  - unpopularity
  - daring and risk taking behaviour
  - impulsivity
  - aggressiveness
  - dishonesty

- neuroticism
- substance abuse
- sensation seeking
- antisociality
- interpersonal callousness
- enduring antisocial traits
- psychopathy
- attitudes supporting or condoning violent behaviour towards women
- anger
- hostility
- jealousy
- revenge-driven attitudes
- rejection
- isolation
- dependency
- dysfunctional coping styles
- emotional instability (Harris et al., 2011; Piquerro et al., 2014; Swogger et al., 2012).

2.8 Criminological theories and violent crime

For many years, criminologists have explained violent and aggressive offenders and sadistic offenders who use gratuitous violence. Although numerous theories exist to explain violent and aggressive behaviour, the four theories discussed below illustrate the link between violence and criminality.

2.8.1 The social control theory

The social control theory holds that poor attachments to parents, to important institutions such as the school, and to one's peers may facilitate and create violent and aggressive behaviour during childhood, adolescence or adulthood (Conklin, 2013). Factors such as negative and criminal associations, poor parental involvement and supervision, poor parent-child bonds, absent parental figures, abusive parents, isolation, poor socialisation practices, and poor academic attainment pave the way to criminality and involvement in violent and aggressive behaviour.

2.8.2 The routine activities theory

According to the routine activities theory, the following three elements are necessary to commit a crime such as armed robbery or vehicle hijacking (Hagan, 2011):

1. a potential offender who inherently has the ability to act violently, to threaten his or her victim(s) and to use lethal force when necessary to achieve the result
2. a suitable target (for example an elderly female who is unarmed, with non-threatening behavioural characteristics)
3. absence of capable guardians (a lack of security systems and/or weapons to defend oneself).

2.8.3 The life-course theory

The life-course theory views a violent and aggressive offender's life from early childhood to adulthood. Various influences (violence and criminality), interpersonal relationships, socialisation, interactions, a support structure, compliance to conventional norms and values (law-abiding behaviour), meaningful long-term goals (education and marriage), and possible employment determine how a person will mature in life.

Life-time exposure to environmental surroundings such as poverty, abuse, absent parents, parental violence and/or criminality, and low educational achievement may create inner conflict and unresolved emotional issues within a person. How one internalises these occurrences may direct one's propensity to engage in violent and aggressive behaviour and crime (Schmalleger, 2011).

2.8.4 The feminist theory

The feminist theory concentrates on socio-political settings to explain violence against women. The core notion of this theory is vested in male power and control and society's ignorance of gender equality. Domestic violence is believed to have emanated from a patriarchal society in which male dominance over women is accepted. Interpersonal violence (that occurs in intimate relationships) is the result of male oppression of women and the batterer's low self-esteem, poor self-control, and personal insecurities – behaviour that is (again) entrenched in a patriarchal society. Women's status in society and better employment opportunities threaten patriarchally inclined men who turn to violent behaviour to control women (Dobash & Dobash, 2003).

CRITICAL REFLECTION

Consult scientific books and publications on criminological theories and find an applicable integrated or life-course theory to explain the behaviour of the so-called 'Modimolle Monster'.

Conclusion

This chapter has reviewed why South Africa is so violent. There seems to be consensus that South Africa is known for its unacceptable high rates of crime and violence. The chapter examined the rationale behind violent offending behaviour, and analysed various South African research on this phenomenon.

The research suggests that the reasons for violence and violent crime in South Africa are multiple and interconnected with a range of political–historical, environmental, social, and individual factors. Violence in South Africa is influenced by the interaction of factors from within, and between, explanations, such as the colonial history and the apartheid legacy of the country, which infused a so-called 'culture of violence' in society. Other explanations – such as substance use and abuse, social exclusion, firearms, gangs, fractured socialisation, and the learned nature of violence – were briefly reviewed in order to sensitise the reader to violent crime in South Africa.

The chapter ended by discussing four theories that attempt to explain violent and aggressive behaviour, to illustrate the link between violence and criminality.

Critical thinking questions

1. Is the notion of a 'culture of violence' still relevant and applicable to South Africa today?
2. Why are so many forms of gratuitous violence linked with brutality and sadism in South Africa?
3. Which cultures in South Africa can you identify that endorse and facilitate gender attitudes and roles that are violence prone and conducive to violence towards women in South Africa?
4. What other personality traits and/or tendencies can you identify from the media snippet about the so-called 'Modimolle Monster'?
5. Access the following and read more on the media and violent crime, and violent crime per se, in South Africa:
   - Coetzer, P. (2013). *Leadership: violent crime in South Africa*. Retrieved July 19, 2013, from http://www.leadershiponline.co.za/articles/violent-crime-in-south-africa.
   - Lancaster, L. (2013). *Is South Africa an inherently violent country*? Retrieved July 19, 2013, from http://www.polity.org.za/article/ is-south-africa-an-inherently-violent-country-.

References

Altbeker, A. (2005). Puzzling statistics: is South Africa really the world's crime capital? *SA Crime Quarterly, 11*, 1–8.

Bezuidenhout, C. (2011). *A southern African perspective on fundamental criminology*. Cape Town: Pearson Education South Africa.

Bonnette a believable witness – judge. (2013, July 15). *News24*. Retrieved July 24, 2013, from http://www.news24.com/SouthAfrica /News/Bonnette-a-believable-witness-judge-20130715.

Bruce, D. (2006). Racism, self-esteem and violence in SA: gaps in the NCPS' explanation? *SA Crime Quarterly, 17*, 31–37.

Bruce, D. (2010a). 'The ones in the pile were the ones going down': the reliability of violent crime statistics. *SA Crime Quarterly, 31*, 9–17.

Bruce, D. (2010b). Anger, hatred, or just heartlessness? Defining gratuitous violence. *SA Crime Quarterly, 34*, 13–20.

Burger, J., Gould, C., & Newham, G. (2010). The state of crime in South Africa: an analysis of the SAPS crime statistics for 2009/10. *SA Crime Quarterly, 34*, 3–12.

Cilliers, S. (2014, April 13). Ma van Zirk se slagoffer wil eis. Maatskaplike werker 'was te onervare vir Bergh-saak'. *Rapport*, p. 9.

Conklin, J. E. (2013). *Criminology* (11th ed.). Upper Saddle River, NJ: Pearson.

Dastile, N. P. (2010). Black female offending in post-apartheid South Africa. *Acta Criminologica, 1*(special edition), 95–106.

Davies, P., & MacPherson, K. (2011). *Why is crime in South Africa so violent? A rapid evidence assessment*. Oxford: Evidentia.

DeLisi, M., & Conis, P. J. (2012). *Violent offenders: theory, research, policy and practice* (2nd ed.). Burlington: Jones & Bartlett Learning.

Dixon, R. (2013). South Africa: Man joins vigilante mob, which burns his son alive. Retrieved April 16, 2014, from http://www.latimes.com/world/worldnow/la-fg-wn-south-africa-vigilantes-20131105,0,3268795.story#axzz2z4N9Yes8.

Dobash, R. P., & Dobash, R. E. (2003). *Violence in intimate relationships*. London: Kluwer.

Frank, C. (2005). Young guns: children in organised armed violence. *SA Crime Quarterly, 14*, 11–15.

Global Peace Index (GPI). (2013). Retrieved July 20, 2013, from http://www.visionofhumanity.org/pdf/gpi /2013_Global_Peace_Index_Report.pdf.

GunSite South Africa. (2014). Another farm attack last night 3 April 2014 – Ermelo, Mpumalanga. Retrieved April 16, 2014, from http://www.gunsite.co.za/forums/showthread.php?46379-Another-farm-attack-last-night-3-April-2014-Ermelo-Mpumalanga.

Hagan, F. E. (2011). *Introduction to criminology: theories, methods and criminal behaviour*. California: Sage Publications.

Harris, G. T., Hilton, N. Z., & Rice, M. E. (2011). Explaining the frequency of intimate partner violence by male perpetrators: do attitude, relationship, and neighborhood variables add to antisociality? *Criminal Justice and Behavior, 38*(4), 309–331.

Hawkins, J. D., Herrenkohl, T. I., Farrington, D. P., Brewer, D., Catalano, R. F., Harachi, T. W., & Cothern, L. (2000). Predictors of youth violence. U.S. Department of Justice. Office of Justice Programmes. Office of Juvenile Justice and Delinquency Prevention. *Juvenile Justice Bulletin*, April, 1–10.

Hesselink, A. E. (2013, January 11). *Monitor: 'Die Van Heerden's moord: Is misdadigers in Suid-Afrika toenemend brutaal, onnodig aggressief en wreed?'* [RSG radio station interview]. Retrieved July 24, 2013, from http://.rsg.co.za/images/upload/sound/klanke/ 20130111 _MONITOR_MOORDE.mp3.

Hesselink, A. E., Herbig, F. J. W., Swart, D. N., Victor-Zietsman, M., Schoeman, M., Morodi, L. R., ... de Neuilly Rice, M. (2009). *Contemporary criminological issues: only study guide for 306N*. Pretoria: University of South Africa (Unisa).

Hesselink-Louw, A. E. (2004). *Criminological assessment of prison inmates: a constructive mechanism towards offender rehabilitation* (Unpublished doctoral thesis). University of South Africa (Unisa), Pretoria.

Hesselink-Louw, A. (2005). The significance of a criminological report in understanding contributory factors to aggressive and violent behaviour: a case study analysis. *Acta Criminologica, 18*(1), 54–67.

Hesselink, A. & Prinsloo, J. (2011). Sex offender assessment procedures: a South African comparison. *Journal of Psychology in Africa (JPA), 21*(3), 451–454.

Holtmann, B. (2008). Why law enforcement is not enough: lessons from the Central Karoo on breaking the cycle of crime and violence. *SA Crime Quarterly, 23*, 13–20.

Institute for Security Studies (ISS) Fact Sheet. (2011/12). *Explaining the official crime statistics for 2011/12*. Pretoria: ISS.

Kotzé 'inherently evil'. (2013, July 17). *News24*. Retrieved July 24, 2013, from http://www.news24.com/SouthAfrica/News/Kotze-inherently-evil-20130717.

Lancaster, L. 2013. *Is South Africa an inherently violent country?* Crime and Justice Hub Manager, Governance Crime and Justice Division, Institute for Security Studies (ISS), Pretoria. ISS (Ed.). Retrieved July 29, 2013, from http://www.polity.org.za/article/is-south-africa-an-inherently-violent-country-.

Loots, S., & Louw, D. (2011). Antisocial personalities: measuring prevalence among offenders in South Africa. *SA Crime Quarterly, 36*, p. 31–36.

Louw-Caarstens, M. (2013, May 30). 'Lewenslank nadat hy sewejarige herhaaldelik verkrag.' *Beeld*, p. 12.

Modimolle co-accused HIV+, court hears. (2013, July 11). *News24*. Retrieved July 24, 2013, from http://www.news24.com/SouthAfrica /News/Modimolle-co-accused-HIV-court-hears-20130711.

'Modimolle monster' blamed wife, says friend. (2012, November 27). *IOLNews*. Retrieved July 24, 2013, from http://www.iol.co.za/news/ crime-courts/modimolle-monster-blamed-wife-says-friend-1.1431655.

MODIMOLLE Monster Johan Kotze was today convicted on charges of murdering his stepson as well as kidnapping, raping and severely assaulting his former wife Ina Bonette. (2013, July 15). *The Citizen*. Retrieved July 24, 2013, from http://www.citizen.co.za/citizen/ content /en/citizen/local-news?oid=448442&sn=Detail&pid=334&-Modimolle-monster--found-guilt.

'Modimolle monster's' accountability to be disputed. (2013, April 16). *Daily News*. Retrieved July 24, 2013, from http://www.iol.co.za/dailynews/news/modimolle-monster-s-accountability-to-be-disputed-1.1500897.

'Modimolle monster' testimony perhaps altered: court told. (2013, April 24). *The Times*. Retrieved July 24, 2013, from http://www.timeslive.co.za/local/2013/04/24/Modimolle-monster-testimony-perhaps-altered-court-told.

Matipa, P. (2014, April 11). Taxibaas by kantoor geskiet. Hy sou glo gou roete bykry. *Beeld*, p. 5.

Muňos, L. C., & Frick, P. J. (2012). Callous-unemotional traits and their implications for understanding and treating aggressive and violent youths. *Criminal Justice and Behavior*, *39*(6), 794–813.

Office of the Presidency. (2010). *The outcomes approach*. Pretoria: Office of the Presidency. Retrieved July 24, 2013, from http://www.thepresidency.gov.za/pebble.asp?relid=1905.

Pauw, J. (2014, April 13). Het ander mans Anene aangeval? *Rapport*, p. 6.

Piquero, A. R., Theobald, D., & Farrington, D. P. (2014). The overlap between offending trajectories, criminal violence, and intimate partner violence. *International Journal of Offender Therapy and Comparative Criminology*, *58*(3), 286–302.

Prinsloo, J. (2012). The problematic nature of the South African crime context. *Acta Criminologica*, *25*(1), 69–78.

Ratele, K. (2010). Watch your man: young black males at risk of homicidal violence. *SA Crime Quarterly*, *33*, 19–24.

Redpath, J. (2010). Using data to make a difference: understanding crime through victimisation surveys. *SA Crime Quarterly*, *32*: 9–17.

South Africa (Republic). South African Police Service (SAPS) (2012). *Crime Statistics. April 2011–March 2012*. Retrieved July 21, 2013, from http://www.saps.gov.za/statistics/reports/crimestats/2012/crime_stats.htm.

Schmalleger, F. (2011). *Criminology today*. Englewood Cliffs, NJ: Prentice Hall.

Silber, G., & Geffen, N. (2009). Race, class and violent crime in South Africa. *SA Crime Quarterly*, *30*, 35–42.

Smith, L. (2014). South Africa: vigilante mob in Rustenburg burn Lesotho foreigner alive. Retrieved April 16, 2013, from http://www.ibtimes.co.uk/south-africa-vigilante-mob-rustenburg-burn-lesotho-foreigner-alive-1435974.

Swogger, M. T., Walsh, Z., Kosson, D. S., Cashman-Brown, S., & Caine, E. D. (2012). Self-reported childhood physical abuse and perpetration of intimate partner violence: the moderating role of psychopathic traits. *Criminal Justice and Behavior*, *39*(7), 910–922.

The so-called 'Modimolle Monster' Johan Kotzé and all co-accused have been found guilty of kidnapping and the gang rape of Ina Bonnette in the North Gauteng High Court in Pretoria on Monday. (2013, July 15). *News24*. Retrieved July 24, 2013, from http://www.news24.com/SouthAfrica/News/Kotze-found-guilty-20130715.

Van Rooyen, F. (2014, April 14). Man dood ná aanval met byl. Rooftog net ná noodvergadering. *Beeld*, p. 1.

Vos, U. (2013, April 17). Geweld by skole neem toe, wys studie. *Beeld*, p. 9.

Zwecker, W. (2013, May 30). Aanval op gesin: seun sal verhoor kan volg. *Beeld*, p. 4.

Zuma, J. (2013). Address by President Jacob Zuma on the occasion of the Official Opening of The National House of Traditional Leaders, 7 March 2013. Retrieved September 8, 2014, from http://www.thepresidency.gov.za/pebble.asp?relid=15021.

Chapter 3

African sea piracy: A twenty-first century enigma

H Fouche

3.1 Introduction

Piracy is a crime. Burnett (2002) describes the ingredients of piracy as hijackings, hostage taking, violent acts of robbery, and cold-blooded murder on the high seas. The difference between piracy and equivalent crimes committed in the terrestrial domain is that piracy occurs at sea. Piracy, however, is subject to the limitation that, in terms of its definition by international convention, it can be committed only on the high seas. The high seas, in turn, are by definition an area beyond the jurisdiction of any state and subject to universal jurisdiction. Should crimes such as the hijacking of a ship, armed robbery, assault or murder be committed within the territorial seas of a state, the perpetrators could not be charged for the crime of piracy, but for crimes under the common law or statute law. Thus a distinction is made as to which charges can be applied in the different jurisdictions.

This chapter will discuss the various maritime zones and will examine the methods that pirates utilise to attack ships on the high seas, as well as the methods employed by robbers to attack ships not sailing on the high seas but in coastal and inland waters. Their motivation will be scrutinised and explained in terms of criminological theories.

Burnett's description of piracy is borne out by a report on the human cost of piracy in 2011. The report notes that in 2011, some 4 514 people were subjected to violent crimes by Somali pirates alone, and that of these 1 206 were held hostage for an average of eight months. The report also reveals that 35 hostages died during 2011; 174 hostages experienced extreme abuse, 371 were used as human shields, and 144 were subjected to abuse and used as human shields (Hurlburt, 2012).

For centuries universal jurisdiction over piracy has been accepted under international law and constitutes an established principle of the world community (Shaw, 1997). This implies that any state may take action against an act of piracy. This makes piracy an exceptional crime in international law, where emphasis is placed upon the sovereignty and the jurisdiction of each state within its own sovereign territory (Shaw, 1997). During the twentieth century most of the attacks against ships took place in territorial waters or inland waters, which constitutes the sovereign territory of a state (Dubner, 2004). In the twenty-first century the world experienced a resurgence of piracy, which in terms of international law can be committed only in areas beyond the jurisdiction of any state.

The problem which arose as a result of the resurgence of this age-old phenomenon was that states were reluctant to prosecute cases of piracy due to, amongst other things, a purported lack of jurisdiction. It swiftly became apparent that to overcome this dilemma, states intending to prosecute pirates would be required not only to criminalise piracy in their domestic legislation, but also to create a framework to extend the jurisdiction of their national courts beyond their sovereign territory. There are no obvious solutions to the jurisdiction and prosecution dilemma; how to deal effectively with piracy remains a tantalising enigma which eludes the world community. In the twenty-first century the total cost of piracy to the global economy has reached staggering proportions. It is estimated to be in the region of between US$7 billion and US$12 billion per year (Oceans Beyond Piracy, 2010).

Piracy is seriously threatening to disrupt the sea lanes of communication around the African continent, and the sea lanes of communication between Africa and Europe. The United Nations (UN) regards the problem of piracy as so serious that it issues United Nations Security Council resolutions on dealing with the problem of piracy off the African continent under article seven of the UN Charter, which applies to situations which pose a threat to international security. The South African Minister of Defence stated in 2011, during a meeting to discuss regional defence, that piracy is potentially one of the most serious problems facing regional security, and that southern Africa's major trade artery in the east coast of Africa is becoming increasingly vulnerable (South Africa (SA), 2011).

3.2 Definitions/key concepts

Whether an attack against a ship in the maritime domain can be classified, and thus prosecuted, as piracy or armed robbery is determined by the particular position where the attack took place. In terms of international law, littoral states have the right to claim different zones at sea in which varying degrees of jurisdiction are applicable. Added to the dilemma of the position of the ship at the time of the attack determining which crime the perpetrators can be prosecuted for, is the nature of the domain itself. At sea there are no mountains, rivers or fences to demarcate borders. These unique features impact on the interpretation of the legal definition of the purported offence. A further feature is that on the high seas, an area to which no state may lay claim, there is no law to enforce. Burnett (2002) describes the situation on the high seas as a state of anarchy where the only semblance of law is the moral authority that humans maintain within themselves.

3.2.1 Piracy

Piracy is any illegal act of violence or detention or depredation committed for private ends, on the high seas by the crew or passengers of a private ship, against another ship or against persons or property on board such a ship. The motive must be for private gain and the attack must be launched from a private ship against another ship. The attack must take place on the high seas or in an area beyond the jurisdiction of any state. The punishment for the crime of piracy, in many jurisdictions, is life imprisonment.

3.2.1.1 Application of piracy legislation by South and East African states

South Africa's definition of piracy is in agreement with the United Nations Convention on the Law of the Sea (UNCLOS) definition of piracy in article 101 (UNCLOS, 1982). The UNCLOS and South African definition of piracy contains the elements that piracy must involve an illegal act of violence, detention or depredation, and that piracy is committed on the high seas or in a place outside the jurisdiction of any state. Thus in South African law, piracy can only be committed on the high seas, or in a place outside the jurisdiction of any state. The area beyond the territorial waters of South Africa, for the crime of piracy, is considered to be an area beyond the jurisdiction of any state. Perpetrators of any act within the territorial waters, which may be considered piratical in nature, such as an armed robbery of a ship, cannot be charged with piracy. Such an act would have to be dealt with by the common laws or statute laws in force in South Africa.

The situation and interpretation in South African law is similar to those on other coastal states on the African continent. Some states, however, such as Kenya and Tanzania, have incorporated the international definition of piracy as well as the offence of maritime violence, as defined in article 3 of the Convention for the Suppression of Unlawful Acts against the Safety of Maritime Navigation (SUA), in their merchant shipping acts,[1] thus covering piratical acts within their territorial waters and beyond the boundaries of their sovereign territory.

Since 2006 Kenya has dealt with 154 suspected pirates; 105 accused were convicted, 17 accused acquitted (in 1 case), and 32 accused are in custody pending trial in 3 cases out of a total of 18 cases (Imbali, 2013).

CRITICAL REFLECTION Establish the penalty for piracy in South African, Kenyan and Tanzanian legislation. Do you believe that the punishment suits the crime? Explain your answer.

3.2.2 Robbery

Burchell and Milton (2000) define robbery as theft of property by intentionally using violence to induce submission to the taking of it from another. They describe the nature and purpose of robbery as theft accompanied with an assault. According to Snyman (1995, p. 474) it is customary to describe the crime of robbery briefly as 'theft by violence'[2] and, although incomplete, such a description does reflect the essence of the crime of robbery. The International Maritime Organisation (IMO) defines 'armed robbery against ships' as follows:

> **2.2 'Armed robbery against ships' means any of the following acts:**
> **.1 any illegal act of violence or detention or any act of depredation, or threat thereof, other than an act of piracy, committed for private ends and directed against a ship or against persons or property on board such a ship, within a State's internal waters, archipelagic waters and territorial sea;**
> **.2 any act of inciting or of intentionally facilitating an act described above (International Maritime Organisation (IMO), 2009).**[2]

The IMO definition of armed robbery has so far been used only in non-treaty IMO documents and makes provision for a wide spectrum of acts which could be classified under armed robbery against ships. Such attacks could include opportunist attacks which target the ship's safe, cash, personal valuables, and anything else that is portable and easily converted to cash. It could also include attacks that are premeditated, highly sophisticated, and extremely violent. Another variant of armed robbery against ships is the hijacking of vessels and kidnapping of crew for ransom (Meija & Mukherjee, 2004).

1 Kenya Merchant shipping Act, 2009. Art 369 Piracy; art 370 Hijacking and destroying of ships Tanzania Merchant Shipping Act, 2003. Art 341 Piracy; art 342 Hijacking and destruction of ships; art 343 Threats and ancillary offences; art 344 Delivery of persons who committed piracy and hijacking to Tanzania for prosecution.

2 Resolution A.1025(26), adopted on 2 December 2009.

3.2.3 Maritime zones

In the case of piracy it is essential to the elements of the crime to establish where the ship was at the time of the attack, to determine whether the perpetrators can be charged with piracy or whether it is necessary to apply charges other than piracy. Bearing in mind that piracy can be committed only on the high seas or in a place outside the jurisdiction of any state, it is necessary to understand the delineation of the sea into maritime zones. The UNCLOS permits littoral states to claim certain zones and demarcates the zones as:

3.2.3.1 Internal waters

Article 8 of the UNCLOS (UNCLOS, 1982) describes internal waters as waters on the landward side of the baseline of the territorial sea as forming part of the internal waters of the state.

3.2.3.1.1 Application

In accordance with the terms of international law the South African Maritime Zones Act (SA, 1994) defines and claims as internal waters, all waters landward of the baselines and all harbours. Any law in force in South Africa, including the common law, will apply in the internal waters and the airspace above the internal waters (SA, 1994).
The main legal reason for a foreign vessel to enter internal waters would be to enter a port. Coastal states, however, have the right to close ports or refuse entry. The right to exit from internal waters and ports, in particular, is also subject to the approval of the coastal state and can be withheld. An example of this is where a vessel has an outstanding account or for other legal reasons (SA, 2003). Perpetrators of attacks against ships in this maritime zone cannot be charged with piracy, but with common law crimes such as assault, robbery, and murder or under any other law in force in South Africa.

3.2.3.2 Territorial sea

Article 3 of the UNCLOS determines that every state has the right to establish the breadth of its territorial sea up to a limit not exceeding 12 nautical miles, measured from the baselines determined in accordance with the convention. The convention describes in article 5 the normal baseline for measuring the breadth of the territorial sea as the low-water line along the coast as marked on large-scale charts officially recognised by the coastal state.

3.2.3.2.1 Application and governance of territorial seas

In accordance with the terms of international law the South African Maritime Zones Act (SA, 1994) defines and claims in section 4 as territorial waters for South Africa the sea within a distance of 12 nautical miles from the baselines. The act states that any law in force in South Africa, including the common law, shall also apply in its territorial waters and the airspace above its territorial waters and that the right of innocent passage shall exist in the territorial waters. In terms of section 14 of the Maritime Zones Act (SA, 1994), the act also applies to the Prince Edward Islands. South Africa's maritime territory thus consists of two separate parts:

1. The mainland part that extends from the Orange River Mouth on the border with Namibia to Ponto de Orro on the border with Mozambique.
2. The second part that consists of the offshore area around Prince Edward and Marion islands, which are situated 2 300 kilometres southeast of Cape Town in the Southern

Ocean (SA, 2003). The responsibility to properly govern the territorial sea can be equated with the governance of the terrestrial territory in that both can be considered sovereign territory.

3.2.3.2.2 Obligations of states in relation to innocent passage in territorial seas

Article 19 of the UNCLOS describes passage through territorial seas as innocent so long as it is not prejudicial to the peace, good order or security of the coastal state. Any activity not having a direct bearing on passage is considered prejudicial to the peace, good order or security. The responsibility to properly govern the territorial sea thus has the added dimension of obligations to shipping on passage through territorial waters. In terms of international law it can be expected of coastal states to ensure an environment in which seafarers and other people active at sea can go about their lawful business in circumstances of safety, security, and fairness (SA, 2003).

Jacobsson (2001) points out that ships of all states enjoy the right of innocent passage, transit passage and archipelagic sea-lanes passage in areas under the sovereignty of a coastal state, and that armed robbery against ships seriously threatens these fundamental rights. Should a coastal state fail to provide the security, by way of policing its territorial waters, for such innocent passage, it would alienate the international community and trade would be disrupted or may be suspended. In 2003, attacks against ships in the Malacca Strait, through which one-third of the global shipping trade and one-half of the world's cargoes pass, reached unprecedented levels. The inability of the states bordering the Malacca Strait to ensure innocent passage to ships transiting the strait caused the joint war committee of the London-based insurance companies to classify the Malacca Strait as a war zone in terms of risk, which resulted in dramatically increased insurance premiums (Whaley, 2009).

Another case in point where a state was unable to ensure innocent passage commenced in 2005 in waters off Somalia, when food aid sent by sea to Somalia by the World Food Programme was disrupted. In such instances states usually join forces to take coordinated action against the perpetrators. This was the case when states bordering the Strait of Malacca (Singapore, Malaysia, and Indonesia) launched coordinated naval patrols in 2004 to stamp out piracy (Yale Global Online, 2013). In the case of Somalia in 2008, the navies of states and several coalitions commenced joint patrols off the coast of Somalia to combat piracy in this region. Somalia's inability to ensure innocent passage through its territorial waters was as a result of the collapse of the state and the consequent absence of a functioning criminal justice system. This resulted in the United Nations Security Council (UNSC) issuing a resolution permitting any state to enter the territorial waters of Somalia in pursuit of pirates (UNSC, 2008).

CASE STUDY: Purported attacks in territorial waters

This case study examines three actual incidents of piracy and armed robbery against ships reported by the International Chamber of Commerce's International Maritime Bureau (ICC-IMB) to have taken place in South Africa in 2000, 2001, and 2003. The three incidents are repeated verbatim as they were reported in the ICC-IMB annual reports for *Piracy and Armed Robbery Against Ships*.

On 03/09/2000 at Berth no 8, Maydon Wharf, Durban. While berthed and discharging two pirates armed with guns boarded and stole ship's stores from the general cargo vessel *Agios Fanourios* (ICC, 2001, p. 55).

On 24/06/2001 near Port Edward. While underway, a speedboat attempted to come alongside the general cargo vessel *Kota Manis*. The crew mustered on deck and the ship altered course to avoid the boat. The pirates aborted the attempted boarding (ICC, 2002, p. 68).

On 19/11/2003 near Port Shepstone. While underway, six pirates in a speedboat trailed the refrigerated cargo vessel *Linares* and attempted to board her. The crew raised the alarm and activated fire hoses. The pirates aborted the attempted boarding and fled (ICC, 2004, p. 93).

CRITICAL REFLECTION

Which of the three incidents reported in the ICC-IMB annual reports in the case study headed 'Purported attacks in territorial waters' would qualify as acts of piracy in terms of South Africa's national laws? Discuss each incident, and in your answer provide an explanation as to the reasons for your answers.

3.2.3.3 Contiguous zone

Article 33 of the UNCLOS permits a coastal state to claim a zone contiguous to its territorial sea, which may not extend beyond 24 nautical miles from the baselines from which the breadth of the territorial sea is measured, in which it may exercise control over infringement of its customs, fiscal, immigration or sanitary laws.

3.2.3.3.1 Application

In terms of section 5 of the Maritime Zones Act (SA, 1994), South Africa claims the sea beyond the territorial waters, but within a distance of 24 nautical miles from the baselines, as the contiguous zone of South Africa. The act states that within the contiguous zone and the airspace above it, South Africa shall have the right to exercise all the powers which may be considered necessary to prevent contravention of any fiscal law or any customs, immigration or sanitary law, and to make such contravention punishable.

As the Maritime Zones Act is also applicable to the Prince Edward Islands, a contiguous zone would also be created around Prince Edward and Marion islands. The territorial sea is now generally accepted as 12 nautical miles with the exclusive economic zone (EEZ) beyond that (subsection 3.2.3.4 below will discuss EEZs).

Although the EEZ overlaps the contiguous zone geographically, the UNCLOS still ascribes enforcement, jurisdiction of customs, fiscal, sanitary and immigration laws in the contiguous zone that is not included in EEZ jurisdiction. Thus, while the zones may overlap geographically, they are functionally distinct (SA, 2003). In terms of article 101 of the UNCLOS, which defines piracy, the contiguous zone is considered to be an area beyond the jurisdiction of any state. Perpetrators of an attack against a ship in this zone could thus be charged with piracy.

3.2.3.4 Exclusive economic zone

The concept of an EEZ was originally put forward by Kenya in 1971. The zone is a reflection of a desire by developing states to gain greater control over the economic resources off their coasts, which were being exploited by developed countries (SA, 2003). Part V of the UNCLOS permits states to establish an EEZ, not exceeding 200 nautical miles from the baselines from which the breadth of the territorial sea is measured, in which that coastal state may exercise sovereignty over the natural resources in that EEZ.

3.2.3.4.1 Application

In terms of section 7 of the Maritime Zones Act (SA, 1994), South Africa claims the sea beyond the territorial waters but within a distance of 200 nautical miles from the baselines, as its EEZ. The act states that subject to any other law South Africa shall have, in respect of all the natural resources in the EEZ, the same rights and powers as it has in respect of its territorial waters. As the Maritime Zones Act is also applicable to the Prince Edward Islands, an EEZ would also be created around Prince Edward and Marion islands. The area of the EEZ covers 1.3 million square kilometres (SA, 2003).

The legal nature of the EEZ has been the subject of considerable debate. One view is that it should become sovereign territory. A fear of so-called 'creeping jurisdiction', however, led to the view that this zone should retain the status of the high seas but with defined rights for coastal states. In the case of South Africa, as with other coastal states, these rights are amplified in article 56 of the UNCLOS, and they involve the right to explore and exploit, conserve, and manage natural resources, whether living (such as fish and plants) or non-living (such as oil, gas and diamonds). As far as policing and maintaining good order are concerned, there are no general rights, but specific rights (such as enforcing immigration, health, customs, and certain fiscal laws and controlling installations) do exist (SA, 2003). For the purpose of prosecuting and charging perpetrators of attacks against ships with piracy, the EEZ would be considered to be an area beyond the jurisdiction of any state.

3.2.3.5 Continental shelf

Article 76 of the UNCLOS (UNCLOS, 1982) defines the continental shelf of a coastal state as comprising the seabed and the subsoil of the submarine areas that extend beyond its territorial sea throughout the natural prolongation of its land territory to the outer edge of the continental margin, or to a distance of 200 nautical miles from the baselines from which the breadth of the territorial sea is measured where the outer edge of the continental margin does not extend up to that distance.

3.2.3.5.1 Application

In accordance with the terms of international law, South Africa defines the extent of its continental shelf in section 8 of the Maritime Zones Act (SA, 1994). In terms of section 8, South Africa also deems the continental shelf to be unalienated state land for the purpose of the exploration and exploitation of natural resources. In terms of section 14, the act also applies to the Prince Edward Islands.

The continental shelf is rich in natural resources. Developing technology is making it possible to exploit resources at increasingly greater distances from the coast and at greater depths (SA, 2003). The type of exploration that will in future be developed and carried out in this extended state land will include oil and gas exploitation, for which platforms will be erected in the ocean far off the coast. Diamonds are also exploited using specially developed vessels to suck diamond bearing gravel off the sea bed. These vessels, when in operation, and the static platforms deep in the ocean may, in future, become prime potential targets for pirates. If such installations are attacked, the issue of jurisdiction in terms of arrest, investigation, and prosecution of perpetrators will become pertinent.

3.2.3.6 High seas

Article 86 of the UNCLOS defines the high seas as all parts of the sea that are not included in the EEZ, in the territorial sea or in the internal waters of a state, or in the archipelagic waters of an archipelagic state. Article 87 declares the high seas open to all states, whether coastal or land locked. Article 87 describes these freedoms as comprising, amongst other things:

- freedom of navigation
- freedom of overflight
- freedom to lay submarine cables and pipelines
- freedom to construct artificial and other structures permitted under international law
- freedom of fishing
- freedom of scientific research.

All states may thus enjoy the freedom of the high seas.

CHECK POINT

- The crime of piracy can be committed only in an area outside the jurisdiction of any state.
- It has to be for private ends.
- This will exclude terrorism which is motivated by political gain.
- Piratical acts committed within the territorial and inland waters of states will be dealt with under the common law or statute law.
- Piracy is a serious offence and it is desirable to charge a perpetrator with piracy, rather than under the common law or municipal law with a lesser offence.

3.3 Extent of sea piracy and armed robbery

3.3.1 Worldwide reported incidents

Piracy and armed robbery against ships occur in maritime locations throughout the world. Piracy is a crime which moves from place to place, creating new hotspots as it moves. In the last century South East Asia bore the brunt of attacks against ships after piracy had moved there from the Caribbean Islands, which were home to pirates in the days when ships were driven by sail through the power of the wind. In 2005, Africa became the new hotspot for piracy. Since 2013, however, incidents in Indonesia have been on the rise to such an extent that it may soon become the hotspot for piracy again. In the case of Africa, interventions by the combined naval forces of various states and coalitions off the coast of Somalia, where most of the attacks took place between 2005 and 2012, forced pirates to shift their field of operations and change their methods.

The ICC-IMB Piracy Reporting Centre began recording incidents of piracy and armed robbery against ships in 1992 (see Table 3.1, which shows statistics accessed from the reports of the ICC-IMB).

Table 3.1 Incidents recorded by ICC-IMB

Year	Number of incidents
1993	103
1994	90
1995	188
1996	228
1997	248
1998	202
1999	300
2000	469
2001	335
2002	370
2003	445
2004	325
2005	276
2006	239
2007	263
2008	293
2009	410
2010	445
2011	439
2012	297

Comment: Piracy reached a five-year low in 2012, compared to the number of incidents reported for 2011. Worldwide figures were brought down by a massive reduction in Somali piracy. East and West Africa, however, remain the worst affected areas, having experienced 150 attacks in 2012 (ICC, 2013).

When the figures in Table 3.1 are considered, it must be borne in mind that they include incidents of armed robbery as well as incidents of piracy. Armed robbery usually occurs at anchorages or in the roadstead and is often conducted by perpetrators armed with hand guns or knives. Worldwide, during 2010, guns were used in 100 incidents, compared to knives in 35 incidents (ICC, 2011).

In 2010 the use of guns to assist in committing crime in the maritime domain thus exceeded the use of knives, which had hitherto been prevalent. At the same time in the terrestrial domain, in crimes of a similar nature (aggravated robberies/

street robberies), a similar trend was observed. The South African Police Service (SAPS) 2008/2009 annual report recorded surprise at a finding that guns had become the weapon of choice (above knives) in street robberies, as knives were traditionally the preferred weapons used in street robbery (SAPS, 2009). This tends to indicate that during robberies, whether committed terrestrially or against ships alongside quays or at anchor, guns have become the weapons of choice, and that attacks of this nature now tend to be more violent with a high risk to seafarers using ports and anchorages. South Africa cannot afford to allow increasingly violent terrestrial crime to spill over into the maritime domain.

Many of these attacks are unreported, particularly in South East Asia (Potgieter, 2012). The IMB has reported in several of its quarterly and annual reports that it is aware of incidents that have not been reported by ships' masters and owners to the IMB Piracy Reporting Centre (IMB-PRC). For example, in the ICC-IMB's *Piracy and Armed Robbery Against Ships. Annual Report for the Period 1 January–31 September 2010* (ICC-IMB, 2010) it is noted that intelligence indicated that in July and August alone there were more than 13 unconfirmed incidents in Nigeria. The IMB points out that many operators are reluctant to report attacks on their vessels due to commercial pressures or fear of reprisals upon their next visit (ICC-IMB, 2011). Shipowners may be reluctant to report incidents due to a fear that their vessels will be delayed unduly during the investigation of the incident, or that the insurance rates on their vessel may rise as a result of the reported attack. In West Africa, the underreporting is accredited to little hope of rescue and an increase in insurance premiums if the incident is reported (Maritime Executive, 2013).

CRITICAL REFLECTION

How serious a crime is piracy, and is it on the increase or decrease worldwide? Motivate your answer with particular reference to piracy off the continent of Africa and the implications it holds for South Africa's national interest.

3.3.2 Types of attack

The majority of attacks worldwide occur in territorial waters whilst ships are at anchor, underway or alongside a berth. Relatively few attacks take place in international waters.

3.3.2.1 Opportunity theft

Ships are vulnerable to opportunity theft when they are tied up alongside a quay in port or at anchor (Maritime International Secretariat Services Limited (Marisec), 2004). Many people have access to the ship during this period and may be tempted to steal anything handy if the opportunity presents itself, and they believe that they will not be caught.

Since 2004, states have been required to implement the International Ship and Port Facility Security Code (ISPS Code), the purpose of which is to provide a standardised, consistent framework for evaluating risk, enabling governments to offset changes in threat with changes in vulnerability for ships and port facilities (ISPS Code, 2004). Increased security in ports worldwide due to the application of the code should lead to a reduction in the opportunity for these types of thefts to be committed without detection.

3.3.2.2 Planned robbery

Ships alongside quays, at anchor or underway are targeted for stealing money, crews' personal effects, and ships' equipment. These planned robberies are often carried out by increasingly organised, determined, and well-armed gangs (Marisec, 2004).

Ships tied up alongside are often approached by a small boat from the seaward side and boarded by robbers who climb from the boat up the side and lower the stolen goods into the boat. Ships at anchor are boarded by robbers who climb up the anchor chain from a small boat. An analysis of the incidents recorded by the IMB-PRC reveals a pattern which usually commences with low-level theft, which gradually increases to gangs robbing ships at anchor, progressing to robbery of ships underway near the ports, and eventually escalating to robbery of ships underway in the territorial waters and beyond. In East Africa in the vicinity of the ports of Mombasa in Kenya and Dar es Salaam in Tanzania, ships have been known to have been targeted for their cargo. In these cases perpetrators will carry out the robbery as agents for sellers who have prearranged the sale of the stolen goods on the black market (Lyman & Potter, 2007).

3.2.3 Permanent hijacking

Ships and their cargoes with crews are permanently hijacked; crews are sometimes murdered, cast adrift or held to ransom (Marisec, 2004). These types of attack are planned in advance, with ships being specifically targeted for the value and easy disposal of the cargo, which together with the ship is usually worth millions of US dollars.

The attacks involve trained pirate gangs armed with knives and automatic weapons, who board the vessel carrying false ship's papers, cargo papers and passports. These pirates are capable of operating the vessel without the assistance of the crews, who are intimidated or subjected to violence and, in a few cases, all murdered.

In some cases the entire ship is renamed, recrewed, and made available in the international maritime trade by the pirates (Mukundan, 2004). The ship takes on a fictitious identity and becomes a phantom vessel. It commences a life of crime that typically involves entering into contracts with unsuspecting cargo owners and then stealing, diverting, and selling their cargoes. This cycle is constantly repeated, inflicting huge economic losses on the ship's owners, cargo owners, and marine insurers, exposing the hijacked crew to situations that could result in injury or death (Mejia & Mukherjee, 2004). After 2001 this type of hijacking decreased due to successes by law enforcement agencies in arresting and prosecuting the pirates and recovering the ship and the cargo. Hijacking gangs convicted in India received severe sentences. After this setback with hijackings of merchant ships to steal the ship and cargo, organised crime gangs turned their attention towards softer targets, such as tugs and barges carrying valuable cargo (Mukundan, 2004).

3.3.2.4 Hijacking for ransom

Another form of hijacking occurs when a ship is hijacked and both the ship and the crew are held by the pirates until a ransom for their release is paid to the hijackers. In 2005 this type of hijacking became endemic off the coast of Somalia, with Somali pirates hijacking passing vessels and sailing them to the coast of Somalia, where they would be anchored. Negotiations would then be opened with their owners for the release of the ship and crew on delivery of a ransom.

In 2012 the tide began to turn against the Somali pirates, and by the first quarter of 2013 this type of hijacking off the coast of Somalia had been successfully contained. This was largely due to interdiction by naval vessels, successful prosecution of pirates, and the application of best practices by shipping transiting the area. When pirate activity in one area is contained, it evolves, adapts its method of operation, and shifts to other areas. In contrast to the decrease and containment of the pirate activity off the coast of Somalia, piracy in the Gulf of Guinea rose vertiginously in 2012. Piracy, like terrorism, when displaced from one area to another, is likely to re-emerge in the new area at the same intensity it left off in the last (ICC, 2012; ICC, 2013).

3.3.2.5 Hijacking to steal cargo

A further form of hijacking occurs when a ship is hijacked with the intention of stealing the cargo, after which the ship is abandoned. Many pirate attacks in the Gulf of Guinea are aimed at stealing the cargo of oil from tankers, as well as valuable items from the ship and the crew. The duration of such attacks is typically between 5 and 10 days, after which the vessel and crew are usually released (ICC, 2013).

CRITICAL REFLECTION

Read through the case study about the cargo vessel *Linares*, and then reflect on the questions posed in the critical reflection box that follows. They cover the possible state of mind of the potential victims, their perceptions regarding what they could expect from the local state authorities, and whether any potential crime could reasonably have been expected.

CASE STUDY: Hijacking of cargo vessel *Linares*

On 19 November 2003 a large refrigerated cargo vessel, *Linares*, was steaming in a choppy sea, less than 12 nautical miles off the coast of KwaZulu-Natal in the vicinity of Port Shepstone, a South African coastal village. With the bridge watch changing at noon and the mates handing over the watch, the piracy alarm was suddenly raised by the crew working on deck. The response was a well-rehearsed action in which the fire hoses were unfurled and primed with sea water. A small speedboat with six occupants was approaching the *Linares* at high speed. With the anti-piracy drill in full swing, the crew activated the fire hoses and directed streams of water at the speedboat, causing it to veer off and abandon what was believed by the crew of the *Linares* to be an attempt to board their vessel with the intention to commit robbery. The master reported the incident to the South African Maritime Safety Authority and the International Chamber of Commerce's International Maritime Bureau's Piracy Reporting Centre in Kuala Lumpur, whose key services are, amongst others, to receive from ships reports of suspicious or unexplained craft movements, boarding and armed robbery, and to alert other ships and law enforcement agencies in the area.

The waters off the coast of Africa at that time had experienced 92 actual and attempted attacks on ships since January 2003. Two years earlier, a similar incident to the one experienced by the crew of the *Linares* was recorded at the Piracy Reporting Centre in Kuala Lumpur as having occurred on 24 June 2001, in the same area, off Port Edward, adjacent to Port Shepstone. In this instance the general cargo vessel *Kota Maris* reported an attempted boarding from the occupants of a speedboat. The master altered course and mustered the crew on deck, which caused the speedboat to abort the attempt. In 2003 South Africans had also experienced their share of being on the receiving end of violence during an attack on their ship.

On 15 April a supply ship, *Maersk Shipper*, crewed by South African seamen, and steaming off the coast of Nigeria, was boarded by pirates, who assaulted the crew and hijacked the ship. The owners paid a ransom for their release.

CRITICAL REFLECTION

Was the crew of the *Linares* in 2003 justified in suspecting that they were in danger from robbers/pirates off the South African coast, and what recourse could they have expected from the state in whose waters they were steaming? If the attack had been successful, what charges could have been formulated against the perpetrators, if any?

3.4 Theoretical explanations for piracy

Criminological theory seeks answers to the causes of criminal behaviour. Such theory takes into consideration the characteristics of individuals and society that result in crime (Lyman & Potter, 2007). In seeking an explanation as to why some people commit the crime of piracy and others in similar circumstances do not, one needs to consider, amongst other things, the reasons put forward by the perpetrators themselves to explain and rationalise their behaviour.

According to a United States Congressional Research Service report in 2010 (Piracy off the Horn of Africa, 2010), Somali pirates frequently link their activities to trends such as illegal fishing and dumping in Somali waters, as a result of Somalia's inability to patrol its waters over time. The report concludes that while these explanations may mask the opportunistic piracy of some, reports suggest that illegal fishing and dumping have disrupted Somalia's coastal economy.

3.4.1 Theory of neutralisation

According to the theory of neutralisation, juridical precepts, such as mitigating circumstances in the law – which include concepts such as 'intent', 'self defence', and 'insanity' – are extended beyond their legal bounds to serve as mechanisms to relieve guilt, thus freeing the person to violate norms. Gresham Sykes and David Matza's techniques of neutralisation include:

- denial of responsibility
- denial of injury
- denial of the victim
- condemnation of the condemners
- appeal to higher loyalties (Brown, Esbensen & Geis, 2004).

In the case of Somali pirates, disclaiming of personal accountability for a law violation by attacking a ship may be attributed to a feeling of justification for the attack, due to purported illegal fishing and dumping in their waters. So, too, the denial of injury could be attributed to not being morally wrong. In the case of the victims of piracy, they may be regarded as being blameworthy for the illegal dumping and illegal fishing purported to have been perpetrated by the governments which may control or manage their vessels. By condemning the condemners as being the actual perpetrators, the pirates may believe that, by comparison, their own misconduct is not blameworthy. In appealing to higher loyalties, the pirates may claim that the offence was committed to obtain money to help their families who are starving, as a result of, amongst other reasons, the depletion of their fishing stocks (Brown et al., 2004).

3.4.2 Rational choice theory

According to the rational choice theory, criminal behaviour occurs when an offender decides to risk breaking the law after considering factors such as the need for money, how well the target is protected, and the efficiency of the police force (Siegel, 2003). Rational choice theory suggests that people who commit crimes do so after considering the risk of being caught and punished for the crimes, as well as the rewards of successfully completing the crime. Crimes are committed for a number of reasons, which include economic, psychological, physical, social, and sometimes political motivations.

In the case of the Somali pirates, targets were initially totally unprotected and transiting an area in which there is no functioning police force or criminal justice system. The rewards for successfully completing the crime in these circumstances are exceptionally huge, with one hijacking netting the criminal equivalent of several years' annual income, and little chance of being caught (Lyman & Potter, 2007).

3.4.3 Deterrence theory

If the decision about whether to commit a crime or not is influenced by the risk of getting caught and the consequences, the theory is that the crime which is being contemplated can be controlled by increasing the actual or perceived threat of criminal punishment.

The general deterrence theory is based on Beccaria's equation that the greater the severity, certainty, and speed of legal sanctions, the lower the crime rate (Siegel, 2003). The special deterrence theory holds that the punishment for criminal acts should be severe enough that convicted criminals will be deterred from ever repeating their acts (Lyman & Potter, 2007).

The IMO maintains that the capture, prosecution and sentencing of pirates and perpetrators of armed robbery against ships are probably the most appropriate deterrent actions governments have available against piracy. The maximum punishment for piracy in South African, Kenyan, and Tanzanian legislation is life imprisonment. Such a penalty is sufficient to act as a deterrent for would-be pirates, provided that pirates are brought to court with good evidence for successful prosecution.

3.4.4 The theory of differential association

Edwin Sutherland proposed the theory of differential association in 1934. The theory is that individuals become predisposed toward criminality because of contact with persons that advocate the commission of crime. The theory is that a person will learn and accept the values propagated by those who condone criminality (Hagan, 2011). The principle of this theory is based on, amongst other things, the idea that criminal behaviour is learnt through association within intimate personal groups with persons who are more inclined to violate the law to express their needs as opposed to satisfying their needs by not violating the law (Brown et al., 2004).

Again, transnational crime committed in the maritime domain comes to mind, as often whole coastal communities are involved in either disposing of the black market goods so obtained or in providing succour to the perpetrators. In such a close-knit group, not only is criminality condoned, but the benefits gained from participation are also tangibly visible.

The theories discussed above are by no means exhaustive. There are many more potential theories to explain the behaviour of persons engaging in piracy. Potential explanations may include combining various theories to explain such behaviour.

CRITICAL REFLECTION Consider an alternative criminological theory or combination of theories to those discussed above in section 3.4 of this chapter to explain the behaviour of pirates.

3.5 Jurisdiction and legislation

Because piracy often occurs in international waters, the question arises as to who will exercise jurisdiction to prosecute. Several countries may have interest in a piracy event, including the flag state and the state whose seafarers have been attacked. A factor also to be taken into account would be the location of the incident.

Between 2008 and 2010, 9 out of every 10 pirates arrested by navies patrolling off Somalia were released without being prosecuted (Lang, 2011). One of the reasons for not initiating prosecutions against the arrested pirates was a purported lack of legislation and jurisdiction to prosecute. On 29 March 2012 the Contact Group on Piracy off the Coast of Somalia[3] took note of the difficulty in initiating prosecutions following naval interdiction, and called on the international community to update existing legislation and other mechanisms to ensure that pirates are prosecuted (Contact Group on Piracy off the Coast of Somalia (CGPCS), 2012). The special advisor on legal issues related to piracy off the coast of Somalia also pointed out in his report that the main reason pirates escape punishment can be attributed to the difficulty of assembling evidence for use in court proceedings. The convention criminalising piracy, as well as its forerunner, will now be discussed.

3.5.1 Geneva Convention on the High Seas

On 29 April 1958, the Geneva Convention on the High Seas (Hedley, 2000–2001) was adopted at Geneva, Switzerland, and came into force on 30 September 1962. As of November 1998, 62 parties had ratified the convention. The principal objective of the convention is to establish a regime for the high seas and to preserve the traditional freedom of the high sea, including the freedom of fishing. Article 15 of the convention defines piracy as consisting of any of the following acts:

> **(1) Any illegal acts of violence, detention or any act of depredation, committed for private ends by the crew or passengers of a private ship or a private aircraft, and directed:**
>
> **(a) On the high seas, against another ship or aircraft, or against persons or property on board such ship or aircraft;**
>
> **(b) Against a ship, aircraft, persons or property in a place outside the jurisdiction of any state.**
>
> **(2) Any act of voluntary participation in the operation of a ship or of an aircraft with knowledge of facts making it a pirate ship or aircraft.**
>
> **(3) Any act of inciting or of intentionally facilitating an act described in sub-paragraph 1 or sub-paragraph 2 of this article (United Nations Convention on the High Seas, 1962, pp. 82–103).**

3 CGPCS, 2010. Contact Group on Piracy off the Coast Of Somalia, based on UNSC resolution 1851, held its first meeting in January 2009 and identified, amongst other things, the task for itself to strengthen judicial frameworks for arrest, prosecution and detention of pirates (*Piracy off the Horn of Africa*, 2010).

The 1958 Geneva Convention on the High Seas was largely superseded by the United Nations Convention on the Law of the Sea (UNCLOS), adopted on 10 December 1982 in Montego Bay.

3.5.2 United Nations Convention on the Law of the Sea

The definition of piracy in article 15 of the Geneva Convention on the High Seas was incorporated as article 101 of the UNCLOS. The Geneva Convention on the High Seas, although to a great extent superseded by the UNCLOS, in 1982, remains in force for those states not party to that convention (Hedley, 2000–2001).

The UNCLOS is the basis on which a littoral state's jurisdiction, rights, privileges, and obligations at sea are built. On 23 April 2011 the UNSC issued Resolution 1976 (United Nations Security Council (UNSC), 2011), on the situation in Somalia, in which it reaffirmed that international law – as reflected in the UNCLOS, and in particular in articles 100, 101 and 105 – sets out the legal framework applicable to combating piracy and armed robbery at sea. The resolution also notes with concern that the domestic law of a number of states lacks provisions criminalising piracy and/or procedural provisions for effective criminal prosecution of suspected pirates, and urges all states to criminalise piracy under their domestic law.

Article 100 of the UNCLOS calls on all states to cooperate to the fullest possible extent in the repression of piracy on the high seas or in any other place outside the jurisdiction of any state. Article 101 defines piracy, and article 105 states that on the high seas or in a place outside the jurisdiction of any state, every state may seize a pirate ship, or a ship taken by piracy and under the control of pirates, and arrest the persons and seize the property on board. According to article 105, the courts of the state which carried out the seizure may decide upon the penalties to be imposed, and may also determine the action to be taken with regard to the ships or property, subject to the rights of third parties acting in good faith.

On 29 February 2012, the UNSC issued Resolution 2039 on the situation in the Gulf of Guinea. The resolution reaffirms that the UNCLOS provides the legal framework applicable to combating piracy and armed robbery, and urges states in the region to establish a legal framework for the prevention and repression of piracy and armed robbery at sea. The resolution also calls for the prosecution of persons engaging in those crimes, and punishment of those convicted.

Jack Lang, in his January 2011 report to the secretary-general of the United Nations, points out for effective prosecution, states need to harmonise their national legislation with the definitions of the UNCLOS and to claim universal jurisdiction over acts of piracy (Lang, 2011).

3.5.3 Defence Act (42 of 2002) (South Africa)

In South African legislation, piracy is defined in Section 24 of the Defence Act (SA, 2002) as:

(a) any illegal act of violence or detention, or any act of depredation, committed for private ends by the crew, including the Master, or the passengers of a private ship or a private aircraft, and directed

  (i) on the high seas, against another ship or aircraft, or against persons or property on board such ship or aircraft;

  (ii) against a ship, aircraft, persons or property in a place outside the jurisdiction of any state;

(b) any act of voluntary participation in the operation of a ship or of an aircraft with knowledge of facts making it a ship or aircraft contemplated in subsection (1); and
(c) any act of inciting or of intentionally facilitating an act contemplated in paragraph (a) or (b).

Any act of piracy committed by the crew of a warship or military aircraft, government ship or government aircraft, which has mutinied and taken control of such ship or aircraft, must for purposes of this section be regarded as having been committed by the crew of a private ship or aircraft.

Any person who commits an act of piracy is guilty of an offence, which may be tried in any court in South Africa designated by the Director of Public Prosecutions, and, upon conviction, is liable to a fine or to imprisonment for any period, including life imprisonment.

3.5.4 International Chamber of Commerce International Maritime Bureau

The International Chamber of Commerce International Maritime Bureau (ICC-IMB) is a specialised division of the International Chamber of Commerce. The IMO, in its resolution A 504 (XII) (5) and (9), adopted on 20 November 1981, amongst other things, urged governments and organisations with an interest to cooperate in exchanging information with each other and the IMB, with a view to maintaining and developing a coordinated action in combating maritime fraud. The ICC-IMB, prompted by concern in the shipping industry at the rapidly increasing number of attacks against ships, established the IMB Piracy Reporting Centre (IMB-PRC) in October 1992 in Kuala Lumpur, Malaysia. The services provided by the PRC to all ships include the issuing of daily status reports on piracy and armed robbery against ships; the provision of updates on pirate activity via internet, Twitter and e-mail alerts; and the publication of comprehensive quarterly and annual reports detailing statistics on piracy and armed robbery against ships (ICC-IMB, 2013).

The UNCLOS definition of piracy and the IMO definition of armed robbery are used by the PRC for statistical purposes to cover actual or attempted attacks, whether the ship is berthed, at anchor or at sea. Petty thefts are excluded unless the thieves are armed.

3.5.5 Convention for the Suppression of Unlawful Acts against the Safety of Maritime Navigation

The SUA convention is the second international treaty which provides for action to be taken against persons committing unlawful acts against ships. These include the seizure of ships by force; acts of violence against persons on board ships; and the placing of devices on board a ship which are likely to destroy or damage it. Similar provisions are contained in the SUA Protocol, relating to unlawful acts against fixed platforms located on the continental shelf (IMO, 2006).

The SUA convention lists the following acts which are offences if committed 'unlawfully' and 'intentionally':

> **1 Any person commits an offence within the meaning of this Convention if that person unlawfully and intentionally:**
> **(a) seizes or exercises control over a ship by force or threat thereof or any other form of intimidation; or**
> **(b) performs an act of violence against a person on board a ship if that act is likely to endanger the safe navigation of that ship; or**

(c) destroys a ship or causes damage to a ship or to its cargo which is likely to endanger the safe navigation of that ship; or

(d) places or causes to be placed on a ship, by any means whatsoever, a device or substance which is likely to destroy that ship, or cause damage to that ship or its cargo which endangers or is likely to endanger the safe navigation of that ship; or

(e) destroys or seriously damages maritime navigational facilities or seriously interferes with their operation, if any such act is likely to endanger the safe navigation of a ship; or

(f) communicates information which that person knows to be false, thereby endangering the safe navigation of a ship.

2 **Any person also commits an offence if that person threatens, with or without a condition, as is provided for under national law, aimed at compelling a physical or juridical person to do or refrain from doing any act, to commit any of the offences set forth in paragraphs 1 (b), (c), and**

(e), if that threat is likely to endanger the safe navigation of the ship in question (International Maritime Organisation (IMO), 2005).[4]

With the exception of (f), the offences require that the act is either likely to destroy the ship or is likely to endanger its safe navigation. The offences listed in article 3 do not have to have to take place on the high seas. Perpetrators of a hijacking in the territorial waters of a state could thus be prosecuted for an offence under this section, if it has been incorporated into the domestic law of that state.

In the case of South Africa, section 231(4) of the Constitution of South Africa, 1996 (SA, 1996) provides that any international agreement becomes law in South Africa only when it is enacted into law by national legislation. Article 8 of the SUA convention defines the roles and responsibilities of the master of a ship, the flag state, and the receiving state in delivering any person believed to have committed an offence under article 3 of the convention to the authorities of any other state party to the convention. Article 12 places an obligation on state parties to assist one another in connection with criminal proceedings brought in respect of offences including, amongst others, the hijacking of a ship. The convention further obliges contracting governments to either extradite or prosecute alleged offenders, subject to international law. The convention does not make provision for the offences of theft and robbery.

In February 2005 South Africa passed the Protection of Constitutional Democracy against Terrorist and Related Activities Act (33 of 2004), which gives effect to article 3 of the SUA convention and article 2 or the 2005 protocol to SUA through section 10 and section 6 of the act. Section 10 of the act makes provision for offences relating to hijacking a ship or endangering safety of maritime navigation. Section 6 of the act makes provision for offences relating to hijacking, destroying or endangering the safety of a fixed platform.

3.6 Human cost

The human cost of piracy is staggering and difficult to document fully. Men and women who go to sea to earn a living are usually away from their families for extended periods. The

4 Article 3.

families are usually dependent on the income earned by the seafarer. It is unacceptable that seafarers be subjected to inhuman treatment at the hands of criminals. According to a report in 2011 on the human cost of piracy, pirates inflict psychological abuse and physical mistreatment when they terrorise hostages, their families, and shipowners to speed up the ransom payment.

This abuse is severe, and includes threats of execution or acting out mock executions and claims that the hostages have been abandoned and will never see their homes again (Hurlbert, 2012). The effect of being held hostage for long periods of time has traumatised some seafarers so severely that they never return to sea, thus denying them and their families their source of income.

CRITICAL REFLECTION

Establish which states on the east coast of Africa have combined the provisions of the UNCLOS and the SUA convention into a single piece of domestic legislation. Consider whether establishing similar legislation would be desirable for South Africa.

CASE STUDY: Motivation for piracy and pirates' view on hostages

This case study provides the motivation of the pirates who hijacked a freighter off Somalia and held the vessel and crew hostage.

In September 2008 Somali pirates hijacked a Ukrainian freighter, the *Faina*, bound for Mombasa on the east coast of Africa. The pirates sailed the hijacked vessel to the coast of Somalia and demanded a ransom for its release.

During the period that the freighter was under the control of the pirates, Jeffrey Gettleman, a journalist representing *The New York Times*, contacted the pirates on board the hijacked vessel via radio telephone link and conducted an interview with their spokesman (Gettleman, 2008).

The responses from the pirates to the questions put to them as to why they had hijacked the vessel indicated that:

1 The motive for the hijacking was to get money to be divided among the pirates to protect themselves from hunger.
2 The pirates were not afraid to die.
3 They do not consider their act as criminal, but rather as the actions of a coastguard protecting their waters against illegal fishing and the dumping of waste.
4 They regard the hostages as people who are doing the illegal activities, such as waste dumping and fishing.

The pirates thus regard the victims, rather than themselves, as the perpetrators, and rationalise their behaviour as being that of guardians of their country's sovereignty.

They also have a sense of entitlement to the ransom money to be paid for the release of the vessel and the hostages. They rationalise this as being due to their livelihood having been stolen from them by the perceived perpetrators in their custody.

The pirates can be expected to act irrationally as they have no fear of dying.

CRITICAL REFLECTION

Consider the following questions:

1. In view of the illegal fishing taking place in Somalia's waters, do you believe that pirates are justified in acting as guardians? Motivate your answer.
2. Utilising the anomie theory, consider what steps could be taken in Somalia to prevent piracy.
3. Consider, from a criminological viewpoint, what guidelines you could provide seafarers with on how to survive a hostage situation, bearing in mind that they will be dealing with perpetrators who are not afraid to die.

Conclusion

The dilemma surrounding piracy begins with the determination of whether the crime in question is piracy or not. This in turn is dependent on where the crime was committed, whether on the high seas or in an area of the maritime domain under the jurisdiction of a particular state. Be that as it may, the debate over the technicalities as to where the offence was committed, or what the motivation for the crime was, has done little for the victims who have suffered loss of life or property (Mejia & Mukherjee, 2004). The full horror of the crimes perpetrated against innocent seafarers, going about their daily task of keeping the wheels of the world's economy turning, was revealed to the world in the report of the One Earth Future Foundation on the human cost of piracy in 2011 (Hurlburt, 2012).

The problem of piracy will not be eradicated by taking action against pirates at sea alone, as the ultimate solution needs to be land based. The action against pirates at sea, however, is of cardinal importance, as no society on earth can stand by and observe crimes being committed with impunity. Piracy thus requires that the resources of states be combined to deal with this manifestation of violent acts of robbery and cold-blooded murder.

Although South Africa has not been subjected to incidents of piracy, it cannot become complacent. As was pointed out by the South African Minister of Defence, piracy is potentially one of the most serious problems facing regional security. The vulnerability of South Africa's east coast to pirate attacks has led to the South African navy's being deployed in the Mozambique Channel continuously since 2010 to prevent Somali pirate attacks and safeguard the east coast of southern Africa (Hes, 2013).

As long as there are ships plying the oceans of the world, there will be crime committed against these targets. The motivation for such crime is as old as humankind, and rests on the human vices of illicit material gain, opportunism, self-justification, and a propensity for violence. Whatever the motivation or the theory surrounding the purported causes of such criminal behaviour, it will continue, as will the need to curtail such acts and punish the perpetrators.

Critical thinking questions

1. Why is the age-old crime of piracy still prevalent today?
2. What, in your opinion, are the causative factors leading to persons deciding to perpetrate piracy?

3. Can you think of any interventions, taking into account the criminological theories explaining the behaviour of pirates, which could be instituted to assist with preventing piracy?
4. What criminological factors would you take into account when debriefing a victim of piracy who had been held hostage for three months with the constant threat of possible death by extreme violence?
5. Do you think that piracy can ever be successfully eradicated?

References

Brown, E. B., Esbensen, F., & Geis, G. (2004). *Criminology explaining crime and its context.* Cincinnati, OH: Anderson publishing.

Burchell, J., & Milton J. (2000). *Principles of criminal law* (2nd ed.). Lansdown: Juta.

Burnett, J. S. (2002). *Dangerous waters: modern piracy and terror on the high seas.* New York: Penguin Putnam Inc.

Contact Group on Piracy off the Coast of Somalia (CGPCS). (2012) Eleventh Plenary Session of the Contact Group on Piracy off the Coast of Somalia, New York, 29 March.

Congressional Research Service (CRS). (2009). *Report for Congress: piracy off the Horn of Africa.* 7-5700. Retrieved November 21, 2013, from www.crs.gov.R40528.

Dubner, B. in M. Meija & P. K. Mukherjee. (2004). Selected issues of law and ergonomics in maritime security. *Journal of International Maritime Law, 10*(4), August–September, 301–325.

Gettleman, J. (2008, September 30). Q & A With a Pirate: 'We Just Want the Money'. *The New York Times.* Retrieved January 7, 2014, from http://thelede.blogs.nytimes.com/2008/09/30/q-a-with-a-pirate-we-just-want-the-money/?ref=africa.

Hagan, F. E. (2011). *Introduction to criminology: theories, methods, and criminal behaviour.* Canada: Sage Publications.

Hes, D. (2013, June 9). SA Navy leads anti-piracy drive. *News24.* Retrieved April 21, 2014, from http://www.news24.com/SouthAfrica/News/SA-Navy-leads-anti-piracy-initiatives-20130609.

Hurlburt, K. (2012). *The human cost of piracy 2011.* Oceans Beyond Piracy – A project of One Earth Future Foundation. Retrieved October 11, 2013, from http://www.oceansbeyondpiracy.org.

Imbali, T. Principal prosecution counsel, office of the Director of Public Prosecutions, Kenya. (2013). *Piracy: Kenyan experience.* Paper presented at the 2nd East African Association of Prosecutors (EAAP) training workshop: Responding to Terrorism, International and Transnational Crimes, Dar-es-Salaam, Tanzania.

International Chamber of Commerce (ICC) International Maritime Bureau (IMB). (2001). *Piracy and armed robbery against ships. Annual report 1 January– 31 December 2000.* Barking: ICC-IMB.

International Chamber of Commerce (ICC). International Maritime Bureau (IMB). (2002). *Piracy and armed robbery against ships. Annual report 1 January–31 December 2001.* Barking: ICC-IMB.

International Chamber of Commerce (ICC). International Maritime Bureau (IMB). (2004). *Piracy and armed robbery against ships. Annual report 1 January–31 December 2003.* Barking: ICC-IMB.

International Chamber of Commerce (ICC). International Maritime Bureau (IMB). (2010). *Piracy and armed robbery against ships. Quarterly report 1 January–31 September 2010.* London: ICC-IMB.

International Chamber of Commerce (ICC). International Maritime Bureau (IMB). (2011). *Piracy and armed robbery against ships. Annual report 1 January–31 December 2010.* London: ICC-IMB.

International Chamber of Commerce (ICC). International Maritime Bureau (IMB). (2012). *Piracy and armed robbery against ships. Annual report 1 January–31 December 2012.* London: ICC-IMB.

International Chamber of Commerce (ICC) International Maritime Bureau (IMB). (2013). *Piracy and armed robbery against ships. Quarterly report 1 January–30 June 2013.* London: ICC-IMB.

International Maritime Organisation (IMO). (2001). *MSC/Circ.4 30 June. Reports on acts of piracy and armed robbery against ships.* Second quarterly report (April to, and including June 2001). London: International Maritime Organisation.

International Maritime Organisation (IMO). (2005). *Consolidated text of the Convention for the Suppression of Unlawful Acts against the Safety of Maritime Navigation and the Protocol of 2005 to the Convention.*

International Maritime Organisation (IMO). (2009). *Code of Practice for the investigation of crimes of piracy and armed robbery against ships* Resolution A. 1025(26). Adapted on 2 December 2009. http://www.imo.org/OurWork/Security/PiracyArmedRobbery/Guidance/Documents/A.1025.pdf.

International Ship and Port Facility Security (ISPS) Code (2004). Retrieved December 26, 2013, from http://www.imo.org/ourwork/security/instruments/pages/ispscode.aspx.

Jacobsson, M. (2001). *EU Presidency Statement – Piracy at Sea,* May 10. Retrieved April 18, 2006, from http://www.europa-eu-un.org/articles/en/article_233_en.htm.

Lang, J. (2011). *Report of the Special Advisor to the Secretary-General on Legal Issues Related to Piracy off the Coast of Somalia.* Annex to UNSC S/2011/30 dated 25 January 2011 from the Secretary-General to the President of the Security Council of the United Nations.

Lyman, M. D., & Potter, G. W. (2007). *Organised crime* (4th Ed). Upper Saddle River, NJ: Pearson Education.

Maritime International Secretariat Services Limited (Marisec). (2004). *Attacks on ships background information.* Piracy Home Page. Retrieved April 20, 2004, from http://www.marisec.org/piracy/background.htm.

Maritime Executive (Marex). (2013, May 29). Nigerian Pirate gangs extend reach off West Africa. Reuters.

Meija, M., & Mukherjee, P. K. (2004). Selected issues of law and ergonomics in maritime security. *Journal of International Maritime Law, 10*(4), August–September, 301–325.

Mukundan, P. (2004). Piracy and armed attacks against vessels today. *Journal of International Maritime Law, 10*(4), August–September, 308–313.

Oceans Beyond Piracy. (2010). *The economic cost of piracy.* Retrieved from www.oceansbeyondpiracy.org.

Piracy off the Horn of Africa. (2010). Congressional Research Service report, April 19. Retrieved November 21, 2013, from www.crs.gov.

Potgieter, T. D. (2012). *Maritime security in the Indian Ocean: strategic setting and features* (Institute for Security Studies paper, 22 August). Pretoria: ISS.

Shaw, M. N. (1997). *International law* (4th ed.) Cambridge: Cambridge University Press.

Siegel, L. J. (2003). *Criminology.* Belmont, USA: Wadsworth/Thompson Learning.

Snyman, C. R. (1995). *Criminal law* (3rd ed.). Durban: Butterworths.

South Africa (Republic). (SA) (1994). Maritime Zones Act, 15 of 1994. *Government Gazette* (No. 37692). Pretoria: Government Printer.

South Africa (Republic) (SA). (1996). Constitution of the Republic of South Africa Act, 1996.

South Africa (Republic) (SA). (2002). Defence Act, 42 of 2002. *Government Gazette* (No. 24576). Pretoria: Government Printer.

South Africa (Republic) (SA). Department of Transport. (2003). *Consolidated Maritime Issues Document Comido 1 (2003/4).* Pretoria: Government Printer.

South Africa (Republic). (2004). Protection of Constitutional Democracy against Terrorist and Related Activities Act, 33 of 2004. *Government Gazette* (No. 27266). Pretoria: Government Printer.

South Africa. (Republic) (SA). 2011. *Address by L N Sisulu, MP, Minister of Defence and Military Veterans at the SADC Extraordinary Meeting on Regional Anti-Piracy Strategy 25 July*. Government online. Retrieved April 21, 2014, from http://www.gov.za/speeches/view.php?sid=20245#top.

South African Police Service (SAPS). (2009). *Annual report of the South African Police Service for 2008/2009*. Pretoria: Government Printer.

United Nations Convention on the High Seas. Signed 29 April 1958 and entered into force 30 September 1962. U.N.T.S. No. 6465, vol. 450, pp. 82–103. Retrieved July 30, 2014, from http://sedac.ciesin.columbia.edu/entri/texts/high.seas.1958.html.

United Nations Convention on the Law of the Sea (UNCLOS). (1982). New York: United Nations.

United Nations Security Council (UNSC). (2008). S/RES/1816(2008) 2 June 2008.

United Nations Security Council (UNSC). (2011). 1976 S/RES/1976(2011) 11 April 2011.

Whaley, F. (2009). *Regional Cooperation's unsung success story. Fighting piracy in the Malacca Strait. Development Asia*. (Asian Development Bank publication No. 3, April.) Retrieved December 27, 2013, from http://development.asia/issue03/cover-05.asp.

Yale Global Online (2013). Indonesia, Malaysia, Singapore launch coordinated patrol of Malacca Strait – *The Jakarta Post* 20 July 2004. Retrieved December 27, 2013, from http://yaleglobal.yale.edu/content/indonesia-malaysia-singapore-launch-coordinated-patrol-malacca-strait.

Conservation crime application – a South African perspective

FJW Herbig

> **For that which is common to the greatest number has the least care bestowed upon it. Everyone thinks chiefly of his own, hardly at all of the common interest.**
>
> ***Aristotle: 384–322 BC***

4.1 Introduction

Characteristically, criminological research throughout the world has been directed towards the more traditional, histrionic, and higher-profile type crimes in society, especially those involving identifiable human victims. Crimes in the conservation remit have lamentably been overlooked and/or awarded considerably less attention by the authorities. The palpable crime occurring in society (including heinous crimes such as rape and murder) is clearly of vital importance, but if so-called 'less significant' crimes such as crimes against natural resources are ignored, one might well speculate what the future of this planet is (not) going to be. The shortage of action taken thus far in this arena gaudily depicts the central thrust, lifestyle, and values of a consumerist society – the perception that humans have a right to exploit all the resources of the planet, that other life forms such as animals (vertebrate or invertebrate) are there to serve our needs, and that humankind has no enduring obligation to future cohorts or the natural world.

Even in schools, teachers often introduce invertebrates used in dissections or experiments in a way that negates a favourable ethical attitude towards them, generally endorsing an instrumental mind-set. Although they are simple organisms which may not suffer in the same way as higher animals, they still deserve respect. Reverence for all animals should be part of the school pedagogy supporting ethical approaches to natural resource assets from an early age. Aggravating this situation in the South African context is the dearth of understanding and awareness of issues such as conservation crime, and a seemingly torpid general disposition amongst South Africans towards such deviance, which in most other countries would collectively be regarded as ethically wrong. Kidd (1998) suggests that the outlook of many South Africans in this regard has to a large extent been enervated by the widespread concern over pervasive everyday criminality which most people regard as more profound than natural resource/conservation/environmental offences. It would appear from anecdotal evidence that little more than supine resistance is tendered by society with regard to conservation crime/criminality in comparison to more conventional type crime (e-toll protests serve as a case in point). Conservation crimes are additionally, on the whole, unobtrusive in nature, with the detrimental effects thereof going portentously overlooked in the short to medium term, often even to the so-called 'trained eye'. Although a well-established discipline that has, through the years, contributed significantly to understanding and addressing the problem of conventional crime and criminality, criminology has barely begun to ponder the questions and challenges presenting in the conservation sphere. The magnitude of natural resource crimes has, over the last decade or so, in concert with a growing global awareness of conservation issues, begun, albeit hesitantly, to receive focused attention from criminological scholars. Even though this gestation period should already have ended, it would seem that conservation crime has not yet received full acclaim as a field of study in criminology. Providentially the antithesis to the chronological decline of wildlife is a hesitant but slowly distending universal appreciation of the importance of conservation, not solely for visual reasons, but also for human fortitude. Society is slowly becoming more aware that today's rapid loss of species is more than just a negligible calamity. It is indeed a reminder of an ailing Earth.

Neither rhinos nor any other endangered species can be considered in isolation from the way in which humankind chooses to view their entire world. Today we stand at a bifurcation. Internationally we can join hands in a genuine effort to redress the immense damage already done to our global environment, or we can continue down the path to destruction. However, the foundations for a gradually embedding and commonly termed 'environmental'/'ecological'/'green' perspective in criminology seem to have already cautiously been laid. What is now required for the dual purposes of innovation and consolidation, and which will be fervently argued for in this chapter, is recognition of this perspective as an unambiguous conservation criminological field, both practically and theoretically.

Furthermore, it is envisioned that this conservation criminological prudence will contribute to enriching and revitalising the theoretical framework of a postmodern conservation criminological imperative, while simultaneously providing students and functionaries alike with a vibrant and resourceful aide-memoir to the envirodrama that is biodiversity perturbation.

4.2 The conservation crime quandary – conflation or conflict?

Environmental and natural resource decrepitude through, amongst other things, illegitimate exploitation has for many years now been of critical concern to those involved with conservation and sustainable utilisation issues. On a regular basis, intercession programmes have, due to pressure group insistence and revile, and even public remonstration, been implemented to redress and restrict environmental perturbation. Alas, most have been directed at protecting those species perceived to possess a higher public value, status, and/or profile, for example abalone (poached in the Western Cape), cycads and ivory (smuggled), and, of late, rhinoceros (the subject of wholesale slaughter and poaching in South Africa's game reserves). Astringently, the geometric tortoise, as well as many other aboriginal and endemic reptile species, shares similar legislative protection status as the endangered rhinoceros and cycad ('*broodboom*' in Afrikaans), but these species are afforded nowhere near the same consideration as those believed to possess more utilitarian, attractive, and anthropomorphic characteristics. This fact casts serious aspersions on the environmental bona fides of those in authority to conserve sustainably South Africa's rich biodiversity heritage.

The mushrooming problem of atrocious and violent crime in South African society has, of course, done little to promote public reproof of conservation-related deviance, and has, in fact, served to relegate natural resource crime issues to the periphery of crime significance. As society lurches under a crime wave that directly affects people's personal safety, their families, and their pockets, the general public becomes, to a large extent, insensate towards issues of conservation crime. To top it all, no virtuous crime category currently exists within which these, and other forms of conservation/natural resource crime, can be grouped. The amplification of explicatory theories for conservation-related deviance has also been ignored, promoting, it is submitted, the view that these crimes are trivial in terms of policing economics. This regrettably only serves to diminish the seriousness of the current state of affairs within this field – only through a greater understanding of why conservation crime endures will a potential solution be revealed.

By the same token, it is submitted that the following have resulted in a somewhat stoical advocacy from within the South African community:

- misperceptions about the sustainability of natural resources
- policy and legislation inconsistency within conservation organisations
- in many cases a total absence of identifiable provincial and/or national strategy regarding specific resources
- inadequate interest in conservation policing
- a low general interest in lower status species (for example insects, reptiles, and other invertebrates).

CRITICAL REFLECTION

Think about the number of daily reports in the mass media regarding conventional crimes. How does this compare with reporting about crimes involving natural resources? Consider possible reasons behind the differences. List at least 10 reasons.

The harm caused by these ignominious acts is, however, palpable and if allowed to continue unbridled will, in all probability, lead to many invaluable natural assets and heritage disappearing from South Africa. This will essentially cannibalise the country's rich natural legacy and impact detrimentally on biotic diversity. Conservation crime militates against society's ethical responsibility in the worst possible way and, therefore, steadfast support is required to surmount the problem. By probing the underlying dynamics and purview of this particular phenomenon and embedding a vibrant conservation and ethical culture, it is anticipated that a valuable contribution can be made in terms of protecting natural resources and restricting this type of deviance for the mutual benefit of humankind. Moreover, such an interrogation will, it is hoped, encourage an interest in conservation criminology, as a furtherance of the mainstream criminological discipline. The criminological range will thereby be uplifted and invigorated, and, furthermore, a reassessment of conventional notions about what qualifies as a serious crime, and what does not, will be facilitated. It is further envisaged that an acceptable explanation for/perspective on crime causation will ultimately produce a valid and reliable framework within which this particular form of deviance can be addressed in the South African context; this will result in the concept of conservation criminology being rightfully afforded its own identity and correctly recognised and applied within the criminal justice domain.

CRITICAL REFLECTION

With due regard to the foregoing section, astutely interrogate the following assertion in a criminological context: 'Advances are made by answering questions. Discoveries are made by questioning answers.'

4.3 Definitions/key concepts: Conservation crime terminology – interpellation or interpretation?

In view of the fact that 'conservation' crime/criminology is a relatively new phraseology representing a schism with more traditional terms such as 'environmental,' 'ecological,' and 'green' crime/criminology, it will be beneficial to provide concise clarification of the use of this preferred term, as presented by Herbig (2008, 2011). Most commonly, natural resource-related crimes and the study thereof are referred to as 'environmental,' 'ecological,' and/or 'green' crime/criminology. This lingua franca, however, has, it is submitted, created some confusion and prevented this type of criminality from being unambiguously defined and addressed. Natural resource crime issues in the criminological context have traditionally been viewed myopically, and dealt with under the diverse and nebulous aphorisms and captions mentioned above. Such arcane terminologies have destabilised the demarcation of coherent and clear-cut parameters with regard to this form of criminality, and have clearly served to sideline focused and dedicated intervention and mitigation in this sphere (Herbig & Joubert, 2006). There is, therefore, an urgent need for the development, formulation and recognition/entrenchment of a viable, parsimonious and mutually exclusive crime category that will effectively encapsulate telluric conservation crime and criminality.

4.3.1 Environmental criminology

'Environmental crime/criminology' can essentially be viewed as a standard label that covers a range of interconnecting perspectives. At the core, the various strands of environmental criminology are bound by a common focus on the role that the immediate environment plays in the performance of crime, and a conviction that careful analyses of these environmental influences are the key to the effective investigation, control, and prevention of (traditional) crime. Consonant with this view, Burke (2009) contends that the contemporary field of environmental criminology includes the following:

- studies of the spatial patterning of crime at different levels of aggregation
- the journey to crime, or the processes by which potential offenders recognise potential crime sites and specific opportunities
- the creation and maintenance of areas of criminal residence.

The term 'environmental crime' and the meaning attributed to it is, therefore, to some extent blemished by the reference to spatial patterning of crime, geographies of crime, and so forth. Although the term might, to the casual observer, seem to describe adequately the study of criminality directed at the natural environment, it is in fact quite the opposite. In criminological circles, environmental criminology refers to a growing field, which explores how actual criminal events involve an interaction between motivated individuals and the surrounding social, economic, legal, and physical environment (Brantingham & Brantingham, 1998).

According to South (in Herbig, 2008), the term 'environmental' within criminology is still principally employed in studies of 'place' (Herbig, 2008, p. 29) and the spatial patterning of crime. The focus is, therefore, on understanding the criminal event and how it relates to individual motivation; to victims and targets; and to the legal, social, psychological, and social milieu. The original or traditional context in which the term has been used, and still is principally being used, has, it is submitted, led to its acquiring the 'tenure' (Herbig & Joubert, 2006, p. 94) of the maxim, and, furthermore, that the transposable usage thereof can quite easily lead to unnecessary confusion and vagueness. The term can simply no longer be used in an obscure manner. Cohen and Felson (1979), moreover, maintain that geographical profiling has its scientific basis in environmental criminology and, more specifically, in routine activity theory and crime pattern theory.

Rossmo (1995) is of the police investigation. Brantingham and Brantingham (1998) maintain that the crime setting or place, the where and when of the criminal act, makes up the fourth dimension of crime (the primary concern of environmental criminology). The roots of this perspective lie in human ecology, Jeffery's bio-social learning approach, and Hirschi's social control theory. By reversing the reasoning and logic of these theoretical models, it may be possible to predict the most probable location of a criminal's residence (Rossmo, 1995). From these arguments, it becomes clear that the term 'environmental crime/criminology' in no way refers to crime involving natural resources, and its use in this remit should, therefore, be terminated forthwith.

4.3.2 Ecological criminology

As was the case with environmental criminology, ecological criminology is, according to Brantingham and Brantingham (1998) and Van Heerden (1988), primarily associated with the study of spatial patterns of crime in an urban context. Williams and McShane (2010) confirm this sentiment by postulating that an ecological study allows researchers to transcend individuality and, through the collection of social data, gain a sense of the characteristics of large groups of people. Once again, it is submitted that so-called 'ownership' of the term has, due to its conventional usage, been 'claimed' by this denotation. Muddying the linguistic waters even further, Aas (2013) talks about eco-global and green criminology as fields which have put issues of environmental crime and justice on the criminological agenda. The question that must be asked is why, in this day and age, we still cannot get simple issues such as crime caste semantics right? Surely criminologists investigating this field can see that blurred (shared) terminologies will do nothing to promote the study and management of natural resource criminality and its adjuncts.

4.3.3 Green criminology

Although the term 'green criminology' is often used to describe collectively the study of crime impacting negatively on natural resources, specifically in the United States of America (South & Beirne, 1998), such use of this term can be considered duplicitous, at the least. Green crime/criminology might easily and inaccurately be associated with the so-called 'greenies' or 'tree/bunny huggers', expressions often used to describe the fanatical, overzealous, activist, and often dictatorial conservation fringe; it immediately conjures up images of the militant environmentalist groups Greenpeace and Sea Sheppard. Lynch and Stretsky moderate the fluidity of aforementioned terminology somewhat by arguing that 'being green implies more than holding values favouring environmental protection; it also entails a political stance wherein it is acknowledged that solutions to environmental degradation may require substantial economic and political reorganization' (2003, p. 231).[1] This viewpoint can be tolerated providing that environmental degradation can be inferred to be a nom de plume for conservation crime.

4.3.4 Conservation crime/criminality

Conservation criminology argues to be well balanced and copasetic and definitely does not favour any particular shibboleth within the natural resource/conservation realm. It deals

1 Copyright © 2003 by SAGE. Reprinted by permission of SAGE.

with a more focused range of issues than those traditionally and simplistically labelled 'green issues', among others, animal rights, animal abuse/cruelty, ecological spirituality, and eco-feminism (Agnew 1998). Swanepoel (1997) even uses the term 'green environmental criminology', clearly indicating the ambiguity of these terms and illustrating that a combination of already vague and non-specific terms does nothing to promote a focused approach to the issue at hand.

Conservation crime can clinically be defined as 'any intentional or negligent human activity or manipulation that impacts negatively on the earth's biotic and/or abiotic natural resources, resulting in immediately noticeable or indiscernible (only noticeable over time) natural resource trauma of any magnitude' (Herbig & Joubert, 2006, p. 96). For obvious reasons, conservation crime can, therefore, be considered the precursor to conservation criminology (Herbig & Joubert, 2006).

Conservation criminology unambiguously deals with, amongst others things:

- the dynamics and nexus between humans and (biotic/abiotic) natural resources on the receiving environment (as a casualty/victim)
- the extent to which natural resource crime encroaches or impacts on the limits of acceptable change with regard to any particular natural resource, or a collection of such resources.

Lending credence to the above arguments, Gibbs, Gore, McGarrell, and Rivers III state that:

> **given the constraints associated with the terms 'green' and 'environmental criminology', we prefer the term 'conservation criminology' to describe our framework. We use conservation criminology as our preferred terminology for several reasons. Environmental or ecological criminology typically refers to the spatial study of criminal events. Green criminology is also problematic due to its association with political perspectives (and the narrow range of associated issues) and its ambiguity. We concur with Herbig and Joubert (2006) that conservation criminology identifies the core theme of this area of study (Gibbs, Gore, McGarrell, and Rivers III, 2009, p. 2).[2]**

The continued misuse of the terms 'environmental', 'ecological' or 'green crime/criminology' can, therefore, further encourage confusion by reinforcing preconceived notions, burdening this new conceptual framework.

CHECK POINT

- There are currently several definitions being used worldwide to delimit natural resource crime and criminality.
- As far as clearly delineating the criminal phenomenon goes, vague and multifarious definitions militate against decisive action in this arena.
- A specific crime type should have its own unique unadulterated designation. If one speaks of environmental or ecological crime, what exactly does it mean? Is there a common understanding within criminological/criminal justice circles?
- Imagine the confusion within the criminal justice field if crimes such as murder, rape, robbery, and the like meant different things to different people.

- The definition challenge expounded on in the section 4.3 above should not be viewed as a mere linguistic exchange, but as an issue that cuts to the very heart of the conservation crime phenomenon and its management.

4.4 Conservation crime aetiology: a theoretical journey

Having succinctly dealt with the origin and semantics of conservation crime the focus of this chapter now shifts towards the identification and chrysalis of a theoretical crime causation model that will sufficiently explicate conservation crime. Scrutiny of the criminological literature pertaining to crime causation theories reveals a host of, often opposing, perspectives and ideologies. None of these, it is submitted, adequately explain or allow for a full understanding of any particular crime or crime category entirely unaided, and they, at most, offer tangential connections. This fact underscores the complex and multidimensional nature of conventional crime and criminality, not to speak of conservation criminality. An interesting, and at the same time perplexing, observation in this regard is the fact that approaches - whilst often based on competing assumptions, and therefore diametrically opposed - can be equally credible and applicable to parallel crime phenomena. Bear in mind that advances are made by answering questions, but discoveries are made by questioning answers. Herein lies the central thrust of a conservation specific criminology.

Seeing as conservation crime, although inimitable in many specific ways, in essence shares certain qualities with conventional crime, the elucidatory model presented will inescapably comprise a fusion of credible fundamental schools of thought that have historically evolved in the criminological discourse; the model will necessarily, therefore, be emancipated in nature. The archetype should at least be punctilious and realistic, and should augment the theoretical repertoire - serving as a means to an end rather than purporting to be an end in itself. The academic pursuit of criminology and the formulation of criminological doctrine can thus be viewed as integral to the development of the discipline, and as the basis for all the activities which are to be embodied in criminal justice.

Bhom states appropriately in this regard:

> **Theory is the foundation of criminology and the basis of action. Everything done in criminal justice is based on theory, although we are often unaware of the theory on which actions are based. We study theory, then, to know why we are doing what we do. People who are uninterested in (or abandon) theory are people who choose to move blindly through life, or, in the case of criminal justice, intervene in people's lives with only vague notions about why they are doing what they are doing (Bhom, in Brown, Esbensen, & Geis, 2001, p. 18).**

To facilitate addressing the issue of crime causation crafting in a holistic, comprehensive, and sequential manner, it is, therefore, considered sensible praxis to provide a succinct overview of those broad schools of thought, as well as their developmental cycle, that have historically dominated the criminological discourse.

So as to understand and explain crime, criminologists have formulated many theories that, at least in their idyllic form, are composed of clearly stated propositions that posit relationships, often of a causal sort, between events and things under study (Schmalleger,

1996), and customarily have their roots in one (or both) of the two dominant theoretical approaches. Through the years, two central ideologies have evolved, by means of which criminologists seek to explain and understand crime and criminality. These two ideologies, or so-called 'schools of thought', namely the classical school and the positivist school, are, paradoxically, characterised by adversative conjecture and diverse policy implications. Despite this obvious and inherent mutual exclusivity, both schools have drawn a wide following and divided support base that essentially remains to this day. It is, moreover, not surprising that these existentialistic, all inclusive and rigid shibboleths have often facilitated the synthesis of elements from both schools in order to create theoretical perspectives that more suitably attempt to explain the complex and multidimensional phenomenon that is crime and criminality.

These two schools have, furthermore, unsurprisingly generated various offshoot explanatory theories or perspectives that are, to a lesser or greater degree, relevant to crime aetiology. However, such offshoots can invariably be linked to the particular temperament and orientation of the criminological scholar. There is no such thing as a so-called 'new' criminology, as each line of thought is a continuation of previous ideas developed through the centuries. The approach to criminology is, therefore, anything but inert; it develops with the changing times, and can be said to be as much influenced by history as by current events. The tenet that typifies each of these schools, their evolutionary or developmental adjuncts, and certain other more prominent theoretical perspectives will be systematically articulated below, serving as a template for the development of an explanatory model for conservation crime.

4.4.1 The classical school

The classical school of criminology was established in the eighteenth century (1755), and is so called because it was the first attempt to reflect logically and formally on criminology (Snyman, 1990). The keystone was founded by Cesare Beccaria and Jeremy Bentham and was developed in response to the primitive and cruel European justice system that existed prior to the French Revolution of 1798 (Glick, 1995; White & Haines, 2001); it effectively usurped earlier views that crime is a supernatural phenomenon (Brown et al., 2001). Unexpectedly, and of course most aptly for this chapter, it was, according to South, Beccaria himself who once pronounced: 'Do not commit any crime and be just with all the things that surround you. Remember that even the smallest creatures, crushed by arrogant and cruel men, are endowed with a little ray of life' (South, 1998, p. 211).[3]

The classical school views human behaviour as basically rational in nature, and suggests that people have the ability to choose right from wrong – in actual fact. It proposes that the major element governing a person's choice of action is the basic human desire to obtain gratification and avoid pain (Bartol, 1995; Glick, 1995; White & Haines, 2001). This theory, therefore, presumes that criminal offenders are mindful agents, not people who are so plagued by internal or external forces that they lose personal sense of reason. Hence, the emphasis within this school falls on crime per se, and not necessarily on the criminal.

Castigation is seen as a major mechanism by which to promote compliance with the law (crime prevention/deterrence), and the notion of equitable chastisement is, therefore, unconditionally endorsed (White & Haines, 2001; Williams & McShane, 2010). For Beccaria (in White & Haines, 2001) the objective of punishment was fundamentally to prevent the criminal from doing further injury to society, and to prevent others from committing

3 Copyright © 1998, SAGE Publications. Reprinted by permission of SAGE.

similar offences by inflicting punishment in such a mode that it would make the strongest and most lasting impression on the minds of others, with the least affliction to the body of the criminal.

According to McReynolds (in Bartol, 1995), Bentham, somewhat incongruously, believed that all individuals are inherently motivated to seek pleasure and avoid pain, without exception, in all situations, and it would, therefore, appear that even Bentham's notion of free will included a good measure of biological determinism, a fundamental tenet of positivist ideology. Despite such paradoxes, the classical school of thought remains popular in criminological academia, and, according to Williams and McShane (2010), it may be safe to say that some 200-year-old ideas are among our most modern policy and theoretical notions.

4.4.2 The positivist school

Even though the classical perspective dominated the thinking and understanding of crime, law, and justice for almost a century, many of the proposals made by the classical theorists had little effect on the crime problem (Glick, 1995). More emphasis was subsequently placed on the existence of certain patterns in the manifestation of crime, drawing attention away from notions of rationalism and punishment, moving towards a scientific investigation of the causes of crime, and stressing in particular the influence of hereditary, psychological, and social factors. White and Haines (2001) stress that the development of positivistic perspectives constituted a major break with the classical tradition that saw crime as primarily a matter of individual choice, due to positivists explaining crime by reference to forces and factors outside the decisionmaking ability of the individual.

The positivistic school, according to White and Haines (2001), was in fact founded upon the conviction that society (civilisation) is progressing ever forward, and that the social scientist can study society, provide a more accurate understanding of how society works, and ultimately provide a rational means of overcoming existing social problems and ills by using scientific methods. Williams and McShane (2010) stress further in this regard that the primary characteristics of positivist criminological thought (essentially empiricism) are a deterministic view of the world, a focus on criminal behaviour instead of on legal issues such as rights, and the prevention of crime through the (individualised) treatment and rehabilitation of offenders. Positivism essentially stressed the idea that much human behaviour is a function of external social forces beyond individual control, and internal forces such as mental capabilities (psychological determinism) and biological make-up (biological determinism) – people were beginning to be viewed and understood as beings who were part of the animal kingdom, whose behaviour was very much influenced (if not determined) by social, cultural, and biological antecedents, rather than as self-determined beings who were free to do what they wanted (White & Haines, 2001).

Positivism is, therefore, related to efforts to adopt natural science methods and concepts in the study of society, basically necessitating the acceptance of certain ideas about human experience, and attempting to enumerate and regulate this experience in the anticipation that expert intercession could obviate or remedy/mitigate specific kinds of social problems. To all intents and purposes, the positivist school (also known as the Italian school), with its emphasis on hard biological determinism and reliance on the use of the senses to gather observable facts and measurements, heralded the beginning of modern scientific criminology (Bartol, 1995). The premise of this school, founded by Cesare Lombroso (1835–1909), is, therefore, deterministic and focuses on the offender whilst seeking to explain criminal behaviour in terms of biological attributes. The positivist orientation, with its exclusive or near exclusive reliance on observable facts, continues to be significant in the study of crime today (Bartol, 1995; Snyman, 1990).

Modern-day positivists, however, define and identify criminality in a manner geared to establishing those people who are so-called 'at risk' of certain behaviour, and there is no longer a one-to-one link between crime and behaviour; rather, certain groups are seen to be more predisposed to crime than others because of biological and social environmental factors – individuals are not born criminal, but are exposed to baseline biological and psychological processes that shape their identity in childhood (White & Haines, 2001).

4.4.3 The neoclassical school

Mainly due to its extreme and inflexible nature, classicism proved to be unrealistic in its assumption of the complete rationality of offenders as well as in its unequivocal opposition to judicial discretion. It was, therefore, gradually modified by neoclassical thought (Brown, Esbensen, & Geis, 2001). This school does not, however, represent any schism with the classical view of human nature; it merely challenges the classical position of absolute free will (Bartol, 1995), subsequently developing rules to cope with extenuating circumstances where individuals could be deemed not to be totally responsible for their actions (White & Haines, 2001). Bartol (1995) maintains, furthermore, that neoclassicists specifically argue that free will can be inhibited by pathology, incompetence, mental disorder, or other conditions that may mitigate personal responsibility. Whereas pure classicists had maintained that humans are totally accountable for their actions, neoclassicists claim that this is not always the case.

As is clear from the above exposition, the distinction between the classical and neoclassical schools is at best obscure, and in essence, they represent a continuum of free will-based deterrence doctrine. As it has been eloquently put:

> **classicism and neoclassical developments are based on a very different set of assumptions and offer a fundamentally more measured analysis of crime and justice, relying, as they do, on humans' capacity for rational thought, rather than assuming an animal instinct of fear (Einstadter & Henry, 1995, p. 43).**

The contrast between these highly similar schools and positivistic criminology, however, remains very sharp.

4.5 Theoretical explanation of conservation crime

Owing to the hybrid nature of the crime threat to natural resources and the intertwined nature of criminological theory, it becomes possible to identify appropriate theoretical ingredients and craft a causational effigy that could tantalisingly become the future default paradigm for explaining conservation crime.

When taking into account the characteristics, features, activities, and nature of conservation crime, the premeditated, lucid, but also underlying positivist, nuances and attributes of this crime category become evident. An apposite explanation for much conservation crime can thus be sought within the existing framework of both the classical/neoclassical and positivist ideologies. This epitome draws on the limited theory and research in the field of conservation crime, and on leading explanatory crime theories in order to develop a comprehensive model concerning the aetiology of conservation crime. This theoretical perspective extorts from and merges, to a greater or lesser extent, elements from the following, in order to extend an explanation of why conservation crime occurs:

- Gottfredson and Hirschi's general theory of crime (classical/neoclassical)
- Bandura's social learning/socialisation theory (positivist)
- Sykes and Matza's neutralisation theory (positivist)
- Cornish and Clarke's rational choice perspective (classical/neoclassical).

These theories have been chosen because they appear to provide a reasonable foundation on which to construct an amalgamated model of conservation crime, given their focus on the factors which ostensibly drive individuals to illegally exploit and manoeuvre natural resources.

4.5.1 Gottfredson and Hirschi's general theory of crime

The general theory of crime (GTC) as proposed by Gottfredson and Hirschi is an all-embracing theory to explain not only all types of crimes, but also many other deviant actions (Moyer, 2001). In congruence with Brown et al. (2001), crime, in terms of GTC, is the result of individuals with low self-control encountering situations or opportunities in which crime will produce immediate gratification with relatively low levels of risk. Gottfredson and Hirschi, according to Brown et al. (2001), Moyer (2001), Siegel and Senna (2000), and Williams and Mc Shane (2010), maintain that self-control is taught in early adolescence, implying that parental discipline and management (child rearing practices) are key factors in explaining deviant and adult criminal offending.

These authors argue further that, according to Gottfredson and Hirschi, not all individuals with low self-control will engage in criminal behaviour, because, although the tendency will be for such individuals to pursue immediate gratification, only when opportunities allowing for use of self-gratifying force arise will these individuals resort to crime. Moyer (2001) highlights in this regard that there must be money or goods that are attractive to the offender, available to the offender, and not rightfully the property of the offender, and that the offender must be insufficiently restrained, for crime to transpire. Moyer (2001), furthermore, importantly mentions that low self-control implies that people differ in the extent to which they are restrained from criminal acts, with individuals possessing less self-control more prone to committing crimes, but, as Gottfredson and Hirschi (1996) argue, crime not being a mechanical or necessary consequence of low self-control.

Winfree and Abadinski (2003) opine that Gottfredson and Hirschi's self-control theory intimates that parental management can be either ineffective or effective with the following upshot. Ineffective parental management can give rise to low self-control and delinquency proneness, whilst effective parenting can yield other levels of self-control and promote conformity proneness.

4.5.1.1 Function in a conservation crime context

Even though this theory is often presented as a complete explanation for crime causation, it is felt that such an application would essentially serve to oversimplify the complex process of crime causation, and GTC, in as much as it stresses deficient self-control and crime opportunities, is, subsequently, in the context of an explanation of conservation crime, viewed as only one, albeit primary, aspect of the total criminal occurrence. GTC as an explanatory theory tends to combine various subsidiary elements – such as rational choice (exercise of free will), hedonism (seeking pleasure), and opportunity (lifestyle issues) – whilst placing a strong emphasis on the inculcation of poor self-control – unmistakably the central thrust of the theory. It is this element of GTC (together with crime opportunities) that is, then, selected as a pivotal constituent of the conservation crime explanation model.

4.5.2 Bandura's social learning theory

While GTC correctly identifies the human trait of greed (self-interest) as being innately present in all human beings, and the establishment of low self-control (in concert with opportunity, hedonism, and rational choice) as being a central premise predisposing individuals towards (conventional) crime, it is felt that there is a further underlying factor that stimulates individuals to partake in conservation crime – essentially non-conventional crime. GTC can indeed be applied as an explanatory theory for many, if not most, forms of conventional crime, but would seem to misfire somewhat in explaining why someone would specifically participate in something as unique as conservation crime.

Self-control deficiencies and opportunities for crime, as discussed above, cannot alone sufficiently explain the incidence of the illegal trade in natural resources, and beg for a further, less arbitrary, mechanism that purports to orientate, sensitise, and/or activate those with a propensity to crime to become involved in conservation deviance. In this regard, it is proposed that Bandura's social learning theory, although specifically developed to explain aggressive behaviour (Bartol, 1995), could provide a satisfactory solution to the issue, and serve as a major approach for integrating the other components of this explanatory perspective.

In terms of social learning theory, all human behaviour is learned in early childhood, by observing (modelling), imitating, and/or interacting with role models, in particular parents and family members, and can be strengthened by reinforcement or weakened by punishment (Bartol, 1995; Glick, 1995; Williams & McShane, 2010).

According to Yablonsky (1990), the community in which offenders grow up is apt to significantly affect their values, ethics, and choices in life – essentially promoting criminal tendencies as a result of the social context within which aberrant behaviour is learnt.

In short, therefore, criminal behaviour is viewed as a learnt response to social conditions and life situations, and subsequently qualifies as positivistic theory. The author is not, however, proposing that the criminal tendency to partake in conservation crime is, in accordance with this theory, learnt per se, but rather that individuals, through the conditioning and socialisation process, acquire and assimilate the general (negative), unbalanced civic stereotype, evident in society to this day, regarding (certain) animals. Drawing on Bandura's theory, the crucial features of the socialisation process are the models people are exposed to, the reinforcements and punishments they receive, and the beliefs they are taught. Persons learn, albeit incorrectly, in their particular communities or neighbourhoods, that certain animals are cold, heartless, invidious, and execrable organisms, which are less significant than humans, and even that they pose a threat to human well-being. Such sentiments are, furthermore, reinforced by, amongst other people, schoolmates and peers, as similar socialisation processes transpire within their own family environments.

Furthermore, Agnew (1998) believes that the media also contribute to this process through their human-like depiction of certain animals, for example buck, rabbits, and lions. Such portrayal could clearly lead people to apportion greater moral consideration to particular types of animals, and, by implication, therefore, less to certain others. Since little or no perceivable punishment or chastisement accompanies these negative sentiments, and conformity with these views realises rewards, in the sense of societal acceptance, this adulterated emotion towards or response to natural resources becomes embedded within the individual's frame of reference and consciousness (Herbig, 2008). Should such individuals also, however, have the misfortune of possessing low self-control, as discussed earlier with regard to GTC, the probability of their becoming involved in conservation crime is likely to increase exponentially, should suitable opportunities present themselves.

It must be emphasised at this point that the socialisation towards animals or nature and a conservation ethos by no means implies that individuals will be forced to engage in conservation crime, but rather that the entrenched stereotype in relation to animals or nature or conservation will influence and shape the decision to partake in such activities, should the individual have an elevated penchant for crime due to low or deficient self-control mechanisms. It should, furthermore, be emphasised that such socialised individuals do not generally display any identifiable personality defects, and are no more emotionally disturbed than the average person – they become more prone to involvement in conservation crime only as a result of the social context in which they learn distorted, prejudiced, and, even, deviant values regarding animals or nature.

In relation to the foregoing it is interesting to note that the Senegalese conservationist Baba Dioum once made the following emotive statement: '[I]n the end, we will conserve only what we love, we will love only what we understand, we will understand only what we are taught!' (Damm, 2002, p. 151).

4.5.2.1 Function in a conservation crime context

Low self-control, opportunities, and deficient socialisation regarding animals or nature are considered as particularly relevant elements for providing a theoretical foundation for, and explaining the origin of, conservation crime for the following reasons, amongst others (Herbig 2003, 2008):

- Ineffective child-rearing practices that lead to low self-control can be anticipated throughout society, from rich to poor communities, as well as in all population groups. Although the nature, frequency and intensity of these deficiencies will, in all likelihood, not be uniform in character, and vary depending on one's position on the affluence continuum, the ensuing low self-control that manifests itself can be regarded as ubiquitous in society. It is, however, anticipated that a higher incidence of low self-control will be evidenced in poverty stricken and deprived communities, due to the presence of a larger number of such communities and the differing hardships, values, standards, and norms applicable within such impecunious units. Yablonsky (1990) argues in this regard that in poverty areas, the values, social pressures, and norms favourable to crime can be considered strong and constant.
- Deficient, distorted, and notably biased stereotypes, regarding especially low order animals such as snakes and lizards, is a phenomenon that is, similarly, ubiquitous throughout society, and something that is not restricted significantly by status and/or demographic precincts. Just as poverty stricken individuals, as representatives of one extreme of the continuum, often indiscriminately utilise natural resources for victuals, subsistence and/or medicinal or traditional purposes, so poachers and illicit traders, as representatives of the other extreme of the continuum, exploit these very resources for greed (financial gain) and/or status reasons. Agnew (1998), however, deduces that the more affluent members of society can be expected, on the whole, to be better educated than their so-called 'poorer' counterparts and subsequently more likely to learn about

the importance of treating or viewing all animals as beneficial, and/or be exposed to beliefs that discourage intolerance and discrimination.

- The rationalisations provided above, furthermore, to a large extent, explain variations in crime – why certain individuals are inclined to partake in conservation crime and others are not. Not all individuals in a community are instilled with low self-control, nor are all individuals exposed to the same degree of socialisation regarding animals and nature. Not all individuals who have low self-control are necessarily prejudiced towards and/or have deficient socialisation regarding certain animals; opportunities are, furthermore, not always present. It is only when there is a confluence of these essential ingredients that conservation crime will quite conceivably result.

These points having been reasoned, it should, however, also be noted that not all illegal natural resource manipulation can be ascribed to a union of the above-mentioned factors, as anomalies are bound to occur.

CRITICAL REFLECTION

Critically evaluate this statement: Opportunistic or accidental crime involving animals or nature can easily arise, or individuals involved in conventional crime could diversify or be exposed to such crime, inadvertently causing them to pursue the abundant opportunities presented.

4.5.3 Sykes and Matza's neutralisation theory

Neutralisation theory, according to Siegel and Senna (2000), contends that damage caused by criminal actions is neutralised in the mind of an offender before a crime is committed, allowing guilt feelings to be eliminated, temporarily freeing a potential offender from the moral constraints imposed by society's rules and laws. Consonant with this sentiment, Fattah (1993) suggests that neutralisation has the cozener (criminal) as its focus, and that its main purpose is to enable the victimiser to overcome the moral and cultural barriers that stand in the way of the victimisation (criminal) act. Fattah (1993) consolidates by stating that the neutralisation process operates to strip the criminal act of its delinquent, illegal or immoral character, making it possible to hurt, injure or harm the victim without feeling bad or guilty about it, and without suffering post-victimisation cognitive dissonance (disharmony).

Sykes and Matza (1996) point out that although neutralisation techniques or justifications or rationalisations are commonly viewed as following deviant behaviour and as protecting the individual from self-blame and the blame of others after the act, there is also reason to believe that they precede deviant behaviour and make deviant behaviour possible. Conklin (2001) appropriately synchronises the above sentiments by stating that individuals can avoid moral blame and maintain self-esteem while violating the law if they tell themselves and others that they had no criminal intent or that their behaviour was justified.

4.5.3.1 Techniques of neutralisation

Five techniques of neutralisation can be distinguished, according to Conklin (2001), Sykes and Matza (in Blackburn, 1993), Sykes and Matza (1996), and Siegel and Senna (2000), namely:

- denial of responsibility
- denial of injury

- denial of the victim
- condemnation of the condemners
- appeal to higher loyalties.

Sections 4.5.3.1.1 to 4.5.3.1.5 cover these techniques.

4.5.3.1.1 Denial of responsibility

Offenders may declare that a criminal or delinquent act was an accident, or assert that it was caused by factors or circumstances beyond their control, such as poverty, a broken home, negligent parents, or wayward friends. Furthermore, Sykes and Matza (1996), aver that delinquents essentially approach a so-called 'snooker ball' conception of themselves in which they see themselves as helplessly propelled into new situations. Criminals, therefore, by learning to see themselves as more acted upon than acting, prepare the way for digression from the prevailing normative system without the necessity of an anterior assault on the medians themselves.

People participating in conservation crime who employ this technique might well argue that the state is failing in its duty to protect the province's or country's natural resource assets, and they are, therefore, fair game – the so-called 'if I don't do it somebody else will syndrome' – or they might reason that certain organisms, such as reptiles, are already so despised by society that their removal is beneficial rather than detrimental. They might even justify their behaviour by reconciling themselves with the fact that crime pertaining to nature is not a major crime, and that participation in it is commonplace.

4.5.3.1.2 Denial of injury

Criminal behaviour is rationalised. Offenders may claim that little or no harm will ensue as a result of their crime, even if they technically violate the law. Those that violate the law may be less sensitive to the effect their behaviour has on victims, or may regard their victims as objects or means to their own ends rather than as individuals (entities) who suffer when victimised.

People using this technique in relation to conservation deviance might well argue that natural resources are so vast and infinite that they can't possibly be depleted by their illegal exploitation efforts, despite such activities running counter to the law. Removal of organisms from their natural environment could be regarded as borrowing from the environment to ensure the safety of the organism, and/or by breeding with poached or rustled (borrowed) organisms, these can be redistributed, in this manner supposedly promoting the conservation of the resource. Due to society's general indifference towards nature, it could well transpire that the conservation delinquent's actions may be tolerated or absolved by the populace, reaffirming, so to speak, the notion that the delinquent's counteraction of social controls by means of meeting the criteria of the norms is an extension of customary practice, rather than a signal of complete resistance.

4.5.3.1.3 Denial of the victim

Offenders might argue that a crime is justified as rightful retaliation against the victim, that is, the victim deserves it. Offenders see the victim as a wrongdoer, rather than seeing themselves as wrongdoers, and use that attitude towards the victim to justify the offence. Sykes and Matza (1996) argue further in this regard that even if delinquents accept responsibility for their deviant actions and are willing to admit that their actions involve an injury or harm, the moral indignation of self and others may be neutralised by an insistence that the injury is not wrong in the light of the circumstances.

Given the negative stereotype and reputation that certain animals enjoy in society, conservation offenders might well deem it acceptable behaviour criminally to manipulate conservation resources. They might further, because of the careless or negligent attitude displayed towards reptile conservation by the authorities, feel that the authorities deserve to lose some of the biodiversity that the authorities have been charged with preserving, or even that they are doing society a favour by removing harmful and despised organisms. Having been apprehended or prosecuted for conservation-related deviance could also leave the perpetrator feeling victimised and abused as a soft target. The perpetrator could subsequently see crime directed at natural resources as a form of retaliation or rebellion – justice for the so-called 'wrong' inflicted on the perpetrator – whilst not experiencing any substantial awareness of a particular victim during the score settling exercise.

4.5.3.1.4 Condemnation of the condemners

The assertion regarding this neutralisation technique is that it is the motives and behaviour of the people who are condemning the offender, rather than the motives and behaviour of the offender, that should be denounced. The blame for the crime is essentially shifted onto others, and any feelings of guilt are suppressed.

Many kinds of offenders justify their actions in terms of this technique. Murderers and bank robbers compare, for example, the harsh punishments they receive with the lack of punishment for politicians who send young men to their deaths in senseless wars. Sykes and Matza (1996) aver further in this regard that delinquents may claim that the condemners are in fact hypocrites and deviants in disguise, or, even, individuals impelled by personal spite.

In a conservation crime context, offenders might argue that those condemning and prosecuting them for conservation crime are not themselves doing much to conserve the resource, and therefore have no place to speak. They might argue further that disparate legislation, lack of coordination, and inefficient sanctions, as well as indifference towards grassroots reptile conservation or policing, for example, are to blame for conservation deviance. They might add that law enforcers (guardians) are themselves commonly involved in illegal exploitation endeavours, seldom paying little more than lip service to the conservation cause.

4.5.3.1.5 Appeal to higher loyalties

This technique encompasses an attempt to justify violation of the law by the demands of a group – the needs of others, such as peers, take precedence. Offenders might well be trapped within syndicates or gangs, and intimidated to conform to standards that may be incompatible with the law. The crux of this technique, according to Sykes and Matza (1996), is that deviation from certain norms may occur not because the norms are rejected, but because other norms – held to be more pressing or involving a higher loyalty – are accorded precedence.

Illegal reptile traders or exploiters might be involved, at some or other level, in a syndicate smuggling fauna and flora, and either cannot, or don't want to, leave the fold. This connection may be the only form of income that the family unit has, and the cessation of such activities would deprive the family unit of an income. Conservation criminals do not necessarily repudiate the requirements of the prevailing normative system, but rather see themselves as caught up in an impasse that must be resolved, unfortunately, at the cost of infringing the law.

4.5.3.2 Ancillary neutralisation techniques

Conklin (2001) is of the view that, besides the above-mentioned generic techniques of neutralisation, the methods discussed in sections 4.5.3.2.1 and 4.5.3.2.2, amongst others, can also be employed to justify crime and delinquency.

4.5.3.2.1 A defence of necessity

Someone could use a defence of necessity to justify a criminal act by saying that it is required under the circumstances; this differs from the denial of responsibility in that the offender accepts responsibility for the act, while claiming that it was necessary. Pilfering natural resources in order to consume them as victuals or sell them for food money might be viewed as exculpatory and justified as a compulsory act for which an offender accepts full responsibility.

Not everyone will, however, partake in such activities, as level of self-control, exposure to crime opportunities, and degree of (negative) socialisation towards natural resources can be expected to differ considerably from person to person. This fact could, furthermore, to a large extent, serve to explain why certain individuals partake in different forms of crime, and why certain others don't become involved in crime at all.

4.5.3.2.2 A view of the violated law as unnecessary, unjust or capricious

An offender could view the law or prohibition being violated as unnecessary, unjust, and/or capricious. This argument may take the form of claiming that particular government interference or protocols with regard to conservation are actually detrimental to conservation or preservation efforts – a subtle variation on the 'condemnation of the condemners' theme. The following would be examples hereof , according to D. G. Malherbe, proprietor of a Die Vonds Snake Park in Noorder-Paarl (personal communication, December 2, 2002) and B. C. Vorster, proprietor of Cape Town Snake Park (personal communication, December 18, 2002):

- short-sighted placement (by government) of a total moratorium on the commercial trade in certain organisms
- prohibition on collection from the wild for breeding purposes
- non-utilisation of rehabilitated so-called 'problem' animals to promote education and preservation.

Regardless of what has been asserted above, it should be borne in mind that some offenders may be so isolated from the world of conformity that techniques of neutralisation need not be called into play. However, that said, techniques are critical in lessening the effectiveness of social controls, and they lie behind a large share of criminal behaviour (Sykes & Matza, 1996).

4.5.3.3 Function in a conservation crime context

A significant, but also ominous, consequence originating from the learning of skewed or biased perspectives towards nature or natural resources is the fact that people become desensitised and fail to perceive these as finite and susceptible to overexploitation. Lower order animals – and, even, plants, shrubs, trees and the soil – are often viewed with disregard, and the resultant antipathy and aversion towards them can serve to promote deviance in this sphere. Deviance can, due to this sentiment, easily transpire, be endorsed, and/or be tacitly condoned in the following two specific ways, amongst others:

- A blunted populace will not necessarily regard illegal acts involving natural resources as reprehensible. Consequently they won't ascribe nearly the same amount of censure towards such misdeeds as they would towards, for example, other more conventional crimes – such as rape, murder, arson and so forth – albeit that conservation crime rapes the country's natural heritage and biodiversity. Conservation crime is resultantly tolerated or allowed to take place with impunity.
- Criminally orientated individuals with a lethargic opinion of nature and its conservation (embedded through social learning) will, as has been mentioned, have a propensity towards conservation crime, should the confluence of required conditions or circumstances be present. The decision to partake in conservation crime is, however, not made on a whim, but is calculated and laced with rationality. Furthermore and importantly, it is justified through the process of neutralisation. Individual differences, with regard to negative socialisation towards nature, can, however, be expected to fluctuate from individual to individual to the extent that they will morally disengage, neutralise, and rationalise the decision to partake in such crime. This fact, it is submitted, will also apply, mutatis mutandis, to self-control (GTC).

Neutralisation techniques are undeniably appropriate in relation to conservation crime, and have, for this reason, been discussed subsequent to an exposition of self-control, opportunities (GTC), and socialisation as causational elements. It is the author's contention that the presence of these factors is a qualification for, fuels, and, to a certain extent, complements the application of neutralisation techniques with regard to natural resource crime and deviance.

CRITICAL REFLECTION

As with many other explanatory theories, the neutralisation theory can be viewed as a functional aid to explain the process of criminal actions, but not necessarily why they occur to begin with. As a criminologist, how would you field a question in this regard?

4.5.4 Cornish and Clarke's rational choice theory

As was alluded to previously, to cite the rational decisions that criminals make in passing is not considered adequate for the purposes of explaining this multifaceted cognitive process in the concatenation of conservation crime. Such downplay only serves to underplay the contribution of this important explicatory element in the total conservation crime performance.

According to Fattah (in Herbig, 2008), Cornish and Clarke's rational choice perspective takes as its point of departure the following assumptions:

- It recognises the mundane, opportunistic, and rational nature of much offending, thus rejecting the view that depicts it as immutably foreign to ordinary behaviour – driven by abnormal motivations, irrational, purposeless, unpredictable, and evil. Much criminal activity is, therefore, viewed as asymptomatic and commonplace.
- It stresses similarities between criminals and non-criminals, rather than whatever differences might exist. Instead of focusing on the irrational and pathological components in some crimes, it examines more closely the rational and adaptive aspects of offending.
- Rather than viewing crime as a unitary phenomenon that could be explained by a far-reaching theory, it calls for crime-specific analysis. The approach intends to provide

a framework for understanding all forms of crime, without attempting to impose a conceptual unity upon divergent criminal behaviour.

- Instead of focusing attention solely on the criminal, his or her attributes, traits, background, and factors governing his or her involvement in particular crimes, it draws attention to the criminal event itself and the situational factors that influence its commission. The rational choice approach explicitly recognises their importance in relation to the criminal event, and, furthermore, incorporates similar influences on decisions relating to involvement in crime.

Rational choice theory focuses, therefore, on the opportunity to commit crime and how the social environment structures criminal choices. Siegel (2007) charges that some irrational or mentally disturbed people may commit crime without thought of potential hazard, but it seems likely that immediate or situational variables determine and guide most criminal behaviour – people commit crime when they view its outcome as beneficial. Another essential ingredient of rational choice theory, and indeed a pillar upon which this theory leans heavily, is that of deterrence. Siegel (2007) is of the opinion that if crime is rational and people choose to commit crime, then it follows that crime can be controlled or eradicated by convincing potential offenders that crime is a poor choice that will not bring them rewards but instead pain, hardship, and deprivation.

Although it is not within the scope of this chapter to provide an exhaustive exposition of the deterrent capacity of this theory, it is, due to the converse essentially being the norm with regard to conservation deviance, deemed prudent to provide a laconic synopsis of the deterrence strategies emanating from it. Siegel (2007) stresses the following in this regard:

- Situational crime prevention: This is aimed at convincing would-be criminals to avoid specific targets. It relies on the doctrine that crime can be avoided if motivated offenders are denied access to suitable targets – in essence increased guardianship, advertising the fact that the potential reward is not worth the risk.
- General deterrence strategies: These are designed to make potential criminals fear the consequences of crime. The threat of punishment is aimed at convincing rational criminals that crime does not pay.
- Specific deterrence: This refers to punishing known criminals so severely that they will never be tempted to repeat their offences. If crime is rational, then painful punishment should reduce its future allure.
- Incapacitation strategies: These attempt to reduce crime rates by denying motivated offenders the opportunity to commit crime. If, despite the threat of law and punishment, some people still find crime attractive, then the only way to control their behaviour is to incarcerate them for extended periods.

4.5.4.1 Function in a conservation crime context

Cornish and Clarke (1987) assert, with regard to the rational choice perspective, that specific crimes are chosen and committed for specific reasons – decisions to offend, in other words, are influenced by the characteristics of both offences and offenders, and are the product of the interaction between the two. This sentiment, in essence, reflects and consolidates the submissions expressed about the rational choice approach's contribution towards the formulation of a comprehensive explanatory perspective of conservation crime. In summary of the foregoing section, it can, therefore, be said that the rational choice approach essentially sees crime as a function of opportunity, rationality, exogenic factors, and the particular situation.

Moreover, it suggests that criminals do not choose their targets randomly, but instead select them based on certain criteria, making it imperative to incorporate the victim in any explanatory model of criminality. Examples of such criteria, it is submitted, are attractiveness, availability, vulnerability (offence characteristics), and, of course, degree of self-control and/or negative socialisation towards natural resources (offender characteristics).

Even though someone contemplating conservation crime is already sensitised towards it, due to the reasons detailed elsewhere, the eventual decision to perform the crime itself remains, it is submitted, a cogent one. It must once again be made abundantly clear at this juncture that potential conservation criminals are in no way *forced* to commit the crime, but that the final decision to continue, displace and/or amend their deviant notions is based solely on economics, that is cost (risk)–benefit considerations (Cornish & Clarke, 1987), and is made entirely independently and coherently.

The rational decisions made by criminals to engage in conservation crime activities, it is submitted, are preceded and complemented by one or more of the neutralisation techniques previously described, and can be viewed as the last stage, so to speak, of the process that sets in motion the actual participation in an illegal act.

It could be said that the neutralisation employed facilitates and augments the decision (further rationalisation) to participate in conservation crime. It would, however, be equally feasible to presume that the decision to partake in conservation crime could result without neutralisation techniques being employed, and only due to the confluence of the factors greed, low self-control, opportunities, and socialisation. The employment of neutralisation techniques prior to involvement in conservation crime is, all things being equal, considered more probable than their non-employment. Manifesting from the preceding discussion, various criminological theories or perspectives or approaches, both classical/neoclassical and positivist, can be merged to explicate and provide an enhanced understanding of the phenomenon of conservation crime. Furthermore, it is implicit in this analysis that there is no readily available panacea or catch-all theory, and that the application of a single theory to produce a result of similar authenticity would be highly unlikely.

Owing to the inimitable and somewhat unconventional nature of natural resource crime, it seems appropriate to use relevant elements from existing theories to create a realistic and pragmatic amalgamated explanation, rather than attempt to force the various elements and characteristics of this natural resource crime sub-type into a corset of conformity.

The theoretical model, which should be viewed as a theoretical explanation rather than an explanatory theory, presented in this chapter, therefore, integrates certain beneficial elements from a number of leading crime theories in order to provide an effective explanation of much conservation crime and deviance. The model, in essence, attempts only to illustrate the causal relationships between the variables or elements at an unmitigated level.

The hypothetical explanation introduced in this chapter should, however, be sufficient to serve as a source for much needed research on the determinants, and interrelatedness, of a wide range of variables of natural resource crime, and to stimulate more focused research on the aetiology of this tremendously neglected topic in the South African context.

Figure 4.1 shows causational DNA and proposed trajectory of conservation crime (adapted from Herbig, 2008, p. 37).

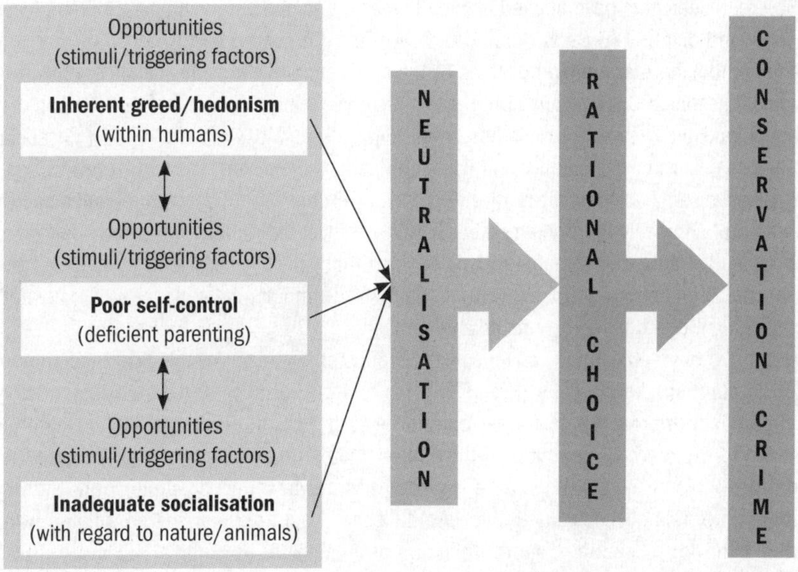

Figure 4.1 Causational DNA and proposed trajectory of conservation crime (adapted from Herbig, 2008, p. 37)

CRITICAL REFLECTION

Having been exposed to the rational choice theory as a fractional explanation for conservation crime, can you think of any other theory or theories that can similarly explain conservation crime. If so, provide a critical argument supporting your view, and if not, list the reasons for your viewpoint.

4.6 Case study: Practical application of criminological theory in addressing conservation crime

This section presents a case study that explores the potential of the routine activities theory to explicate the phenomenon of conservation crime in a South African context.

CASE STUDY

In order to demonstrate the utilitarian value of criminological theory to explain crime in the conservation arena, Herbig (2011) cites an authentic example (case study) involving several high profile South Africa nature reserves or game reserves. This qualitative enquiry examined the efficacy of routine activities theory to explain poaching in South Africa. Data collected at conservation areas threatened by poaching were analysed via the theory. To identify the causes of poaching and develop solutions, past research focused on this problem. Studies attributed poaching to poverty in African communities resulting in individuals hunting for food or profit (Jackson, 2008; Knecht, 2006), or overseas demand for exotic animals as live pets or their parts for use as traditional medicines and decorations (Warchol, Zupan, & Clack, 2003).

Several researchers have applied economic theories to understanding the problem, focusing on supply and demand (Bulte & Horan, 2002; Wilkie & Carpenter, 1999). Other studies, though fewer in number, have examined poaching by the application of criminological theory focusing on offenders (Eliason, 2003; Eliason & Dodder, 1999). While this has assisted understanding of what motivates individuals to poach, less has been done to examine why the protected conservation areas are so easily penetrated and the wildlife populations victimised on a regular basis. Therefore this qualitative study takes an alternative approach by examining the potential of routine activities theory to explain poaching in South Africa. Data were collected via interviews and observation at seven conservation areas threatened by poaching, and analysed via routine activities theory. Several causal factors were isolated with the analysis, with their related policy recommendations for controlling illegal hunting on conservation areas.

Notably, though poaching is a crime, explanations of it using criminological theory are more limited in number. Eliason (1999), pointing this fact out, discussed different methodological and theoretical approaches to further contribute to the literature. Neutralisation theory was employed to explain how poachers in the United States rationalised their actions (Eliason & Dodder, 1999; Forsyth, 1993) and as 'a cognitive dissonance reduction strategy, and individuals who use it are able successfully to alleviate guilt that would normally be associated with law violating behavior by neutralizing any definition of themselves as criminals' (Eliason, 2003, p. 225).[4] Neutralisation theory was also used to explain poaching in Canada, finding that violators avoided and manipulated existing laws, and that poaching became a part of the social structure (McMullan & Perrier, 1997, 2002). General deterrence theory was used by Milner-Gulland and Williams (1992) to model poacher behaviour. They found that organised hunters were deterred only at very high levels of enforcement, and concluded that penalties should be related to the 'quantity of output of a poacher' (Milner-Gulland and Williams, 1992, p. 397).[5] The longitudinal study by Hilborn et al. (2006) found that since 1977, expanded law enforcement budgets and anti-poaching patrols in the Serengeti National Park in Tanzania had allowed populations of certain animals to rebuild. While these studies have contributed to understanding various types of illegal hunting, the existing literature has been somewhat fragmented in providing the academic community and policymakers with a comprehensive understanding of the juxtaposition of all the elements contributing to poaching. Another approach may help to facilitate a better understanding of the phenomena.

Routine activities theory (Cohen and Felson, 1979) contends that crime is opportunistic and dynamic in nature. Routine activities are defined as 'the day to day activities that characterize a particular community. In disorganized communities, the routine activities are such that they practically invite crime' (Walsh & Ellis, 2007, p. 66). The theory is centred on three key elements: motivated offenders, suitable targets, and the lack of capable guardians of those targets. According to the theory, for crime to take place there must be the convergence of these three elements. Motivated offenders are the opportunistic criminals nearly always present in socially disorganised communities. The term 'suitable target' refers to the value or desirability of the property target, and includes access, visibility, and physical size. Capable guardianship is the amount of protection afforded the target by a person (such as a police officer) or physical deterrent (such as a fence or security system). It is further argued that the lack of any one of these elements will prevent the completion of crime (Cohen & Felson, 1979). As a result, crime rates will vary based on changes in capable guardianship and suitable targets.

The theory is based in part on the rational choice model (Cornish & Clark, 1987), in which one of the core assumptions is that individuals make rational decisions to commit crimes (Walsh & Ellis, 2007), weighing both the benefits and risks associated with crime before deciding to engage in the event. Unlike other theories that may concentrate on the offender, routine activities theory treats the motivated offender as only one element of the criminal event, and looks at other factors that contribute to the crime equation. First, it is premised on crime occurring in a social system (Winslow & Zhang, 2008), where criminals feed on and depend upon the patterns of everyday life. It also looks at the structural conditions that may explain the distribution of crime in society. Furthermore, it is not concerned with the personal histories of offenders. Instead it considers the crime's situational characteristics and the involvement of particular persons or objects, and the target's degree of attractiveness in the context of levels of guardianship (Cohen & Felson, 1979). Its focus on the three key elements of the criminal event has led to its application to explain a variety of offences. For example, Wright and Decker (1994) examined residential burglary via routine activities theory. Mannon (1998) applied the theory in his study of domestic violence, while Messner and Tardiff (2006) analysed via routine activities theory how socio-demographic characteristics in conjunction with time of day, week, and month related to urban homicide. Finally, studies have expanded the theory to focus on offenders, and not just on the nature of victimisation (Gilbertson, 2006; Meith & Meier, 1994).

It is contended that routine activities theory may provide a suitable and unique theoretical framework for examining poaching from conservation areas. South Africa's game reserves are located in close proximity to human populations, often with high rates of unemployment and crime providing a pool of motivated offenders. The field ranger staff and the natural and man-made barriers in the conservation areas are capable guardians. Finally, the wildlife are suitable targets. As is the case with humans, wildlife follows very predictable patterns of behaviour during their day to day activities.

Motivated offenders

The concept of motivated offenders was operationalised as poachers, who included both employees who pilfer from the reserves and outsiders who illegally enter a reserve to hunt. According to Cohen and Felson (1979) motivated offenders, with which they are not particularly concerned (Williams & McShane, 2010), were a product of socially disorganised areas. While routine activities theory did not focus on offenders (they were assumed as present by Cohen and Felson), the author believes a description is warranted, given that this study was the first to assess the potential of the theory to explain illegal hunting in South Africa. Therefore, some descriptive information on the nature and motivations of these offenders is helpful for this and future studies of poaching.

The interview and secondary data showed that motivated offenders were present at or near all of the research sites. This was partly a function of the following:

- large human populations living in close proximity to the conservation areas with desirable wildlife
- very high unemployment rates (Statistics South Africa, 2007)
- views that wildlife is a resource to be used rather than protected (Warchol et al., 2003)
- the formal claims on some parks contending that they were once tribal land (Herrington, 2008).

The Kruger National Park (KNP), for example, has approximately four million people living in villages and towns in close proximity to the park on all four sides, providing an ample amount of motivated offenders and a ready market for the illegally hunted bushmeat. The KNP's own literature acknowledges the presence of a significant bushmeat poaching problem (SANParks, 2008). A similar situation was found near the other reserves where large human populations were also present, though not to the same extent as at the KNP. An open air market selling bushmeat was found. Bushmeat was also observed at open air stalls in the neighbouring town. Evidence collected at the sites indicated that some of the game meat sold at these markets came from the nearby reserves. While the existence of offenders was a constant, considerable variation was found in their motivations and methods, and in the types of wildlife being poached. Offenders included the following:

- subsistence and commercial poachers of bushmeat
- ivory or rhinoceros poachers supplying buyers (middlemen) with tusks or horns for eventual resale to foreign syndicates
- abalone poachers in the Western Cape
- private collectors poaching rare plants, insects, and other natural resources.

Data revealed that subsistence hunters of bushmeat were the most common type of poacher at most of the sites. Subsistence poachers of bushmeat were typically lower income or unemployed black South Africans or Mozambicans possessing good hunting skills, who illegally entered the parks and killed game to feed themselves and their families. Most of these poachers were local residents who poached in close proximity to the sites, often walking to the conservation area. They hunted mainly by setting small numbers of snares, and occasionally hunted with small calibre firearms or bows and arrows. Also present were commercial poachers of bushmeat, who supplied the local market with wild game meat – an item in great demand (Traffic, 2002). Demographically similar to subsistence poachers, they operated alone or in small groups, employing larger numbers of snares or firearms (for larger game such as hippos), sometimes combined with dogs to drive game into a killing zone.

Ivory and rhinoceros hunters were sometimes individual offenders, but were more typically groups of poachers using larger calibre military weapons (SANParks, 2008). These poachers were found mainly in the lager parks.

Abalone poachers, present only at the coast, comprised a range of offenders. Abalone is in very high demand both for the South African market and for shipment to Asia. These poachers were described as a mix of opportunistic local fishermen, white South African certified divers, and, more commonly, gangs of untrained divers desperate for income and recruited from the large and impoverished informal settlements in nearby areas. The purchase of and thriving trade in abalone was mainly the domain of several Chinese Triads operating in the area, informally known as the Abalone Coast (Redpath, 2001; Warchol et al., 2003).

Private collectors were individuals motivated by the desire to increase their own collections of rare species – mainly plants, insects, and small reptiles. They were primarily men and women from Eastern Europe and Asia. These individuals were described as educated foreigners working in small groups of two or three. Recent arrests of plant poachers have revealed that several were well-known biologists and academics.

An interesting finding was that motivated offenders also included park employees poaching for bushmeat, ivory and rhinoceros. These individuals were motivated by the opportunity to earn money from selling game meat to local villagers or ivory or horn to traffickers. In one premier park, staff illegally hunting has been recorded. In one of the more serious cases, a park ranger was arrested for shooting 20 white rhinoceros, and another admitted to killing nearly 4 dozen over a

12-year period to pay gambling debts. In another instance, two interpretive guides on a so-called 'day walk' with a group of tourists spotted a white rhinoceros on their tour. They later returned after dropping off their guests and shot the animal for its horn. Evidence of complicity between rangers and poachers in the parks has also been reported. Another strategy that is employed was described as follows:

> **The ranger calls his family and tells them where his unit will deploy for the patrol. They [his family] tell the poachers who target other areas. Others use their mobile to tell them where the animals are. The ranger gets a share of the meat or the profits. Simple (Herbig & Warchol, 2011, pp. 10–11).**

It was established that management practices on some private commercial game farms also contributed to the creation of motivated offenders. Private commercial game farms in South Africa are primarily operations owned by white people. Some owners live on the site and manage daily operations, while others in the area were absentee landlords. Some of these owned multiple properties and employed managers to run the daily operations of their farms. It was, however, far more likely that farms with absentee owners and/or inefficient or corrupt managers would be targeted by poachers. In fact, the data revealed that there have been cases in which game farm managers have actively participated in illegal hunting by working with a poaching gang for a share of the profits. An owner summed it up by stating: 'Ninety-nine percent of game farm poaching is due to bad management. Too many farmers aren't concerned about security. If the landlord is truant, the farm manager can tell them anything' (Herbig & Warchol, 2011, p. 11).

Finally, how the manager compensated employees was also identified as a motivating factor in employee-based poaching. It was revealed that farm employees were often paid in both cash and groceries. However, few managers provided employees with quality game meat from common species, even though it was highly desired. An employee also noted:

> **Blacks typically get very little from the game farms – low pay and the worst part of any animals, if they get any. If a white wants to kill a lion, he can afford to do so, legally. If a black wants to hunt warthog traditionally, common for them, he has to do it illegally (Herbig & Warchol, 2011, p. 11).**

As a result, employees of some private farms poached game from their owners – a form of employee pilferage. Simply by providing his workers with quality surplus game, one owner alleviated some of the employee poaching pressure on his farm, and summed it up by stating: 'They want protein, good meat. Slaughter a couple impala and give it to them every month and it keeps them from poaching two or three times as many' (Herbig & Warchol, 2011, p. 11).

One park administrator stated: 'Where there is wildlife, there will be poaching' (Herbig & Warchol, 2011, p. 11). This statement confirms the view of others that the combination of the high demand for protein, population increases, unemployment, and severe poverty among many rural black South Africans near the sites were very significant motivating factors for poachers to hunt for bushmeat. This was also apparent with the abalone poachers at the coast. Many of the desperate township residents, who lacked any training in diving, literally risked their lives in search of income.

Furthermore, the lure of a potentially high payoff for a rhinoceros horn or elephant tusk, even among field rangers charged with protecting these species, was identified as another strong factor motivating poachers to take the chance of killing either of these animals and trying to sell its parts. Employee poaching illustrates a unique occurrence, that is, instances of capable guardians of the wildlife becoming the motivated offenders. Finally, the desire among foreign collectors, some of whom were professors and scientists, to have those rare plant or insect species motivated them to steal.

Suitable targets

Cohen and Felson defined suitable targets as things that are or at least appear valuable and therefore worth stealing (Williams & McShane, 2010). The concept of suitable targets was operationalised in the study as the desired wildlife species sought after by poachers. These include the full range of wildlife, from common mammals such as antelope or hippo for the bushmeat trade, to rhinoceros and elephant for their horns and ivory, abalone, and rare and endangered plants and reptiles. All of the wildlife species were considered very valuable commodities for consumption and trade in the local and international market. All sites had problems with poaching, though it varied by locale due to species (or suitable target) availability. Data revealed that several parks were under heavy pressure from organised gangs of poachers striking on a regular basis. Wildlife populations which included hippo were very attractive targets for bushmeat poachers, given the large amount of meat hippo provide. Data from 2005 revealed that the hippo population had declined dramatically in just two years. It was found that the protection of valuable animals was paramount over protecting the common grazing species, which were nevertheless a target of poachers. Yet, due to the extensive amount of protection afforded these high value species, the owners and rangers of certain private parks stated that poachers had not been able to kill any type of animal. In regard to poaching, several parks reported serious problems that they attributed to their very small field ranger staff and subsequent inability to thoroughly patrol the parks.

All the sites offered a diverse array of suitable targets that had significant monetary or personal value to the motivated offender. These included the smaller mammals for bushmeat consumption and sale; elephant and rhinoceros for the international trade in ivory and horn; abalone in demand in both South Africa and Asia; and the small reptiles, plants and insects sought after by collectors. Variation was found in the size of the suitable target populations by site and also by species.

The absence of capable guardians

The final component of routine activities theory is capable guardianship, which refers to the amount of protection afforded the target by a person or a physical barrier. In this study, the concept of guardianship was operationalised as having three components. These were:

1 game fences
2 natural obstacles, including terrain and dangerous wildlife
3 the field rangers, including their supervisors.

The first guardian that may be encountered by poachers coming from outside a park, even prior to their encountering a game fence, could be a natural barrier. Only one park served as an example of a location with an external natural barrier providing a level of guardianship. Its northern border is on a river, across which is a neighbouring country, the home to many poachers who target the reserve. Park staff revealed that during the wet season, when the river is high, crossing is more difficult, thereby deterring offenders from that country. Conversely, it was repeatedly mentioned that the absence of this capable guardian during the dry season influenced poaching, leading to more losses of wildlife. However, the other sites lacked any significant external natural barriers and could be approached by simply walking or driving up to the game fence.

CRITICAL REFLECTION

An ideal situation would be to make the very community from which the poachers originate the guardians of the selfsame natural resources being poached. How do you think the local community or communities can be persuaded or incentivised to fulfil such a guardianship role and reduce or prevent poaching?

Game fences

As soon as any external natural barriers have been overcome, the next guardian encountered by an intruder was the game fence, which was used at all sites. Fencing defines ownership and the boundary of a location, but provided only a limited deterrent to access in the sites, as the fences were mainly designed to prevent animals from leaving. Fencing that did exist at all sites typically consisted primarily of heavy gauge wire fencing that stood several meters in height, supported by wooden posts. Sections of the game fence were sometimes electrified to prevent animals from leaving rather than to keep intruders from entering. The majority of the fence lines also had standoff zones – an area of approximately three meters on each side of the fence where the brush was cut back, allowing for the unobstructed surveillance of the perimeter. Even though these fences were quite high and occasionally electrified, they had a very limited deterrent effect on humans. Data revealed that they represented only a minor obstacle to the motivated offender. It was robustly stated that entering a protected area offered little challenge to the poacher. Electric fences were not always functional and even if they were, intruders simply shorted them out and cut the wire or dug a shallow depression under the fence to gain access to the park. Other techniques included tearing down entire sections of fence. Additionally, overgrown brush close to the fence in some sections impaired surveillance of the perimeter, combined with the fact that there were usually not enough guard forces to engage in proactive patrols. Even more surprising was that bushmeat poachers, who commonly rely on snaring to capture animals, would make their snares out of wire they cut from the fence.

Natural obstructions

Once inside the park, the intruder may encounter more natural barriers hindering movement. Examples of this were found in both a private reserve and the KNP. The private reserve's terrain is very sandy, making travel slow and arduous and leaving a clear trail that is easily observed and followed by field ranger staff. This feature contributed to the lower levels of poaching in this park. Poachers simply targeted the neighbouring reserve, where the terrain was less challenging. A second example was found in the southern part of the KNP, where the Lower Sabie River also inhibited access to the region during the wet season. At flood stage, this large and fast river presented a significant barrier for the intruder in this section of the park.

Existing wildlife – including predatory or aggressive animals such as lion, leopard, and buffalo – also provided a limited amount of natural capable guardianship deterring some poachers. Avoiding the thick bush that often exists in the parks, poachers commonly follow game trails. Some predators also regularly use these trails in search of the same species that poachers are seeking. At the same time, large game – such as buffalo – use these game trails to travel to grazing areas. It was reported that on more than one occasion, intruders, who included suspect poachers and illegal migrants from a neighbouring country, were attacked and sometimes killed by these animals. On the other side of the coin, the lack of these species serves as an incentive to some poachers. For example, private commercial game farms may not have predatory animals such as lions or leopards. Rangers at these sites reported that the lack of predators was perhaps one factor that made their sites more attractive for bushmeat poachers, thereby requiring close guardianship by field rangers.

Field rangers

The primary source of capable guardianship, and the one that was most influential on the level of poaching, were the field ranger units which operated at all sites, though with interesting differences. Staff commonly made the point that the field ranger force at some of the sites was insufficient in size; this influenced poaching.

CRITICAL REFLECTION

Staff shortages are a reality and will probably persist for some time to come. In the context of preventing or combating conservation crime, critically discuss the truism 'working smarter, not harder'.

Almost all parks stated that they lacked sufficient personnel adequately to patrol, and to respond to and investigate offences. On the whole, the field rangers were found to be quite capable guardians. They were very enthusiastic about their jobs, eagerly recounting incidents where they spotted poachers, and even pursuing them into the neighbouring communities. In the case of private parks, the rangers' actions were a function of their core business. Their financial survival depended on the revenue generated from wildlife. Since these animals were intended for sale to other game reserves that comprise part of South Africa's lucrative tourism industry, any losses would have directly impacted the farm's profit, and perhaps the guards' employment status.

It was also found that poachers engaged in a variety of tactics to defeat the effectiveness of the field rangers. Data revealed that poachers employed diversionary tactics such as setting snares in obvious locations meant to be found by rangers. Field rangers would then establish an observation point in one area, only to have the poachers hunt in a different area that lacked capable guardians. In another example, a field ranger supervisor reported that several armed poaching gangs were regularly hunting in the reserve. When field ranger units responded to intrusions in one section, the poachers would leave to hunt in another region. This went on continuously, with field rangers constantly reacting to the intrusions, often after wildlife had been killed. Another, more insidious, tactic involved poachers threatening field rangers' families, thereby rendering the rangers ineffective. As one field ranger explained: 'The guy [poacher] was threatening the field rangers' families – rape, theft, arson – he would do it unless he [the ranger] cooperated' (Herbig & Warchol, 2011, p. 12).

Another problem identified was the influence of a poor work ethic on poaching among some field rangers. This was especially prevalent at a certain park which includes a long coastline with a marine sanctuary that is targeted nearly daily by poachers mainly seeking abalone. Unlike the case in other parks, the field rangers were responsible for a range of duties in addition to law enforcement. These included fire control, assisting with research projects, and infrastructure maintenance. The supervisor reported some instances of field rangers who, on days of poor weather (certainly not uncommon in the area), would spend their entire shift in warming huts rather than on patrol. It was reported that on these days abalone poachers would often strike, knowing that the field rangers were less likely to be on patrol. Abalone poachers, acting as recreational sport divers, were also reported to be poaching during good weather, but leaving their catch in bags tied to underwater rocks adjacent the shoreline. During poor weather, they would return to retrieve their catch, again aware that they were unlikely to be observed.

Conclusion

Whereas much research has been done on the crime of poaching, only a limited amount has applied criminological theories. Therefore, the objective of the inquiry featured in the case study in this chapter was to build upon the existing criminological literature by completing a pioneer examination of the crime of poaching in South Africa from the theoretical perspective of routine activities theory. In particular, it focused on how the interaction of motivated offenders with preferred wildlife, and the corresponding lack of capable guardianship, resulted in poaching in certain of South Africa's protected conservation areas. The findings support the author's view that routine activities has significant potential as an appropriate theoretical construct to understand better the nature of illegal hunting on conservation areas and develop solutions. Based on assimilated data, the three components of routine activities theory – motivated offenders, suitable targets, and the absence of capable guardians – were identified at the research sites. First, the presence of motivated offenders was a function of social and economic factors in the communities in close proximity to the conservation areas. These factors included high unemployment, land claims on the parks, viewpoints about wildlife being a resource to exploit indiscriminately, and high demand for wild game as food. All the conservation areas reported a clear and ongoing threat from poaching. Second, the conservation areas all contained suitable targets consisting of a wide range of common and rare species. While suitable targets were generally omnipresent and predictable in their patterns of behaviour, there was some variation in poaching observed in the conservation areas, due in part to the types and populations of wildlife. Third, the absence of capable guardianship was also documented. This occurred as a result of insufficient manpower to patrol a site thoroughly; field rangers who were absent due to time off or a poor work ethic; field rangers who were actively involved in or complicit with criminal consortia; and managers who were absentees, refused to recognise seasonal game-demand changes that required enhanced patrol, or were also directly involved in poaching. All of these issues contributed to leaving a site's wildlife vulnerable to poaching. Most notably, the data additionally revealed instances in which motivated offenders converged with suitable targets that lack capable guardianship and poaching occurred. In contrast, when the guardianship was dexterous, the data indicated that poaching was far less of a dilemma. The results point toward some pragmatic policy implications focused on guardianship, including target hardening. While capable guardianship consisted of three elements – boundary fences, natural barriers including terrain and dangerous or predatory wildlife, and the field ranger units – each had an influence, but the latter was the most significant. Fences were an easily overcome obstacle that, at most, temporarily slowed offenders, indicating that minimum effort should be placed on enhancing these as a deterrent against human intruders. However, the natural guardians of difficult terrain, high rivers, and the presence of predatory animals did deter some poachers from hunting in these parks, either completely or depending on the season. As a result, for example, field ranger patrols in areas with these features can be modified, with fewer rangers in selected areas, depending on the season. This could be critical for areas that are short staffed.

It is important to mention that the research is not without limitations. Whereas the study used several sites, a non-probability sample was employed, detracting from the ability to extrapolate accurately and generalise from the results to the population.

Moreover, the data on offenders was sourced from those charged with preventing poaching, not from the poachers themselves. Every attempt was, however, made to authenticate the validity of the offender data by cross-checking the interview responses against one another, the observations, and the secondary data on poaching incidents. While this cannot guarantee complete accuracy of the data on offender motivations from the field rangers and their supervisors, little or no variation in responses was found. However, this project was not intended to be the definitive application of routine activities theory on poaching. Instead it was designed to offer a first look at the efficacy of using this approach to explain this crime. The results indicate this theoretical approach offers promise for identifying additional causes beyond the known ones and developing new conservation policy.

It is hoped that it will lead to future studies employing alternative methodologies or theoretical approaches in different research sites to develop and test new wildlife conservation law strategies and contribute to the theoretical explanations of illegal hunting. These may include a comprehensive study via routine activities theory at one location that includes data gathered directly from offenders to thoroughly document their decisionmaking process, or one that matches several private and public game reserves located in proximity to one another for an interesting comparison. Furthermore, some conservation areas in South Africa are implementing new technologies for field rangers and the use of remote sensing and ultra-light aircraft for patrols. It would be of value to assess the impact of these enhancements of guardianship on poaching. The practical application of criminological theory, it would certainly seem, has considerable scope in the conservation and allied realms.

Critical thinking questions

1. Can you think of any other criminological theories that could explain conservation crime, generally or in a specific sphere?
2. Weigh up the argument of reactive conservation initiatives against proactive conservation initiatives in the context of actual preservation of natural resources (reactive success versus proactive failure).
3. After reading this chapter, what will your approach be to the use of the terms 'environmental crime' or 'ecological crime' or 'green crime' to refer to crime in the natural resource remit?
4. In your view, why is rhino poaching and the poaching of other conservation resources still prevalent in this day and age, and when do you think it will be reduced or come to an end?
5. Why, in your opinion, do conservation authorities, academics, and other relevant organisations not pool their knowledge and resources to combat the conservation crime scourge?

References

Aas, K. F. (2013). *Globalization and crime* (2nd ed.). Thousand Oaks, CA: Sage Publications.

Agnew, R. (1998). The causes of animal abuse: a social-psychological analysis. *Theoretical Criminology, 2*(2), 177–209.

Bartol, C. R. (1995). *Criminal behaviour: a psychosocial approach* (4th ed.). Englewood Cliffs, NJ: Prentice Hall.

Blackburn, R. (1993). *The psychology of criminal conduct: theory, research and practice.* Liverpool: John Wiley & Sons.

Brantingham, P. J., & Brantingham, P. L. (1998). Environmental criminology: from theory to urban planning practice. *Studies on Crime and Crime Prevention, 7*(1), 31–60.

Brown, S. E., Esbensen, F., & Geis, G. (2001). *Criminology: explaining crime and its context* (4th ed.). Cincinnati, OH: Anderson.

Bulte, E. H., & Horan, R. D. (2002). Does human population growth increase wildlife harvesting? An economic assessment. *Journal of Wildlife Management, 66*(3), 574–580.

Burke, R. H. (2009). *An introduction to criminological theory* (3rd ed.), Portland, OR: Willan.

Cohen, L., & Felson, M. (1979). Social change and crime rate trends: a routine activities approach. *American Sociological Review, 44*, 588–608.

Conklin, J. E. (2001). *Criminology* (7th ed.). Boston: Allyn and Bacon.

Cornish, D., & Clark, R. (1987). Understanding crime displacement: an application of rational choice theory. *Criminology, 25*, 933–947.

Damm, G. R. (2002). *The conservation game: saving Africa's biodiversity.* Rivonia: Safari Club International African Chapter.

Einstadter, W., & Henry, S. (1995). *Criminological theory: an analysis of its underlying assumptions.* Fort Worth: Harcourt Brace.

Eliason, S. L. (1999). The illegal taking of wildlife: toward a theoretical understanding of poaching. *Human Dimensions of Wildlife, 4*(2), 27–39.

Eliason, S. L. (2003). Illegal hunting and angling: the neutralization of wildlife law violations. *Society & Animals, 11*(3), 225–243.

Eliason, S. L., & Dodder, R. A. (1999). Techniques of neutralization used by deer poachers in the western United States: a research note. *Deviant Behavior, 20*, 233–252.

Fattah, E. A. (1993). The rational choice/opportunity perspectives as a vehicle for integrating criminological and victimological theories. In R. V. Clarke & M. Felson (Eds.) *Routine activity and rational choice: advances in criminological theory.* (pp. 225–258). New Brunswick: Transaction.

Forsyth, C. J. (1993). Chasing and catching 'bad guys': the game warden's prey. *Deviant Behavior, 14*, 209–226.

Gibbs, C., Gore, M. L., McGarrell, E. F., & Rivers III, L. (2009). Introducing conservation criminology. *British Journal of Criminology, 1*, 1–21.

Gilbertson, T. A. (2006). Alcohol-related incident guardianship and undergraduate college parties: enhancing the social norms approach. *Journal of Drug Education, 36*(1), 73–90.

Glick, L. (1995). *Criminology.* Needham Heights, MA: Allyn & Bacon.

Gottfredson, M. R., & Hirschi, T. (1996). Criminality and low self-control. In J. E. Conklin (Ed.). *New perspectives in criminology.* (pp. 39–50). Boston: Allyn and Bacon.

Herbig, F. J. W. (2003). *The illegal reptile trade: a criminological perspective* (Unpublished doctoral thesis). Pretoria: University of South Africa.

Herbig, F. J. W. (2008). Conservation crime causation – towards proactive compliance management. *Acta Criminologica, 21*(2), 27–39.

Herbig, F. J. W. (2011). Informant application in South African conservation crime management: criminological affordances. *Acta Criminologica, 24*(3), pp. 97–112.

Herbig, F. J. W., & Joubert, S. J. (2006). Criminological semantics: conservation criminology – vision or vagary? *Acta Criminologica, 19*(3), 88–103.

Herbig, F. J. W., & Warchol, G. (2011). South African conservation crime and routine activities theory: a causal nexus? *Acta Criminologica, 24*(2), 1–16.

Herrington, S. (Producer). (2008, November 10). *50/50.* [Television broadcast]. Zululand Wildlife E-Forum - Second Appeal. Johannesburg. South African Broadcasting Service.

Hilborn, R., Arcese, P., Borner, M., Hando, J., Hopcraft, G., Loibooki, M., ... Sinclair, A. R. (2006). Effective enforcement in a conservation area. *Science, 314*(5803), 1266.

Jackson, T. (2008). Coming of age. *Africa Geographic, 16*(4), 29–33.

Kidd, M. (1998). Environmental crime: time for a rethink in South Africa. *South African Journal of Environmental Law and policy, 5*(2), 181–204.

Knecht, G. B. (2006). *Hooked: pirates, poaching and the perfect fish*. Emmaus, PA: Rodale.

Lynch, M. J., & Stretsky, P. B. (2003). The meaning of green: contrasting criminological perspectives. *Theoretical Criminology, 7*(2), 217–238.

Mannon, J. (1998). Domestic and intimate violence: an application of routine activities theory. *Aggression and Violent Behavior, 2*(1), 9–24.

McMullan, J. L., & Perrier, D. C. (1997). Poaching vs. the law: the social organization of illegal fishing. In J. L. McMullan, D. Perrier, S. Smith, & P. Swam (Eds.). *Crimes, laws and communities*. Halifax: Fernwood.

McMullan, J. L. & Perrier, D. C. (2002). Poaching and the ironies of law enforcement. *Law & Society Review, 36*(4), 679–718.

Meith, T. D., & Meier, R. F. (1994). *Crime and its social context: toward and integrated theory of offenders, victims and situations*. Albany: State University of New York Press.

Messner, S., & Tardiff, K. (2006). The social ecology of urban homicide: an application of the 'routine activities approach.' *Criminology, 23*(2), 241–267.

Milner-Gulland, E. J., & Williams, N. L. (1992). A model of incentives for the illegal exploitation of black rhinos and elephants: poaching pays in Luangwa Valley, Zambia. *Journal of Applied Ecology, 29*(2), 388–401.

Moyer, I. L. (2001). *Criminological theories: traditional and nontraditional voices and themes*. Thousand Oaks: Sage Publications.

Redpath, J. (2001). *The hydra phenomenon, rural sitting ducks and other recent trends around organized crime in the Western Cape*. Institute for Human Rights and Criminal Justice Studies, Technikon South Africa, Gauteng.

Rossmo, D. K. (1995). Place, space and police investigations: hunting serial violent criminals. In J. E. Eck & D. L. Weisburd (Eds.), *Crime and place: crime prevention studies* (Vol. 4) (pp. 217– 235). Monsey, NY: Criminal Justice Press.

SANParks. (2008). *Conservation at South African National Parks*. Retrieved June 9, 2008, from http://www.sanparks.org/conservation/investigations.

Schmalleger, F. (1996). *Criminology today*. Englewood Cliffs, NJ: Prentice Hall.

Siegel, L. J. (2007). *Criminology: theories, patterns, and typologies* (9th ed.). Belmont, CA: Thomson.

Siegel, L. J., & Senna, J. J. (2000). *Juvenile delinquency: theory, practice, and law* (7th ed.). Belmont, CA: Wadsworth.

South, N. (1998). A green field for criminology? A proposal for a perspective. *Theoretical Criminology, 2*(2), 211–233.

South, N., & Beirne, P. (1998). Editors' introduction. *Theoretical Criminology, 2*(2), 147–148.

Snyman, H. F. (1990). The development of criminology. In M. G. T. Cloete & R. Stevens (Eds.). *Criminology*. (pp. 3–19). Halfway House: Southern.

Statistics South Africa. (2007). *March labour force survey*. Retrieved March 1, 2008, from http://www.statssa.gov.za/PublicationsHTML/P0210March2007/html/P0210March2007.html.

Swanepoel, G. (1997). The illegal trade in rhino horn as an example of trade in an endangered species. *Acta Criminologica, 10*(2), 47–57.

Sykes, G. M., & Matza, D. (1996). Techniques of neutralisation. In J. Muncie, E. McLaughlin, & M. Langan (Eds.). *Criminological perspectives: a reader*. (pp. 206–213). London: Sage Publications.

Traffic. (2002). *Food for thought: the utilization of wild meat in eastern and southern Africa*. Nairobi: World Wildlife Fund, TRAFFIC East/Southern Africa-.

Van Heerden, T. J. (1988). *Introduction to police science*. Pretoria: Unisa.

Walsh, A., & Ellis, L. (2007). *Criminology: an interdisciplinary approach*. Thousand Oaks, CA: Sage Publications.

Warchol, G., Zupan, L., & Clack, W. (2003). Transnational criminality: the illegal wildlife trade in southern Africa. *International Criminal Justice Review, 13*, 1–27.

White, R., & Haines, F. (2001). *Crime and criminology: an introduction* (2nd ed.). South Melbourne, Australia: Oxford.

Wilkie, D. S., & Carpenter, J. F. (1999). Bushmeat hunting in the Congo Basin: an assessment of impacts and options for mitigation. *Biodiversity & Conservation, 8*(7), 927–955.

Williams, F., & McShane, M. (2010). *Criminological theory* (5th ed.). Upper Saddle River, NJ: Prentice Hall.

Winfree, L. T., & Abadinsky, H. (2003). *Understanding crime: theory and practice* (2nd ed.). Belmont, CA: Thomson-Wadsworth.

Winslow, R., & Zhang, S. (2008). *Criminology: a global perspective*. Upper Saddle River, NJ: Pearson Publishing.

Wright, R., & Decker, S. (1994). *Burglars on the job: streetlife and residential break-ins*. Boston: Northeastern University Press.

Yablonsky, L. (1990). *Criminology: crime and criminality* (4th ed.). Grand Rapids: HarperCollins.

Chapter 5

Substance abuse and drug-related crime in South Africa

B HÄEFELE

5.1 Introduction

A 2005 United Nations (UN) report on Crime and Development in Africa concluded that 'Africa may have become the continent most targeted by organized crime'. Among other things, it states: 'International drug seizures indicate that Africa is increasingly being used to route drugs destined for other markets.' The region used to be a transhipment point for drugs originating from South East Asia and South America, en route to the markets of North America and Europe. In recent years, the cultivation, smuggling, and consumption of drugs has become the greatest organised crime concern to sout0hern Africa. Simultaneously, domestic consumption in South Africa of so-called 'hard' drugs – including methamphetamine, heroin and cocaine – has escalated in the last decade (Hübschle, 2011, p. 3).[1]

The increase in substance abuse in South Africa caused major social implications for the country. The harms associated with substance abuse dependency include:

- poverty
- unemployment
- a drain on the healthcare system
- the disintegration of family systems
- child abuse
- an increase in teenage pregnancies and drug-related crime (Häefele & Ovens, 2013).

The annual release of South Africa's crime statistics once again draws attention to the country's substance abuse problem. The numbers show that, while there has been a general increase in drug-related crime across the country, the Western Cape Province continues to be the most affected (South African Police Service (SAPS), 2012).

This chapter will discuss the extent of substance abuse and drug-related crime reported annually to the South African Police Service (SAPS) since 2004. Special attention will be given to the history and origin of substance abuse in the South African context. The history of alcohol abuse on the Cape wine farms (the so-called '*papsak/dop* system'), and the forced removal during apartheid due to the implementation of the Group Areas Act to the Cape Flats, will form part of the discussions on the origin, history, development, scope, and extent of the substance abuse problem. The incidence of foetal alcohol syndrome (FAS) in South Africa is one of the highest in the world. FAS is a medical diagnosis, made by physicians who have received specific training in the assessment of birth defects. When FAS is diagnosed, there is a known or strongly suspected history of maternal use of alcohol. Any amount of alcohol is damaging (FAS, 1995).

---

1 Reprinted by permission of the ISS.

This phenomenon will also be discussed to emphasise the impact on the social environment. Statistics will highlight the so-called 'hotspot' areas for drug-related crime reported to the SAPS.

There are a number of theories in the criminological literature to explain substance abuse. The focus here is on the explanation of anomie theory and social disorganisation theory to provide better understanding of the substance abuse problem in South Africa. These theories are singled out as the most applicable to explain the substance abuse problem. Mitchells Plain, situated on the Cape Flats in the Western Cape Province, has the highest drug-related crime reported figures in the whole of South Africa (for the past 10 years) and is used as a case study to illustrate the practical application of criminology. A number of substance abuse addicts are used as case studies to explain how their addiction impacts on women's pregnancies, their daily life, families, social environment, employment, and crime.

The chapter concludes by reflecting on the social implications of substance abuse on families and leaves the reader with a few critical questions on how to deal with this growing phenomenon in South Africa.

5.2 Definitions/key concepts

5.2.1 Drug/substance

The *National Drug Master Plan (2006–2011)* broadly defines a drug as a 'substance that is used with the intention of bringing about change in some existing process or state be it psychological, physiological or biomedical' (South Africa (SA) Department of Social Development (DSD), 2007, p. 5). This

> **indicates that a variety of substances from a wide range of sources can be considered as drugs, and they can be divided broadly as follows ...:**
>
> **Naturally occurring substances: Certain plants and animal tissue have psychoactive effects; in some cases the crude material is used as a drug preparation while in other cases the psychotic substances are extracted and purified [for example cannabis (dagga), tobacco and khat (a herbal drug with mildly hallucinogenic qualities)].**
>
> **Semi-synthetic drugs: Chemical manipulations of psychoactive substances that have been extracted from natural materials may result in drugs with different properties. Examples are cocaine, alcohol and heroin.**
>
> **Synthetic drugs: These involve psychoactive agents neither found in nature nor derived from natural psychoactive agents. They are created entirely by the laboratory manipulation of two or more relatively simple chemicals, which are themselves usually psychoactively inert. Examples are methylenedioxymethamphetamine (MDMA) (ecstasy), methaqualone (Mandrax), methamphetamine and methcathinone (SA DSD, 2007, p. 5).**

5.2.2 Drug addiction

The American Psychiatric Association defines drug addiction as 'a chronic, relapsing disease that results from the long-term effects of drugs on the brain' (Jasper, 2011, p. 1).[2]

5.2.3. Drug abuse

The concept 'abuse' means the 'persistent or periodic excessive drug use inconsistent with or unrelated to acceptable medical practice' (SA DSD, 2008, p. 1).

5.2.4 Drug-dependent personality

This is a personal trait characterised by a pervasive psychological dependence on mood-altering substances (Siegel, 2011).

5.2.5 Operational definition for substance abuse

For the purpose of this chapter and for clarity, substance abuse means the chronic abuse of drugs such as Methamphetamine and alcohol and the subsequent impact on family life.

5.3 Origin of the crime phenomenon/criminological field

It is widely believed that in most of southern African organised crime markets evolved during the 1980s. The tightly controlled security situation and discriminatory apartheid laws made it difficult for foreigners to make contact with local criminal groups and to find markets in South Africa during this period. However, after 1994 and the advent of democracy, South Africa's border controls became less strict. Organised criminal syndicates saw South Africa as a key area for the smuggling of illegal commodities (weapons, drugs, stolen vehicles, and the like).

5.3.1 Forced removals

One of the most frequently quoted causes for drug trafficking and substance abuse in South Africa originates with the apartheid, colonial past and the forced removals from District Six to the Cape Flats. The Cape Flats was born with the passing of South Africa's Group Areas Act (41 of 1950), which saw thousands of people forced from Cape Town's suburbs to an area which is now home to the city's poorest communities. Families found themselves being uprooted and moved from family homes to cramped council houses and flats in what became Hanover Park, Grassy Park, and Mitchells Plain, among others (Leggett, 2004). This relocation led to the destruction of extended and nuclear family structures in the community.

5.3.2 Disintegration of family structure

With the forced removals during apartheid in the background, it is also important to focus on the structure of the family in the pre-apartheid (first generation) and post-apartheid (second generation) era. The Group Areas removals in the Western Cape had a destructive impact of coloured families and communities:

> **One of the first casualties was the extended family, resulting in the isolation of nuclear families within small housing units. The removals had destroyed the way the [so-called] 'street, the corner shop and the shebeens [local drinking places] in**

2 The contribution of Jasper, K. is gratefully acknowledged.

> **the "old" areas had provided the residents with a great measure of communal space' (Pinnock, 1985, p. 32). This in turn placed increasing strain on the nuclear family as it had to serve as the sole focus of solidarity, as well as compensate for the diversity of relationships previously provided by neighbours and wider kin. As pressures on the nuclear family increased, working-class households were not only isolated from the outside. Isolation in turn bred fear and mistrust (Emmett, 2003, p. 7).**

After the forced removals and post apartheid, the family structure on the Cape Flats changed. Historically, women had been able to access state grants and housing. However inadequate this may have been and still is, it gave them some independence from working-class men, while also forcing women into more masculine roles (Gibson, 2004). In this respect Salo (2000) argues that the contestation between institutionalised masculinities prescribed by the dominant state and the subordinate masculinities of gangs and working-class husbands was physically articulated on (the bodies of) working-class women. The conflict concerned the state institutions' control over women, and its intervention in the private household sphere, a sphere that had previously been the domain of working-class males (Salo, 2000).

As a result of their reliance on state assistance, women could to some extent financially support unemployed men and youth through their access to welfare grants and housing. They were nevertheless also perceived as unwilling and disloyal allies in the struggle against impoverishment. These have changed women's role into the more masculine role of the dominant figure in the family. Through gender violence, domestic conflict, and substance abuse, frustrated unemployed men have tried to regain control over women and the family (Salo, 2000). Thus, the structure of the once nuclear family has disintegrated into turmoil, leaving destitute families on the Cape Flats.

5.3.3 '*Papsak/dop* system'

Another potential causal factor contributing to the substance abuse problem is the so-called '*dop* system' (or '*papsak* system'). As Leggett explains:

> **Due to their presence in the Western Cape's wine growing areas, many ... people have historically worked in the vineyards. As a result of the so-called '*dop* system' in which labourers were paid part of their wages in wine, alcoholism ... [became and still is problematic] in certain parts of the community ... The *dop* system is diabolical in its ability to keep labour submissive and dependant, and has the side effect of promoting violence, dysfunctional families and foetal alcohol syndrome [FAS] (Leggett, 2004, p. 24).[3]**

Research confirms that excessive alcohol use will increase the likelihood of violence being committed. It has also shown that many victims and offenders of violence had high levels of alcohol in their systems (Shaw & Louw, 1997). Furthermore, considering the number of liquor outlets, one would assume that a considerable amount of alcohol is consumed in the Western Cape. There are, for example, 227 known liquor outlets in Mitchells Plain alone (Transformation Research Project, 2003).

---

3 Reprinted by permission of the Editor, *SA Crime Quarterly*.

5.4 Current substance abuse trends in South Africa

This section deals with the major substance abuse trends in South Africa and the effect of prenatal substance abuse on the foetus.

5.4.1 Alcohol abuse

Alcohol and its primary metabolite, so-called 'acetaldehyde', are known tissue toxins, which may interfere directly with cellular growth and metabolism. When a pregnant woman consumes alcohol, for example, it is carried to all her organs and tissues, including the placenta. The placenta functions to protect the foetus and provides nourishment from the mother to the foetus. Alcohol is able to cross the placental membrane, and is then transported directly to all developing tissues of the foetus (Clarren, Olsen, Clarren, & Astley, 2000).

FAS is a permanent birth defect caused by maternal consumption of alcohol during pregnancy. It is a clinically defined syndrome, characterised by growth deficiency, central nervous system (CNS) damage and dysfunction, and a unique cluster of minor facial abnormalities (Davies & Bledsoe, 2005). These adverse effects of alcohol on the developing foetus are characterised by an array of disorders, termed Foetal Alcohol Spectrum Disorders (FASD). They include structural anomalies as well as behavioural and neuro-cognitive disabilities. Children at the severe end of the spectrum are defined as having the FAS. The following are some facts about FAS (Clarren et al., 2000):

- An estimated 25 000 babies are born with FAS every year in South Africa.
- South Africa has the highest frequency of FAS reported in one population anywhere in the world.
- The prevalence of FAS in countries such as America varies from 0.1 per cent to 0.8 per cent , whereas in South Africa FAS is as high as 12.2 per cent in some areas.
- The prevalence rate of foetal alcohol exposure is far higher than the recorded FAS rate (three to five times higher).
- FAS is the largest cause of mental retardation in most industrial nations.
- FAS is found amongst all races and across all socio-economic groups.
- Alcohol during pregnancy, regardless of quantity, can cause permanent brain damage.
- FAS is 100 per cent preventable.
- There is no cure for FAS (World Foetal Alcohol Syndrome (FAS) day, n.d.).

Today, alcohol is available in most communities, and in some areas licensed and unlicensed outlets are plentiful. According to the then MEC for Finance, Economic Development and Tourism in the Western Cape, Alan Winde, in 2012 there were an estimated 25 000 illegal liquor outlets in the Western Cape (Province begins crackdown on illegal liquor sales, 2012). The ethanol in the wine could be responsible for more damage to the foetus than the ethanol alone (*Foetal Alcohol Syndrome Spectrum Disorders in Cape Town, South Africa*, 2008).

In South Africa, research related to FAS has been limited to a few at-risk areas, namely the Northern Cape and Western Cape. According to the CEO of the Foundation for Alcohol Related Research (FARR), excessive alcohol ingestion stunts foetal growth, damages neurons and brain structures – which can result in psychological or behavioural problems – and causes other physical damage (Nyathikazi, 2011).

5.4.2 Methamphetamine abuse

Methamphetamine is commonly known as 'tik' in South Africa. It is a white, odourless, bitter-tasting crystalline powder that easily dissolves in water or alcohol. The drug was developed early last century from its parent drug, amphetamine, and was originally found in nasal decongestants and bronchial inhalers. Like amphetamine, methamphetamine causes increased activity and talkativeness, decreased appetite, and a general sense of well-being. However, methamphetamine differs from amphetamine in that at comparable doses, much higher levels of methamphetamine get into the brain, making it a more potent stimulant drug (*The naked truth. Methamphetamine/Tik*, n.d.).

Since 2003, the Western Cape has seen a dramatic increase in the use of methamphetamine (tik), as a primary or secondary drug of abuse. As Hübschle explains:

> **Traditionally ingredients for tik, such as ephedrine, have been imported into South Africa from Asia and the final product is made in factories and then distributed to gangs in the Western Cape ... A growing trend, however, is that tik is produced locally from household ingredients, such as bleach. The increasing involvement of gangs producing their own tik means that the product is more readily available and gangs no longer rely on foreign connections (Hübschle, 2011, p. 31).[4]**

Kapp reports that 'the Medical Research Council (MRC) estimates that there could be as many as 200 000 tik users in and around Cape Town' (Kapp, 2008, 193).[5] Methamphetamine comes in many forms and can be smoked, snorted, injected, or orally ingested. In the Western Cape the preferred method is to smoke it through a light bulb. Users place the bitter white powder in a light bulb from which the metal threading has been removed, heat it with a lighter, and smoke the fumes. The name of tik – also known as 'tuk-tuk' – is derived from the noise it makes when smoked. Immediately after smoking or injecting it intravenously, the user experiences an intense rush that lasts only a few minutes and is described as extremely pleasurable. As is the case with similar stimulants, methamphetamine is often used in a so-called 'binge and crash' pattern, because the pleasurable effects of methamphetamine disappear even before the drug concentration in the blood falls. Significantly, users try to maintain the high by taking more of the drug. In some cases, abusers indulge in bingeing (heavy episodic drinking with the primary intention of becoming intoxicated), forgoing food and sleep while continuing abuse, sometimes for days without end (*The Naked Truth. Methamphetamine/Tik*, 2011).

The rush methamphetamine users experience includes feelings of enhanced well-being, heightened libido, increased energy (sexual), and suppression of appetite. Psychological effects observed with methamphetamine use include euphoria, paranoia, agitation, mood disturbances, violent behaviour, anxiety, depression, and psychosis. Cheaper than cocaine, its stimulant effects are also longer lasting. Users begin 'tweaking' – a term describing a dangerous combination of restlessness, anxiety, irritability, fatigue, and dysphonic behaviour. Further use of methamphetamine temporarily improves the symptoms and further reinforces the addiction. Eventually, after days of sleeplessness, users crash into a non-restful sleep (Lineberry & Bostwick, 2006).

---

4 Reprinted by permission of the ISS. Reprinted by permission of the ISS.

5 Reprinted from *The Lancet*, Vol. 371(9608) Kapp, C. Crystal meth boom adds to South African health challenges. *The Lancet*, 371(9608), 193-194. Copyright C 2008, with permission from Elsevier. Retrieved April 11, 2011, from http://www.thelancet.com/journals/lancet/article/PIIS0140-6736%2808%2960120-8/fulltext

Methamphetamine abuse during pregnancy can result in prenatal complications, including low birth weight, birth defects, increased rates of premature delivery, and abnormal infant behaviour (Michael, 2006). Further, 'problems at birth may include difficulty sucking and swallowing, hypersensitivity to touch and excessive muscle tension. Long-term risks may include developmental disorders, cognitive deficits, learning disabilities, poor social adjustment and language deficits' (Michael, 2006, p. 25).[6]

University of California, Los Angeles (UCLA) scientists scanned the brain structure of 61 children, including 21 whose mothers has used methamphetamine before delivery and 13 whose mothers drank heavily. They found that children whose mothers used methamphetamine or alcohol had notable different structural changes in their brains, and in some cases the children of methamphetamine mothers had even more dramatic changes than babies whose mothers use alcohol. For instance, the caudate nucleus, which helps process learning and memory, was smaller in babies exposed to methamphetamine than those exposed to alcohol. A part of the brain called the 'cingulated cortex', which involves emotion processing and conflict resolution, was larger in methamphetamine exposed babies. Either scenario – smaller or larger brain growth – could be detrimental in children with prenatal drug exposure. These drugs are likely altering the trajectory of development and clearly not in a good way (Sowell et al., 2010).

The use of methamphetamine has also been found to be associated with sexual risk behaviours. A Cape Town study (Plüddemann, 2008, in Kurian, Brown, Carney, Peterson & Wechsberg, 2011) found that adolescents who had engaged in methamphetamine use within the past 30 days were significantly more likely to have had vaginal, oral or anal sex, and experienced a pregnancy, when compared with adolescents who never used methamphetamine (Kurian et al., 2011). However, there is no statistical evidence to suggest that methamphetamine abuse has led to an increase in teenage pregnancies. A Cape Town Health Director said that 5.5 per cent of births in Mitchells Plain in 2005 were attributed to teenagers, and 5.4 per cent in 2006. He further stated that methamphetamine abuse 'among pregnant women led to low birthweights, and the infants were often described as irritable, but not enough was known about the longer-term side effects on children' (Kapp, 2008, p. 194).[7]

5.4.3 Mandrax abuse

South Africa is the largest consumer of Mandrax in the world. Statistics show that Mandrax with cannabis (dagga) is still the drug of preference in the largest parts of South Africa (Moeng, 2012). The active ingredient in Mandrax is methaqualone. Mandrax is mainly sold in the form of a tablet and is highly addictive. In the 1960s and early 1970s these tablets were prescribed as sleeping medication. In 2010 the price of a Mandrax tablet is between R25 and R65, depending on the availability, demand, and quality (*Drug wars-about drugs. Mandrax*, 2010).

The Mandrax tablet is usually crushed and mixed with dagga and then smoked in a dagga pipe, better known as a 'bottle neck'. Mandrax has added and stronger side effects than dagga, such as:

- serious emotional problems
- depression

6 © Child Welfare League of America Inc.

7 Reprinted from *The Lancet*, Vol. 371(9608) Kapp, C. Crystal meth boom adds to South African health challenges. *The Lancet*, 371(9608), 193-194. Copyright C 2008, with permission from Elsevier. Retrieved April 11, 2011, from http://www.thelancet.com/journals/lancet/article/PIIS0140-6736%2808%2960120-8/fulltext

- drastic weight loss
- headaches
- stomach cramps
- insomnia
- epilepsy
- aggression
- toxic psychosis (*Drug wars-about drugs. Mandrax*, 2010).

Mandrax is packed in 1 000 tablet packets by the producers. It is then exported on a large scale and brought into South Africa in false panels in cars, spare wheels of trucks, false fuel tanks, and containers, among other things (*Drug wars-about drugs. Mandrax*, 2010). It is then taken to distribution areas and repacked in bank bags in quantities of 200s, 100s and 50s. It is then sold at street level to individuals (*Drug wars-about drugs. Mandrax*, 2010).

Pregnant mothers who use Mandrax may bear children who suffer from problems such as breathing difficulties, eating and sleeping disorders, and increased risk of fevers and other illnesses (*'We do recover,' Mandrax addiction types*, n.d.).

5.4.4 Heroin abuse

Heroin (diacetylmorphine) is a semi-synthetic opiate which acts as CNS depressant and an analgesic. It is produced from morphine, which is extracted from the Asian poppy (*Papaver somniferum*). Historically, the main mode of heroin use has been through injection. Improvements in the purity of heroin and the fear of HIV/Aids have resulted in more new users snorting or smoking it. The latest trend in the Western Cape is to smoke or inhale heroin combined with methamphetamine (*Drug use in South Africa-Fact sheet*, n.d.).

Heroin acts on the opioid receptor sites in the brain, resulting in feelings of intense pleasure and a dulling of pain. This rush includes a flushing of the skin, a dry mouth, and heaviness in the limbs, and may involve nausea, vomiting, and severe itching. These initial effects are accompanied by feelings of relaxation and drowsiness, dulling of mental functions, and slowed breathing and cardiac functions. The rush occurs within seven to eight seconds of intravenous heroin use, and within a couple of minutes of snorting or smoking heroin (*Drug use in South Africa-Fact sheet*, n.d.).

With chronic use of heroin, psychological and physical addiction occurs, and tolerance of and craving for the effects of heroin develop. Injecting drug users risk developing the following from the use of unsterile or blunt needles:

- bacterial infections of the blood vessels, heart valves, and heart lining
- collapsed veins
- skin abscesses
- wound botulism
- tetanus.

Respiratory problems – such as pneumonia and tuberculosis – may develop. Indirect and direct sharing of injection equipment places the user at high risk for contracting HIV and other blood-borne viruses such as hepatitis B, C and G. Heroin use during pregnancy may place the child at risk for developmental difficulties. There is an increased risk of miscarriage, low birth weight, and foetal abnormalities (*Drug use in South Africa-Fact sheet*, n.d.)

5.4.5 Cocaine abuse

A large part of southern African cocaine trafficking occurs in Mozambique, where the drug arrives via Brazil from producer countries in Latin America. The volume of cocaine trafficking has increased in the past four years. It is mostly affluent individuals throughout South Africa who use cocaine, the price per gram of which is US$25 to US$60 (Hübschle, 2011).

Cocaine is a CNS stimulant extracted from the leaves of the coca plant (*Erythroxylum coca*). There are two chemical forms of cocaine: cocaine hydrochloride (HCL) – which has the appearance of a white, crystalline powder – and freebase cocaine. Crack is a specific form of freebase cocaine, which is processed from cocaine HCL by the addition of an alkaline substance (for example bicarbonate of soda), to form smokeable rocks. Cocaine HCL is usually administered intranasally (sniffing/snorting) or, less frequently, intravenously, through injection. Crack cocaine is mainly ingested through smoking or inhaling (*Drug use in South Africa-Fact sheet*, n.d.).

Cocaine is a stimulant which causes the pulse rate to increase and blood pressure to rise. It leads to changes in neurotransmitter functioning, resulting in feelings of euphoria, self-confidence, heightened awareness, and alertness. In large doses, cocaine may lead to paranoia, violent and erratic behaviour, dizziness, and dilated pupils (*Drug use in South Africa-Fact sheet*, n.d.).

According to the Organisation of Teratology Information Services (OTIS), during the early months of pregnancy, cocaine exposure may increase the risk of miscarriage. Later in pregnancy, cocaine use can cause placental abruption, which can lead to severe bleeding, premature birth, and foetal death. Babies who are exposed to cocaine later in pregnancy may be born dependent and suffer from withdrawal symptoms such as tremors, sleeplessness, muscle spasm, and feeding difficulties. Some experts believe that the child may experience learning difficulties later on in life (*Using illegal street drugs during pregnancy*, 2011).

5.4.6 Cannabis (dagga) abuse

The main cannabis products are herbal cannabis and cannabis resin. Herbal cannabis refers to leaves and flowers of the plant, while the pressed secretions are known as cannabis resin or hashish. Drug consumers mostly use herbal cannabis. 'Cannabis is cultivated in many African countries. It is smuggled and traded within Africa, but the majority is destined for the … lucrative markets of North America and Europe' (Hübschle, 2011, p. 23).[8]

Studies of cannabis in pregnancy reveal that most women who smoke dagga also use tobacco and alcohol. Smoking dagga increases the levels of carbon monoxide and carbon dioxide in the blood, which reduces the oxygen supply to the foetus. It can also increase the chance of miscarriage, low birth weight, premature births, developmental delays, and behavioural and learning problems (*Using illegal street drugs during pregnancy*, 2011).

CRITICAL REFLECTION

Thus far this chapter has discussed potential causes (origins) of the substance abuse problem in South Africa as part of organised crime. It has focused on the forced removals during apartheid, disintegration of family structure and '*dop/papsak* system'. With this in mind, what is your opinion of the potential causes of the substance abuse problem in South Africa? Can you think of any other potential causes to the substance abuse problem?

8 Reprinted by permission of the ISS.

This chapter has also cited the current substance abuse trends in South Africa, and identified alcohol, methamphetamine, Mandrax, heroin, cocaine and cannabis abuse as the main types of abuse. Are you aware of any other substances currently being abused in South Africa?

5.5 Drug-related crimes

5.5.1 Drug-related crimes reported to the South African Police Service

Drug-related crimes (these cover the use of, possession of, and dealing in drugs) report under the SAPS crime category of 'crimes heavily dependent on police action for detection'. Other crimes that report under this category include illegal possession of firearms and driving under the influence of alcohol and drugs (SAPS, 2010).

Crime statistics provide a basis on which to measure and monitor change in crime rates over time. There are, however a number of limitations in using official crime statistics. These limitations include official crime statistics which measure only reported crimes. Thus, crimes which are not reported or detected by the police (the so-called 'dark figure' of crime) are not measured. Drug-related crime is primarily a victimless crime, which is usually not reported to the police by members of the public. This type of crime draws attention primarily as a result of police actions such as roadblocks. An increase in these crimes may actually indicate that the police are more active, whereas a decrease may indicate reduced police activity. Decreases may also be the result of a change in strategy among drug dealers relocating or avoiding roadblocks, an actual decrease in these phenomena, or the impact of campaigns on people's alcohol and/or drug abuse (SAPS, 2010).

Table 5.1 shows the results of using a quantitative approach to analyse SAPS crime statistics (April to March annually from May 2005 to December 2011) on drug-related crimes reported to the police in South Africa.

Table 5.1 Drug-related crimes reported: April to March 2004/5 to 2011/12 (SAPS, 2012)

Province	2004/5	2005/6	2006/7	2007/8	2008/9	2009/10	2010/11	2011/12
Eastern Cape	9 061	7 511	7 231	8 003	8 437	8 946	9 566	11 654
Free State	4 063	5 074	5 462	4 525	4 561	5 110	4 209	4 463
Gauteng	10 722	14 202	12 582	12 742	13 574	14 729	16 457	25 949
KwaZulu-Natal	19 290	23 206	26 228	24 100	23 819	28 693	32 457	37 415
Limpopo	1 786	1 977	2 178	3 198	3 316	4 837	4 634	5 254
Mpumalanga	1 714	1 794	2 068	1 770	1 642	2 041	3 178	4 153
North West	4 383	5 053	5 759	6 610	7 109	7 704	7 166	7 678
Northern Cape	2 550	2 085	2 114	2 201	1 933	2 371	2 418	2 672
Western Cape	**30 432**	**34 788**	**41 067**	**45 985**	**52 781**	**60 409**	**70 588**	**77 069**
RSA Total	**84 001**	**95 690**	**104 689**	**109 134**	**117 172**	**134 840**	**150 673**	**176 307**

SAPS statistics reveal that the Western Cape has the highest number of drug-related crimes reported to the SAPS in South Africa. Nearly half of the entire country's drug-related crime is reported in this province. The only other provinces that also reflect high figures for drug-related crimes reported are KwaZulu-Natal and Gauteng (SAPS, 2012).

What causes the linkage between drugs and crime? According to Siegel (2011, p. 371), drug use interferes with maturation and socialisation. Substance abusers are more likely to drop out of school, to be unemployed, to engage in premarital sex, and/or to become unmarried parents. These factors have been linked to a weakening of the social bond, which could lead to antisocial behaviour.

Thus, although the connection between drugs and crime is powerful, the relationship is still unsure, because many users have a history of criminal behaviour before the inception of their substance abuse.

CHECK POINT

- There are a variety of drugs in use in South Africa, and alcohol remains a major problem.
- Substance abuse and drug-related crime have increased during the past 10 years in South Africa, with the Western Cape being the province with the highest amount of drug-related crime reported to the SAPS.
- There is no single cause of substance abuse. Some people, however, have a predisposition to it.
- In South Africa there is strong link between substance abuse, gangs, and crime. People who become addicts may increase their illegal activities (crime) to support the habit. Others, for example gangs, engage in violence as part of their drug-dealing activities.

5.5.2 Why are drug-related crime figures so high in the Western Cape?

Possible explanations for the high figures for drug-related crime in the Western Cape are inward migrations, unemployment, population composition, and the introduction of methamphetamine to the Western Cape. The Western Cape, and specifically the city of Cape Town, has experienced a large growth in population in the recent past, mainly due to migration from other provinces, especially the Eastern Cape. During the period 2001–2006, the Western Cape gained an estimated 240 000 people, mostly from the impoverished Eastern Cape (Marindo, Groenewald, & Gaisie, 2008). This in-migration is challenging industries to increase job creation. The 18 per cent unemployment level in the Western Cape is substantially lower than the 25 per cent found in Gauteng (Marindo et al., 2008). However, the huge population growth, coupled with unemployment levels in the Western Cape, might be a catalyst for people to become involved in substance abuse.

Section 5.4.2 has already mentioned the trend for local production of tik from household ingredients by gangs, and its consequences (Hübschle, 2011).

According to a South African Community Epidemiology Network on Drug Use (SACENDU) Research Brief,

> **the most common primary substances of abuse reported by 26 specialist treatment centres/programmes participating in the project between January and June 2011 were methamphetamine ..., alcohol, cannabis and heroin (together comprising 94%**

> **of all admissions) ... Overall, 2 927 patients were treated across all 26 treatment centres/programmes in the 1st half of 2011, increasing compared to the 2nd half of 2009 (Dada et al., 2011, p. 1).**

Most of the patients were coloured (86 per cent) and 73 per cent were male (Dada et al., 2011).

5.6 Theoretical explanations

There are many different views of why people take drugs, and no theory has proved completely adequate in explaining all forms of substance abuse. Recent research efforts show that drug users suffer a variety of family and socialisation difficulties, have addiction-prone personalities, and are generally at risk for many other social problems. It is known that the risk of using dangerous substances may increase by first engaging in recreational drugs such as cannabis (Siegel, 2011, p. 370). Recreational drugs are chemical substances taken for enjoyment, or leisure purposes, rather than medical reasons. Alcohol, tobacco and caffeine can be classified as recreational drugs (*Recreational drugs*, n.d.).

A number of theories in the criminological literature attempt to explain substance abuse. The focus here is on the anomie theory and social disorganization theory explanations. These theories are selected as the most applicable to explain the substance abuse problem, with specific reference to prenatal substance abuse in Mitchells Plain on the Cape Flats.

5.6.1 Anomie theory

According to Robert K. Merton's anomie theory, substance abuse takes place when avenues to material success are blocked off. The theory argues that in a competitive, materialistic, achievement-orientated society, success is encouraged as attainable to all members. However, it is attainable to only a small proportion of the society. Individuals who do not succeed must devise deviant or disapproved adaptations to deal with their failure. Those who have given up on achieving society's materialistic goals, whether by approved or disapproved means, become so-called 'retreatists.' According to Merton (Siegel, 2011, p. 151), chronic drunkards and drug addicts fall in this category. An extension of this theory embraces the idea that a person most likely to become a drug addict has already attempted to use both legal and illegal means to achieve success, and has failed at both (retreated into the undemanding world of addiction) (Siegel, 2011, p. 151).

Merton's theory received much criticism relating to the explanation of substance abuse. One should be cautious in being too harsh with judgments. What is drug dealing if not innovative attempts to maintain the goal of achieving material success by engaging in an illegal deviant enterprise? Drug dealing is an innovative adaptation to blocked or frustrated material success for many members of society who have learned to expect success, but who live in an environment in which high levels of achievement are all but impossible. Mitchells Plain on the Cape Flats is a good example of an area in which high levels of achievement seem almost unattainable. The anomie theory focuses greatly on one major aspect of substance abuse, namely drug dealing.

Mitchells plain is known for its drug dealing activities. Most of the drug addicts are unemployed and have given up attempts at finding any employment. Substance abuse and drug dealing are ways not only to escape from the society's expectation to be successful, but to make a living. The following case study illustrates this element of the anomie theory in practice.

CASE STUDY

This case study evaluates and interrogates the family and living circumstances surrounding Evelyn and Plankies, a young couple addicted to substances, living in Mitchells Plain, Cape Town. Attention is given to Evelyn's drug addiction during her pregnancies, and to the impact of their substance abuse on their children's upbringing. The couple reflects on treatment centres and the reasons behind their drug addiction (Häefele and Ovens, 2013, pp. 29-30).

Evelyn and Plankies

Evelyn and Plankies, an unmarried couple, live with Evelyn's mother in Beacon Valley, a neighbourhood in Mitchells Plain. The three bedroom house is small with barely any furniture (most furniture had been sold to buy drugs). Evelyn is 29 years old and Plankies 30. Both are unemployed. Evelyn left school at grade 10; Plankies has matric. (He was one of the best 10 students in matric.) Plankies, a boilermaker at an engineering company, was recently retrenched, due to the owner's sudden death. He is now unemployed and a drug dealer. Plankies is also a tik and Mandrax addict. Evelyn (unemployed) has three children: a son of 13 years, a daughter of 6 years and another daughter of 4 years (all from different boyfriends). One child died after birth and, according to Evelyn, this triggered her to start using tik again. Evelyn is five months pregnant with Plankies's child. She has been addicted to substances for the past 14 years. Evelyn started initially with Mandrax abuse, followed by tik for the past five years.

The price of tik ranges between R30 and R60, depending on the quality and quantity. Plankies buys tik and Mandrax from known dealers in the neighbourhood, mostly gang members. He uses some of the drugs and resells the rest. Both stated that they are able to quit drugs, but they don't want to because of their poor state of affairs (unemployment, no support base, and the environment, among others). By no support base they mean nobody to turn to. They said tik helps them to relax and forget reality. Both said alcohol and tik together are not a good combination; that is why they do not consume alcohol. Alcohol apparently makes them aggressive. Both stated that using both drugs (alcohol and tik) together allows a person to consume alcohol for hours without getting intoxicated. They also said that they will definitely keep drugs away from their children. (This means they are aware of the dangers of drugs, but are not able to, or do not want to, quit drugs.)

Evelyn uses Tik every second and third day, depending on her mood swings. According to her, there are no side affects or danger to the foetus in using tik. Evelyn is a tiny woman (almost fragile), and although she is five months pregnant it is hardly noticeable. According to Evelyn, she is having a normal pregnancy with no side effects or complications. She also used tik previously during her pregnancy with Lientjie, who is now four years old. Lientjie was born prematurely (six months). It was a natural birth.

Although Lientjie looks like any other four-year-old toddler, she is a small girl. According to her mother, Lientjie is hyperactive and very intelligent. The hyperactivity and high intelligence of tik babies as unique characteristics were also mentioned during other interviews with teachers and family members. Both Evelyn and Plankies said that Lientjie is never sick and has a normal appetite, like any other child. Both said that Lientjie is intellectually 'advanced' and she is able to remember things that happened months ago (good memory). According to Evelyn, Lientjie knows everybody in their street by name, which for them is quite remarkable for a toddler of four years. (Both Evelyn and Plankies overcompensated for their substance abuse by stressing how intelligent and 'advanced' Lientjie, as a tik child, is.)

When asked about the dangers of tik during pregnancy, Evelyn said she is aware of them. However, with Lientjie and her current pregnancy, she feels that there were no complications that will prompt her to stop using tik. Even the premature birth of Lientjie at six months was not sufficient to alert Evelyn to the danger and potential side effects of tik on the foetus. When asked if they are aware of FAS babies and their characteristics, both said they know FAS babies in the neighbourhood and that Lientjie as a tik child does not have any of the FAS characteristics. As has been mentioned, they almost see Lientjie as a 'gifted' child.

Evelyn is aware of drug counselling services in Mitchells Plain but feels that there is no need for her to go for treatment. She said she feels in control and capable of handling her drug addiction. Evelyn mentioned that she was 'booked' at the hospital for a medical check-up and prenatal session, but cancelled because she felt no need as she is able to quit tik if she wants to. She said she did stop using tik previously for three months, but started again after the death of her baby. When asked if she does not think that her tik abuse could have contributed to the death of the baby, she denied it. Evelyn said another reason for her not going for treatment or counselling for tik addiction is the fact that medical personnel and councillors have a preconceived and judgmental attitude towards pregnant tik mothers: 'They make us feel ashamed.'

Reflecting on the case of Evelyn and Plankies

Both Evelyn and Plankies mentioned the following as contributing factors to the substance abuse problem:

- easy availability of drugs
- unemployment
- escape from reality
- peer pressure
- boredom
- family breakdown
- people feeling marginalised
- general feelings of helplessness regarding the dire living conditions in Mitchells Plain.

However, the main reason both gave for the substance abuse problem is the poor economy in the area and the promise of quick and easy money.

It was evident during the interview with how much ease and self-belief both Lientjie and Plankies talked about their substance abuse addiction. Both expressed society's preconceived attitude towards and judgment about their drug addiction, but simultaneously did not have a desire to change their lives for the better.

With reference to the anomie theory, both Evelyn and Plankies retreated to the world of substance abuse and drug dealing because they felt they did not succeed in meeting society's expectations. Both are unemployed, and drug dealing provides a means to survive. They also feel like 'outcasts' and have failed society's expectations.

Furthermore, the fact that Evelyn feels ashamed to go for treatment because of medical personnel's judgmental attitudes shows that she cannot conform to society's expectations of acknowledging the addiction, take responsibility, and go for treatment. She failed society's expectations and therefore retreated into the undemanding world of drug addiction.

Other considerations

- Having Lientjie and Evelyn's being pregnant while using tik will make neither Evelyn nor Plankies take responsibility for their addiction or seek treatment for the sake of the children. They don't want their children to use drugs but don't care about the example they set as role models.
- Lientjie and Evelyn denied the danger pregnant tik mothers' addiction represents for the foetus by stressing how healthy and above average Leintjie's intelligence is. The fact that they denied this makes one realise how uninformed drug addicts are about their personal health and that of their children.
- Are pregnant tik addicted mothers just ignorant about the dangers of drug abuse, or is it a case of selfishness?

CRITICAL REFLECTION

Does substance abuse cause crime?

Consider this statement: substance abuse causes crime. Is this fact or fiction?

It is fiction. Most substance abusers have a history of antisocial behaviour before they became addicted to drugs. However, drug abuse strengthens the frequency of potential involvement in crime.

5.6.2 Social disorganisation theory

Most social disorganisation studies focus primarily on intra-neighbourhood influences on crime, without considering the larger urban political and economic context (Bursik & Grasmick, 1993). The social disorganisation theory is a branch of social structure theory that focuses on the breakdown, in inner-city neighbourhoods, or institutions such as the family, school and employment (Siegel, 2011, p. 463). According to Shaw and McKay (1942), political and economic decisions may have direct effects on community crime rates, for example by increasing the level of unemployment and poverty (through deindustrialisation and disinvestment), residential instability (via housing, construction, and demolition policies), and population density (through public housing or zoning policies) (Siegel, 2011, p. 144) .

Mitchells Plain was chosen as a case study because of the area's history, high drug-related crime figures, and socio-economic situation. Parts of Mitchells Plain quickly deteriorated into little more than so-called 'urban ghettoes.' Many families relocated to Mitchells Plain from District Six, when the latter was razed to the ground, and today Mitchells Plain is an area swamped with gangs and drugs (*Things to do in Mitchells Plain*, n.d.).

The township is approximately 20 kilometres from the city of Cape Town. It is located on the Cape Flats near the False Bay coast between Strandfontein and Khayelitsha (*Mitchells Plain. Serving history*, n.d.). Mitchells Plain is economically divided into east and west: the western half of Westridge, Rocklands, and Portlands, and eastern half of Tafelsig, Beacon Valley, and Eastridge (*Things to do in Mitchells Plain*, n.d.). Mitchells Plain is isolated due to its distance from the city; transport costs are high and commuters have to travel for a long time each day. It is situated far from the centres of economic opportunity. The provision, running, and maintenance of public facilities are inadequate, resulting in stretched operating budgets and the inability of authorities to ensure the appropriate service levels (*Communications and marketing strategy for the Urban Renewal Programme*, 2011).

By far the most developed commercial area in Mitchells Plain is the Mitchells Plain CBD. It includes a 58 000 square metre retail plaza, a smaller shopping centre in the railway station, an extension of the town centre, two major transport interchanges, and improvements to public spaces in the area. The informal sector is an important employer in Mitchells Plain; however, informal traders face many constraints. Helping informal business to formalise would help them to increase turnover and employ more people (*Communications and marketing strategy for the Urban Renewal Programme*, 2011).

5.6.2.1 Different ethnic groups

Another element of the social disorganisation theory is the mixture of different ethnic groups. Mitchells Plain's has approximately 1 million people living in an area 110.2 square kilometres in size, most of it urban (*Things to do in Mitchells Plain*, n.d.). The population density is 3 618 persons per square kilometre. Some 22 per cent of households live in informal houses. About 58 per cent of households comprise four persons or more. Almost 62 per cent of the population is younger than 29 years of age. Afrikaans is spoken by 57 per cent of the population, with isiXhosa (9 per cent) and English accounting for about 40 per cent (*Communications and marketing strategy for the Urban Renewal Programme*, 2011).

5.6.2.2 Employment level

Nearly 49 per cent of the Mitchells Plain population can be defined as economically active. Of this group, 36 per cent were employed at the time of the survey and 13 per cent unemployed looking for work. The mean household income in Mitchells Plain is R3 451 for an average household size of five persons per household (*Communications and marketing strategy for the Urban Renewal Programme*, 2011).

5.6.2.3 Educational level

Twenty-four per cent of the population indicated that they have completed grade 12, with 18 per cent having completed grades 1–7. Most (92 per cent) of the people between 16 and 19 were enrolled in school. There are 15 secondary schools, 43 primary schools, and 53 early childhood development centres in Mitchells Plain. Very few people in Mitchells Plain have access to higher education. Almost 40 per cent of people aged 5 to 24 do not attend school. The most important reason provided for leaving school is either to work or to look for work (*Communications and marketing strategy for the Urban Renewal Programme*, 2011).

5.6.2.4 Living conditions

After the forced removals and post apartheid, the family structure on the Cape Flats changed dramatically. Today, the structure of the once nuclear family has disintegrated into turmoil, leaving destitute families on the Cape Flats. Many residents in Mitchells Plain are living in two bedroom flats or houses, leaving little room to expand as families grow. As a result, Mitchells Plain is characterised by high concentrations of overcrowded houses and unemployed people. Mitchells Plain is now home to a vast number of people and families who exist outside the formal economy - what social scientists refer to as being 'socially excluded' (Standing, 2003, p. 2).

According to the social disorganisation theory, residents of communities with high rates of crime often lack the skills and resources to assist others effectively. They are poor, and many are single parents struggling with family responsibilities. Hence they often face problems in socialising their children against crime and providing them with a stake in conformity, for example the skills to do well in school or the connections to secure a job.

These residents are also less likely to have close ties with their neighbours and to care about their community (*Crime causation: sociological theories-social disorganisation theory*, n.d.)

It is in this context that one finds depressing social features shared by numerous urban ghettoes that have emerged worldwide in the last 30 years. Most noticeable are the following:

- ill health
- stress
- substance abuse
- family fragmentation
- school truancy
- exceptionally high levels of inter-personal conflict
- domestic violence
- assaults involving knives and guns
- high rates of crime (Standing, 2003).

5.6.2.5 Gangsterism

The forced removal from District Six brought together young men who had previously lived in different communities, creating a sudden competition for limited resources and territory that facilitated the growth of gangs (*The numbers*, n.d.). With little room inside the home, youths (second generation) in Mitchells Plain spend a lot of time on the streets. The initial playgroup outside the home becomes a kind of surrogate family, but with a different set of norms. When the street gang becomes more important for the individual than the norms at home are, gang formation takes place (Häefele, 2003).

Gangsters and drug dealers are a common sight in Mitchells Plain. Different types of gangs exist, such as the street gang, the Mafia style family structure, and syndicate gangs. However, the so-called 'number' and name gangs are the most notorious. From the Cape Flats and Mitchells Plain, gang members sell crystal methamphetamine to a constant stream of customers, the most regular users appearing to be themselves (*In-depth: Youth in crisis. Coming of age in 21st century South Africa: Gang culture in Cape Town*, 2007). Well-known gangs (approximately 13–20) in Mitchells Plain include the Americans, the Junky Funky Kids, the Sexy Boys, the Yakkies, the Wonder Boys, the Dixie Boys, and the Hard Living Kids. Most gang members are initiated between the ages of 13 and 15, and are immediately armed with guns. Younger members are expected to assume front-line duties during gang wars over turf and drug deals, to prove their mettle (solidarity) to senior members. For some, membership may last until the age of 40 or 50 (*The numbers*, n.d.).

A brief explanation of the criminal economy, although not delving too deeply into the gangs and the organised crime phenomenon, will lead to an understanding of the substance abuse problem versus community dependency on the criminal economy in Mitchells Plain (Häefele, 2003).

The criminal economy – meaning criminal networks (white-collar crime, organised crime and state crime) intertwined with each other, and representing a major sector of the local economy (Standing, 2003, p. 3) – in the Cape Flats resembles the model of the 'Sicilian Mafioso' developed by Henner Hess. It comprises a series of 'criminal domains,' each centred on a powerful individual commonly referred to as a 'gang leader,' a 'crime boss' or more flatteringly as a 'drug lord' (Standing, 2003, p. 3). Each of these domains has a supporting base of followers-similar to what Hess refers to as a '*cosca*.' For the most part, the base comprises a loose association of street gangs and career criminals, all commonly labelled as gangsters. In addition to the base, each of the criminal elites/high flyers relies on enduring partnerships with various professionals, foreign criminal entrepreneurs, and corrupt members of the state: for example police, judges, and local politicians. The sum of these corrupt associations was termed by Hess as the '*partito*' – an area of the criminal economy where the distinctions between white-collar crime, organised crime, and state crime blur and overlap (Standing, 2003).

The number of criminal domains is difficult to establish and will change over time. However, there seem to be roughly 10 to 20 men who lay claim to being in control of significant areas of the Cape Flats (Mitchells Plain included) and who share the characteristics of the criminal elite/high flyers/drug lords. The careers of these men tend to follow the same pattern. All originated from poor communities and remain attached to the areas where they grew up. Though most subsequently moved away from the Cape Flats, buying property and living in some of the more affluent areas of Cape Town, they remain firmly attached to the regions of the Cape Flats where they have power and are well known to locals. They typically own one or several houses, which are used as centres (so-called 'shebeens') from which alcohol and drugs are sold and consumed (Standing, 2003).

Their considerable personal wealth is achieved by assuming a critical position in the local criminal economy. They control the distribution and sale of alcohol and drugs in their areas. Some also control the local sex industry, the stealing of vehicles, and other illegal criminal activities. Not all of them are gang leaders. Some may be ex-gangsters and employ a large number of specialist personnel who fall outside the gang structures. Most of the criminal elite, however, are closely related to the prison gangs known as the 26s, 27s and 28s (Standing, 2003).

The base of each criminal domain comprises members of numerous street gangs. The street gangs are affiliated to a criminal domain, and they are responsible for the selling and distribution of drugs. Communities show ambivalent feelings towards the criminal elite/high flyers. The starkest social contradiction of the criminal economy relates to the income it provides. Many unemployed in the community are involved in the underworld economy, from brothels, shebeens, stolen goods, and the drug trade to money laundering industries such as taxis and tow-trucks. Many people live around drug lords, or houses benefit by having their silence bought. They are assisted with rent payments, contributions are made to funerals, and sometimes their sons are employed as gangsters and their daughters as prostitutes. In return, a so-called 'parcel' of drugs or weapons could be hidden in their homes (Häefele, 2003).

5.6.2.6 Substance abuse versus community dependency on the criminal economy

It is within the criminal economy that substance abuse (drug trafficking) is prevalent and alive in Mitchells Plain. The trafficking in substances provides an income to people suffering from poverty and unemployment. Some community members, however, have a misconception about their role and place in the criminal economy. By supporting, assisting, buying, and selling substances and illegal commodities from a drug lord, they actually do not benefit, but are dragged deeper into the misery of substance abuse and poverty (communities are under the impression they benefit and some might even benefit in the short term, but most are losing out in the long term). It is the drug lords/merchants/elites that benefit financially with their illegal criminal activities. By providing money to help establish a community centre that feeds local school children, buying school uniforms, paying rents, and offering training to the unemployed, the drug lords buy support from the community (Häefele, 2003).

These acts of generosity may be symbolic of the depressing reality of life in some areas in Mitchells Plain; for an impoverished community that provides few cases of celebrated success, the crass actions of the obscenely wealthy drug lord can easily assume centre stage (Standing, 2003).

The following case study illustrates elements of the social disorganisation theory in practice.

CASE STUDY

This case study evaluates the extent of maternal substance abuse of 16 prenatal substance abuse addicts in Mitchells Plain. The evaluation includes demographic information such as race, age, educational achievements, and employment. Attention is also given to the sixteen prenatal substance abuse addicts' social environment (living conditions), their attitude towards their addiction and treatment, the type of substances they used during pregnancy, and their connection to crime.

Sixteen prenatal substance abuse addicts

The sample consists of sixteen mothers who used methamphetamine, heroin, and alcohol respectively during pregnancy. A quantitative research approach was used, with the interview-questionnaire technique as method of data collection. A total of 56 questions were asked during each interview-questionnaire.

Two community workers in Mitchells Plain organised and set up the interviews with the mothers. The snowball sampling technique was applied, where one mother would inform the community workers about another pregnant mother addicted to substance abuse. The mother was then contacted and the purpose of the research explained to her. Upon agreement, the community workers set up an interview schedule with the mother. Due to the sensitivity of the matter, respondents would be assured of anonymity, and participation took place on a voluntary basis.

Collectively, demographic data reflected that all the respondents were from the coloured population, mostly in the age group 25–30, half of them completed grades 8–10, most of them were unemployed, more than half were single, and a small percentage (31.2 per cent) were financially supported by a husband or partner. All the respondents lived in dire socio-economic conditions with little access to basic life necessities. All the mothers used methamphetamine during their pregnancies; other drugs used included cannabis (31.2 per cent), alcohol (25 per cent), Mandrax (25 per cent), cocaine (18.7 per cent), and heroin (18.7 per cent). With reference to substance abuse by other people residing with the mothers, half of the mothers stated that their fellow residents also used substances, mostly methamphetamine, followed by alcohol, Mandrax, and heroin.

The 16 mothers had 38 children altogether, 14 boys and 24 girls, ranging from 1 to 17 years of age. Most of the women stated that they had normal pregnancies and normal births while abusing substances. One mother explained that two of her four children were born prematurely, but with the last one she experienced high blood pressure due to her substance abuse. Another mother explained that her oldest daughter was born prematurely at eight months, while she was abusing substances.

More than half (62 per cent) of the mothers stated that they never mistreated their children. However, 18.7 per cent admitted that they had mistreated their children due to their substance abuse and that was why their children were in foster care or staying with family members. Most of the mothers (69 per cent) admitted that they never received any assistance in developing effective parental skills during pregnancy, neither from medical staff nor family members. Some mothers explained that their children had stayed with family members since birth, due to their substance abuse addiction.

Most of the mothers (69 per cent) were of the opinion that their substance abuse interferes with their responsibilities towards their children. The following are some direct quotations from the mothers:

- 'My mother and I do not have a good relationship. She looks after my children and I am staying with the gangsters, but I miss my children.'
- 'My two-year-old boy is in foster care because I can't look after him.'
- 'I neglected the children and was aggressive, did not feed the children properly.'
- 'I see my children only weekends because they do not stay with me.'
- 'I was at times aggressive towards them; my children are in foster care.'
- 'I am a sex worker, my five children is in foster care.'
- 'I am impatient with my child.'

The direct quotations from the mothers reflect the mothers' acknowledgement that their substance abuse interferes with their responsibilities towards their children. Most of them are unable to look after their children. The children are either in foster care or with family members. An interesting observation made during the interview process was that mothers and grandmothers of these women were playing a considerable supportive role in the upbringing of the children.

In most cases a mother or grandmother fed the children, took them to school and the clinic, and basically looked after them.

Most of the women acknowledged that their substance abuse during pregnancy had had an effect on their children. The following are some of the direct quotations from mothers:

- 'I have twins; the boy has asthma and the girl bandy legs.'
- 'My boy is two years old, but acts as a one-year-old.'
- 'My child looks normal but his drivel all the time and he has bad teeth.'
- 'My second child's eyes are squint. She went for an operation and wears glasses.'
- 'Her hair used to fell out. In the beginning she struggle at school but it is going a bit better now.'
- 'My two youngest daughters have eczema.'
- 'My child has asthma and a weak immune system.'
- 'My oldest daughter was born premature at eight months.'
- 'My child has got a low self-esteem and the other children at school talks about his tik mother.'

The responses from the mothers perhaps explain their haphazard attitude towards the potential damaging effect of substance abuse on the foetus. They are aware of the dangers of substance abuse during pregnancy, but continued using it, believing that the foetus would not be affected.

The findings in this research correspond with elements of the social disorganisation theory. The 16 respondents in Mitchells Plain came from low economic neighbourhoods where different ethnic groups live together. Their family life consisted of disrupted broken homes, unemployment, and difficult financial circumstances. There are a number of prominent gangs in Mitchells Plain with continuous gang wars over the drug trade and territory. Some of the respondents had close links with gangs, with some gang members being the fathers of their children. One pregnant respondent was shot by an opposing gang member; the unborn baby was instantly killed. More than half of the mothers (62.5 per cent) had been in conflict with the law, convicted of crimes ranging from possession of drugs to drug trafficking, assault, possession of a stolen vehicle, theft, and shoplifting. Their sentences varied from imprisonment to suspended sentences and the imposition of fines.

Most of the mothers (63 per cent) stated that they did not have access to treatment due to monetary constraints. The rest (37 per cent) said they had access to treatment. The following are some of the direct quotations reflecting mothers' attitude towards treatment:

- 'Rehabilitation is not successful. They come out crazier than before.'
- 'I feel ashamed to go for treatment.'
- 'I am scared for the judgment from the community.'
- 'There is a waiting list.'
- 'I don't like the gossiping from the community because I am doing tik.'
- 'I am scared people will point fingers and criticise me.'
- 'Money is the problem; you must first pay before you go for treatment.'
- 'I am afraid they will take my children away if I go for treatment.'
- 'Nothing really prevents women to go for treatment, if they really want to go there is help available.'

It seems that mothers felt ashamed to go for treatment due to the fear of judgment and rejection from community workers. The high financial cost of going for treatment was another prohibiting reason for not seeking help.

CRITICAL REFLECTION

The issue of prenatal abuse as a crime is a controversial matter, as society tends to take two stands regarding the use and abuse of substances during pregnancy, namely:

- the so-called 'harm reduction approach', which views prenatal substance abuse as a social welfare problem
- the punitive approach, which views the abuse of substances during pregnancy as a crime and calls for the criminalisation of drug use by pregnant women.

Limited research may account for the absence of South African legislation providing for prevention of prenatal abuse and drug policies. Chapter 1 of the Prevention and Treatment of Substance Abuse Bill 2008 sets out the rights of substance abusers and persons affected by substance abuse. Section 7(1) states that substance abusers and persons affected by substance abuse enjoy the rights contemplated in Section 9 of the Constitution of the Republic of South Africa, 1996, including the right to fair access to existing public care, treatment, and rehabilitation. It is this part of the bill that could be applied to protect the rights of the unborn child, as the foetus can be defined as 'persons affected by substance abuse' (Ovens, 2010, p. 45).

What is your opinion on these two viewpoints?

CRITICAL REFLECTION

Imagine you have accepted a position as a research assistant in a Community Development Programme in one of South Africa's main cities. You are tasked with initiating a project to show that government can reduce substance abuse and drug-related crime. The area that is chosen is a large township in the south of the city, with approximately 2 million people. This township is well known for substance abuse, drug trafficking, poverty, unemployment, family turmoil, and violence. There are more or less 20 gangs in the area, fighting over drug territory and terrorising citizens. The school and other community programmes have failed to provide educational and job opportunities sufficient to prevent young people from joining gangs. Stores, homes, public buildings, and schools are deteriorating fast, and commercial enterprises are leaving the area.

Furthermore, there are racial tensions between the various ethnic groups living in the township. Xenophobic attacks occur on a regular basis, because residents feel that foreigners are involved in drug trafficking. Residents feel unsafe in the area and have lost hope about bringing their neighbourhood back to life. One of the major problems has been the large block of flats that government built to provide housing after the forced removals from the city centre. These are now overcrowded and dilapidated. Gangs control these blocks of flats and residents live in fear for their own safety.

Thinking like a criminologist

Write a proposal outlining a development programme to rejuvenate the area and eventually prevent substance abuse and drug trafficking. Describe how the government, public sector, and private sector can assist in tackling this problem. What programmes would you recommend to break the cycle of substance abuse, drug-related crime, and poverty?

5.7 Government's plan to beat substance abuse

According to the Department of the Premier (Provincial Government of the Western Cape), the R100-million rand per annum spent on drug and alcohol abuse prevention programmes in the past can be described as ineffectual, fragmented, and out of kilter with international best practices. Programmes were often devised to benefit politically connected people under the pretext of tackling substance abuse. Poor coordination between provincial government departments resulted in duplication, repeated funding of non-performing programmes, and policy gaps. Furthermore, no needs analysis was done to determine gaps, and there was an almost complete absence of aftercare and reintegration services provided for people emerging from treatment (relapse of 60 per cent). Finally, an untargeted and weak approach to prevention most focused on flawed, once-off awareness campaigns has not produced any measurable results, despite the millions of rand spent (Department of the Premier, 2011).

The Department of the Premier established a new comprehensive plan to prevent substance abuse, focusing on young people with psycho-social support, over and above awareness and education. The plan includes some of the following interventions (Department of the Premier, 2011):

- Conducting a comprehensive survey of substance abuse in schools to prioritise those with the most serious drug and alcohol problems (drug testing might be included).
- Increasing after-school programmes in partnership with NGOs and community-based organisations to keep learners off the streets in the afternoon.
- Increasing the availability of social workers by 400 per cent to serve schools and communities.
- A new focus on drug and alcohol intervention and treatment programmes in rural areas.
- Proceeding to shut down the province's approximately 30 000 illegal shebeens.
- Increasing roadblocks to close the net on drunk drivers and drug trafficking.
- Establishing more youth intervention and treatment facilities.
- Increasing the availability of aftercare services for people who have completed rehabilitation programmes.
- Increasing funding to non-profit organisations in the sector with a proven record of providing quality services.

According to the premier's department, this plan is the most comprehensive governmental response to substance abuse in South Africa (Department of the Premier, 2011). The plan's implementation, however will not alleviate the drug crises in the Western Cape overnight.

The National Drug Master Plan (2013–2017) was approved by cabinet on 26 June 2013, and is to be implemented with immediate effect by the Central Drug Authority (CDA). This plan serves as South Africa's blueprint for preventing and reducing alcohol and substance abuse and its associated social and economic consequences for South African society. It places emphasis on four pillars: prevention, early intervention, aftercare, and reintegration. The CDA will use the National Drug Master Plan to drive alcohol control legislation to promulgation, in order to save lives on the roads and to reduce the incidence of FAS. More than 6 000 people, many of them children, die on South African roads every year because of alcohol abuse. The CDA wants a zero tolerance policy on drinking and driving and appropriate health warnings on all alcohol products (Department of Social Development (DSD), 2013).

The following prevention and service agencies are involved in the substance abuse sector in South Africa:

- Central Drug Authority (CDA) – (http://www.dsd.gov.za/cda/)
- Cape Town Drug Counselling Centre (CTDCC) – (http://www.drugcentre.org.za)
- South African National Council on Alcoholism and Drug Dependence (Sanca) – (http://www.sancanational.org.za)
- Soul City Institute for Health and Development Communication – (http://www.soulcity.org.za)
- Khulisa Crime Prevention Initiative – (http://www.khulisaservices.co.za)
- DSD and United Nations Office on Drugs and Crime – (http://www.dsd.gov.za).

CRITICAL REFLECTION

- What is your opinion of this comprehensive plan to beat substance abuse in the Western Cape?
- Do you have any innovative ideas to add to this plan?
- Do you think the National Drug Master Plan will have an effect on the incidence of substance abuse in South Africa?

Conclusion

This chapter began by explaining what is meant by substance abuse and drug-related crime in the South African context. The concept 'substance abuse' in the South African context means persistent or periodic excessive drug use inconsistent with or unrelated to acceptable medical practices. It is the intention of bringing about change in some existing process or state, be it psychological, physiological, or biomedical. This indicates that a variety of substances from a wide range of sources can be considered as drugs, such as naturally occurring substances (for example cannabis), semi-synthetic drugs (for example cocaine) and synthetic drugs (for example methamphetamine).

Drug-related crime (which covers both the use and possession of and dealing in drugs) is primarily a victimless crime, which is usually not reported to the police by members of the public. This type of crime draws attention primarily as a result of police actions like road blocks or police raids.

The chapter continued by covering the current substance abuse trends in South Africa. It was explained that in South Africa, the main substances abused are methamphetamine, alcohol, cannabis, Mandrax, heroin, and cocaine. Although substance abuse is prevalent throughout South Africa, the Western Cape Province – specifically Mitchells Plain – has had the highest level of drug-related crime reported to the SAPS for the past ten years. Recently there has been a dramatic increase in treatment demand for abuse, related to, for example, cannabis, Mandrax, cocaine, heroin, and methamphetamine. Methamphetamine has been linked to risky sexual behaviour and sexually transmitted infections, including HIV. Thus, methamphetamine has immense public health implications for South Africa.

The chapter then went on to consider the historical context of substance abuse in South Africa in order to foster an understanding of the origin of this crime problem.

It was explained that it is widely believed that the origin of substance abuse escalated after 1994 with the advent of democracy in South Africa. South Africa's borders became less strictly policed, and organised crime syndicates saw South Africa as a key area for the smuggling of illegal commodities such as drugs. One of the most quoted causes for drug trafficking originates with apartheid, the colonial past, and forced removals from District Six to the Cape Flats. The relocation led to the destruction of extended and nuclear family structures in the community. Furthermore, many people historically worked in the vineyards, and wages were paid in wine, called the '*dop* system or '*papsak* system'. This system is diabolical in its ability to keep labour submissive and dependent, and has the side effect of promoting violence, dysfunctional families, and alcohol abuse.

The chapter went on to discuss the anomie theory to explain how people 'retreat' into drugs and alcohol. It was explained that, according to Merton's anomie theory, substance abuse takes place when avenues to material success are blocked off. The theory argues that in a competitive, materialistic, achievement-oriented society, success is encouraged as attainable to all members. However, it is attainable to only a small proportion of the society. Individuals who do not succeed must devise 'deviant 'or 'disapproved adaptations to deal with their failure'. Those who have given up on achieving society's materialistic goals, whether by approved or disapproved means, 'retreat' into the undemanding world of addiction. According to Merton, chronic drunkards and drug addicts fall in this category.

Finally, the chapter described the association between social disorganisation and substance abuse. It was explained that residing in a deteriorated area is often correlated with entry into substance abuse, and that social disorganisation theorists see a link between urban political and economic decisions and substance abuse. The issues of unemployment and poverty (deindustrialisation), residential instability (housing, construction, forced removals), different ethnic groups, gangsterism, and population density though public housing or zoning policies were considered in relation to substance abuse. Mitchells Plain was presented as a case study to explain how elements of the social disorganisation theory are present in this area, which has the highest drug-related crime figures in South Africa.

The levels of substance abuse are on the increase among South Africans, and this is a growing concern, considering the contribution of substance abuse to social and health problems. To address substance abuse, it is important to recognise that the causal factors are complex and multifaceted – it requires a multisectoral and holistic approach. Substance abuse prevention is not the responsibility of government alone; non-governmental and civil organisations also have a role to play in addressing this growing phenomenon.

Critical thinking questions

1. Have you ever perceived anomie? What causes anomie?
2. Could the element of 'retreat' lead to substance abuse among college or university students?
3. Is there an area in your town or city that is well known for drug trafficking? If so, think about the social disorganisation theory's explanation of substance abuse, and identify elements present in your town or city's drug trafficking area.
4. Do you know any students at your college or university who abuse substances? What do you think is the reason behind their substance abuse?
5. Is there a way to prevent and stop substance abuse?

References

Bursik, R. J. (Jnr), & Grasmick, H. G. (1993). *Neighborhoods and crime: the dimensions of effective community control.* Lexington publishers. Retrieved February 4, 2012, from http://www.books.google.co.za/books/about/neighborhoods_and_Crime.

Communications and marketing strategy for the Urban Renewal Programme. (2011). Retrieved June 19, 2014, from http: mitchellsplain.files.wordpress.com/2011/07/urp._comms_and_marketing_strategy_final_17Aug2.pdf.

Clarren, K., Olsen, H. C., Clarren, S. B., & Astley, S. J. (2000). A child with Fetal Alcohol Syndrome. In M. J. Guralnick (Ed.), *Interdisciplinary clinical assessment of young children with developmental disabilities.* (pp. 307–326). Baltimore, MA: Paul. H. Brookes Publishing Co. Retrieved April 5, 2011, from http://www.depts.washington.edu/fasdpn/pdfs/child/pdf.

Crime Causation: sociological theories-Social Disorganisation Theory. (n.d.). Retrieved March 29, 2011, from http://www.law.jrank.org/pages818/Crime-Causation-Sociological-Theories-Social-disorganisation.

Dada, S., Plüddemann, A. Parry. C, Bhana, A., Vawda, M., Perreira, T. ... Weimann, R. (2011). *Monitoring alcohol & drug abuse trends in South Africa (July 1996–June 2011)* (South African Community Epidemiology Network on Drug Use (SACENDU) Research Brief, Vol. 14(2)).

Davies, K., & Bledsoe, J. M. (2005). Prenatal alcohol and drug exposures in adoption. *Pediatric Clinics of North America, 52,* 1369–1393.

Department of the Premier (Provincial Government of the Western Cape). (2011, January 11). *A comprehensive plan to beat substance abuse*. Retrieved April 7, 2011, from http://www.capegateway.gov.za/eng/your_gov.

Drug use in South Africa-fact sheet. (n.d.). Medical Research Council. Retrieved from http://www.healt-e.org.za/uploaded.

Drug wars-about drugs. Mandrax. (2010). Retrieved July 19, 2013, from http://www.drugaware.co.za/mandrax.

Emmett, T. (2003). *Organisational contributions. Social disorganisation, social capital and violence prevention in South Africa*. Retrieved from www.unisa.ac.za/.../ASPJ2003-1-2-02-Social-disorganisation-social-capital-and-violence.pdf.

Foetal Alcohol Syndrome (FAS). (1995). Retrieved from http://www.lcsc.edu/education/fas/DefFAS.html.

Foetal Alcohol Syndrome Spectrum Disorders in Cape Town, South Africa. Policy Brief. (2008). Retrieved February 6, 2008, from http://www.research.newsbeat.co.za/projects.

Gibson, D. (2004). *Rethinking domestic violence: case studies from the Western Cape, South Africa* (Working Paper No. 04/08). Amsterdam: Amsterdam School of Social Research. Retrieved June 10, 2007, from http://www.researchgate.net/publication/242688076¬_RETHINKING_DOMESTIC-VIOLENCE._Case_Studies_from_the_Western_Cape_South_Africa.

Häefele, B. W. (2003). Gangsterism in the Western Cape. Criminal economy, gangs and child abuse in the Western Cape. *Community Safety Monitor, 1*, 5–34.

Häefele, B. W. & Ovens, M. (2013). Effect of substance related disorder on family dynamics and subsequent child abuse. *Child Abuse Research: A South African Journal, 14*(2), 26–36.

Hübschle, A. (2011). *Organised crime in Southern Africa: first annual review*. Pretoria: Institute for Security Studies.

In-depth: Youth in crisis. Coming of age in 21st century South Africa: Gang culture in Cape Town. (2007). Retrieved February 5, 2012, from http://irinnews.org/indepthmain.aspx.

Jasper, K. (2011). *Sociological theory of drug abuse*. Retrieved June 8, 2011, from http://www.ehow.com/about_5393359_sociological-theory-drug-abuse.html.

Kapp, C. (2008). Crystal meth boom adds to South African health challenges. *The Lancet, 371*(9608), 193–194. Retrieved April 11, 2011, from http://www.thelancet.com/journals/lancet/article/PIIS0140-673%2808%2960120-8/fulltext.

Kurian, K. M. S., Brown, F. A., Carney, T., Petersen, P., & Wechsberg, W. E. (2011). Exploring the intersecting health risks of substance abuse, sexual risk and violence for female South African teen dropouts. *Journal of Psychology in Africa, 21*(1), 15–26.

Leggett, T. (2004). Still marginal: crime in the coloured community. *SA Crime Quarterly*, 7, 21–26.

Lineberry, T. W., & Bostwick, J. M. (2006). *Methamphetamine use: a perfect storm of complications*. Mayo Foundation for Medical Education and Research. Retrieved April 11, 2011, from http://www.171.67.112.83/content/81/1/77.full.

Marindo, R., Groenewald, C., & Gaisie, S. (Eds.). (2008). *The state of the population in the Western Cape Province*. Cape Town: HSRC Press.

Michael, J. (2006). Growing up with meth. *Children's voice: Child Welfare League of America, 15*(1), 22–28. Retrieved March 4, 2012, from http://www.cwla.org/voice/0602meth.html.

Mitchells Plain (n.d.). Serving History. Retrieved March 24, 2013, from http://www.servinghistory.com/topics/Mitchells.

Moeng, K. (2012, July 23). Cops nab Mandrax dealer. Retrieved June 7, 2013, from http://www.sowetanlive.co.za/news/2012/07/23/cops-nab-mandrax-dealer.

Nyathikazi, S. (2011). Welcome to the world's FAS capital. Retrieved May 5, 2011, from http://www.citypress.co.za.

Ovens, M. (2010). A criminological perspective on the prenatal abuse of substances during pregnancy and the link to child abuse in South Africa. *Child Abuse Research in Southern Africa, 11*(2), 38–48.

Province begins crackdown on illegal liquor (2012, April 2). *Cape Times*. Retrieved April 30, 2013, from http://www.iol.co.za/capetimes/province-begins-crackdown-on-illegal-liquor.

Recreational Drugs (n.d.). Retrieved from http://www.patient.co.uk/health/recreational-drugs.

Salo, E. (2000). Gangs and sexuality on the Cape Flats. *AGI Newsletter, 7*, 1–6.

Shaw, C., & McKay, H. D. (1942). *Theoretical perspectives on race and crime* (Section 3). Sage Publications. Retrieved on April 6, 2013, from http://www.sagepub.com/upm-data/40397_3.pdf.

Shaw, M., & Louw, A. (1997). The violence of alcohol: crime in the Northern Cape. *Crime and Conflict, 9*, 6.

Siegel, L. J. (2011). *Criminology: the Core* (4th ed.). Wadsworth: Cengage Learning.

South Africa (Republic) (SA). Department of Social Development (DSD). (2007). *National Drug Master Plan (2006–2011)*. Pretoria: Government Printer.

South Africa (Republic) (SA). Department of Social Development (DSD). (2008). *Department of Social Development Substance Abuse Programme Concept Paper*. Pretoria: Government Printer.

South Africa (Republic) (SA). Department of Social Development (DSD). (2013). *Central drug authority ready to implement national drug master plan*. Retrieved July 23, 2013, from http://www.dsd.gov.za.cda.index.php.

South Africa (Republic). South African Police Service (SAPS). (2012) *Crime statistics: 2012*. Retrieved April 5, 2013, from http://www.saps.gov.za/statistics/reports/crimestats.

South Africa (Republic). South African Police Service (SAPS). (2010). *The crime situation in South Africa*. September. Retrieved August 10, 2011, from http://www.saps.gov.za/statistics/reports/crimestats.

Sowell, E. R., Leow, A. D., Bookheimer, S. Y., Smith, L. M., O'Conner, M. J., Kan, ... Thompson, P. M. (2010). Differentiating prenatal exposure to methamphetamine and alcohol versus alcohol and not methamphetamine and discriminant analysis. *Journal of Neuroscience, 30*(11), 3876–3885. Retrieved October 13, 2012, from http://www.jneurosci.org/content/30/11/3876.

Standing, A. (2003). *The social contradictions of organised crime on the Cape Flats* (Occasional Paper no. 74). Pretoria: Institute for Security Studies.

The naked truth. Methamphetamine/Tik. (n.d.). Retrieved March 31, 2011, from http://www.tnt.org.za/index.php?option=content&view=article.

The numbers (n.d.). Retrieved October 9, 2010, from http://www.worldofgangs.com.

Things to do in Mitchells Plain (n.d.). Retrieved February 2, 2012, from http://www.sa-venues.com/attractionswc/mitchells-plain.

Transformation Research Project. (2003). *Mitchells Plain*. Unit for Religion and Development Research (URDR): University of Stellenbosch. Retrieved February 3, 2010, from http://www.stbueb02.stb.sun.ac.za.urdr/downloads/ Mitchells Plain.pdf.

Using illegal street drugs during pregnancy. (2011). American Pregnancy Association. Retrieved June 8, 2011, from http://www.americanpregnancy.org/pregnancyhealth/illegaldrugs.html.

'We do recover,' Mandrax addiction types. (n.d.). Retrieved July 21, 2013, from http://www.wedorecover.com/addiction/addiction-types/mandrax.html.

World Foetal Alcohol Syndrome (FAS) day. (n.d.). Retrieved May 5, 2011, from http://www.skills-universe.com.

Chapter 6

Cybercrime[1]

A MINNAAR

6.1 Introduction

Peter Grabosky, an Australian academic and one of the early pioneers of research on all aspects of cybercrime, has succinctly outlined the problems and issues regarding cybercrime:

> **The connectivity of computing and communications has provided new opportunities for crime, including theft of services; information piracy, counterfeiting and forgery; the dissemination of offensive materials; electronic money laundering; electronic vandalism and terrorism; telemarketing fraud; illegal interception; and electronic transfer fraud (Grabosky, 1998, Abstract).**

This quotation highlights all the different forms of crime associated with the computer-driven electronic/digital information age we now live in. From the list of crimes mentioned, one can see exactly how diverse and widespread these electronic crimes can be. Since the time (1998) when Grabosky first formulated this list, additional definitions and terms have been used to describe and label the new and innovative ways of committing crime online. Another aspect that needs to be highlighted in Grabosky's definition is the provision of 'new opportunities' for the commission of so-called cyber-, compu-, e- or online crime.

One of the major facilitators for this growth in cybercrime has been the technological development in equipment, in terms of size, cost, and portability. When equipment is considered, it should be noted that smartphones and tablets and are now almost hand-held computers, and as such are labelled as mobile devices. Both smartphones and tablets enable users to undertake all kinds of electronic transactions, from banking to connecting to the internet. An additional facilitating factor for the exponential growth of cybercrime over the past two decades has been the innovation of wireless connectivity (Wi-Fi) and satellite transmission, which in turn have led to global dissemination of and ease of access to information. In other words, what has driven this so-called 'electronic revolution' has been the convergence of computing and communications.

Finally, it needs to be noted that cybercrime affects everyone and is not confined merely to the internet, hi-tech industries or businesses; its impact is felt right down to the ordinary members of the public in all walks of life. Cybercrime has become a global crime phenomenon of staggering proportions, containing the elements of many different types and categories of crime. The central linking thread is their perpetration in cyberspace with the foundational action largely being e-fraud.

---

1 The contributions of Shandre Sissing and Merlyn Barkhuizen are gratefully acknowledged.

6.2 The global extent of cybercrime

It is statistically quite difficult to put monetary figures on the costs of cybercrime or its full extent, due to under-reporting or lack of knowledge of what exactly constitutes cybercrime, and its hidden costs – for example reputational damage, loss of sales, and the time spent (work hours) in combatting and preventing it. But general trends on the extent, size, and number of cyber- and hackattacks have been generated by various global cybersecurity firms, such as Symantec, Verizon, Microsoft and Google.

For the year 2011 it was estimated in a survey conducted with online active adults in 24 countries that the total bill for cybercrime was US$388 billion. This estimate placed the total costs of cybercrime as being bigger than the global black market in marijuana, cocaine, and heroin combined ($288 billion) and approaching the value of all global drug trafficking ($411 billion). In this survey, victims valued the time they lost to cybercrime at over US$274 billion, and the direct monetary losses (money stolen by cybercriminals plus time spent on resolving cyberattacks) at US$114 billion (Symantec, 2012). In October 2013, the United States Federal Bureau of Investigation (FBI) estimated that within the next two to three years the proceeds from cybercrime, given its exponential increase over the previous five years, would outweigh those from all other forms of white-collar crime combined (SAPA, 2013).

The 2013 *Norton Report*, compiled by the cybertech firm Symantec, indicated that while the number of online adults who have experienced cybercrime had decreased (over the previous reporting year), the average cost per victim rose by 50 per cent from US$197 in 2011 to US$287 in 2012 (Symantec, 2012, p. 6; Symantec, 2013, p. 8). For 2012 it was estimated that every day 1,5 million people were victims of some sort of cybercrime or cyberattack (556 million cybercrime victims a year) (Symantec, 2013).

Who is most affected by cybercrime? Victims are more likely to be male than female (64 per cent, compared to 58 per cent) and these victims would be mobile device owners (63 per cent) and social network users (63 per cent). Moreover, the cybercrime was more likely to occur at a public internet connection (for instance an internet café) or unsecured Wi-Fi so-called 'hotspot' (68 per cent). These victims are also more likely to live in an emerging market country (68 per cent) than in developed countries. In addition, these victims of cybercrime were most likely to have experienced cyberattacks such as malware, viruses, hacking, **scams**, fraud, and theft. Interestingly, the three highest numbers (percentage-wise) of cybercrime victims per country are found in Russia (85 per cent), China (77 per cent) and South Africa (73 per cent) (Symantec, 2013).

6.2.1 Data hacking breaches

A further indication of the size of penetration of cybercrime in the global e-markets is that in 2012 it was reported by Verizon in its annual *Data Breach Report* (for 2011) that 174 million records were compromised in a total of 855 data breaches, in what was called 'an all-time low' for protection against data breaches (Verizon Risk Team, 2012, p. 2).

The Verizon report further outlined that 96 per cent of firms that were required to comply with the Payment Card Industry Data Security Standard (PCI DSS) and that fell victim to data breaches recorded in Verizon's own caseload from 2011, were 'not compliant with the security standards' (Verizon Risk Team, 2012, p. 56).

In its *2013 Data Breach Investigations Report* (for the 2012 reporting year), Verizon analysed more than 47 000 reported security incidents and found that there were 621 'confirmed data disclosures' where at least 44 million records had been 'compromised'. More than half of these data disclosures involved hacking, and malware/crimeware (see the definitions in Section 6.3 below) was present in 40 per cent of the 2012 data disclosure cases. In addition, Verizon disclosed that in 76 per cent of all the cases 'weak or stolen credentials' helped enable these network intrusions. Verizon's data breach analysis also revealed that financial motives were the predominant single driver behind these data breaches, whilst 71 per cent of cases involved the targeting of user devices (including smartphones and tablets). In most (69 per cent) of the analysed cases the breaches were identified as having been perpetrated by external parties, such as internet service providers and external organised crime hacker cybercriminals, rather than from within the organisation experiencing the breach. But more frightening, from a cybersecurity perspective, was the fact that in two-thirds of the cases the breaches had taken months to uncover and be reported. This last factor is extremely significant, since it goes to the heart of combatting all forms of cybercrime via improved cybersecurity measures (see the section later in this chapter on this) (Verizon Risk Team, 2013, pp. 6–9).

6.2.2 Global estimated costs

In 2012 it was estimated that annually consumer cybercrime globally cost US$113 billion (2011 costs estimated at US$110 billion). The countries (out of 24 surveyed) most affected were:

- China: US$37 billion (2012); US$47 billion (2011)
- United States of America: US$38 billion (2012); US$21 billion (2011)
- European Union countries: US$13 billion (2012); US$21 billion (2011)
- India: (US$4 billion: 2012); US$8 billion (2011)
- Brazil: (US$8 billion: 2011 and 2012)
- Mexico: (US$3 billion: 2012); US$2 billion (2011)
- Australia: (US$1 billion: 2012); US$2 billion (2011)
- Russia: (US$1 billion: 2012); US$2 billion (2012)
- Japan: (US$1 billion: 2012); US$0,5 billion (2011)
- South Africa: US$0,3 billion (2011 & 2012) (at 2013 exchange rates this represents a loss to the South African economy in excess of R3 billion)
- New Zealand: US$0,2 billion (2012) (Symantec, 2012; Symantec, 2013).

As evidenced from the above list, considerable sums are being lost every year to consumer cybercrime. Comparatively, in terms of size of economy, the annual loss of US$0,3 billion for South Africa would have greater economic impact than some of the other countries' losses. For example, the US$1 billion Russian loss in 2012 is for an economy five times larger than South Africa's.

6.2.3 Overview of cybercrime in South Africa

All three of the Symantec *Norton Cybercrime Report*s for the years 2011, 2012 and 2013 highlighted specific trends for South Africa in the perpetration of cybercrime:

- First, South Africa – like Brazil, where physical crimes are among the highest in the world – is clearly emerging as a country with high levels of cybercrime.
- Second, South Africa – like China and Singapore – is a country with high levels of free antivirus software users, with the associated risks of large numbers of people accessing the internet and becoming cybercrime victims via mobile devices (free antivirus software is not necessarily safe and secure, since these software programmes are often targeted

by cybercriminals to hide malware inside the free software that often pops up unsolicited on mobile devices).

In October 2013 the FBI had listed South Africa as globally the sixth most active country in terms of the occurrence of cybercrime (SAPA, 2013). By the end of 2013, according to the PricewaterhouseCoopers (PWC) South African edition of the *Global Economic Crime Survey*, South Africa had become (in terms of extent and relative to size of population) the world leader in money laundering, bribery and corruption, procurement fraud, asset misappropriation, and, notably, cybercrime. In this PWC survey, the South African respondents reported that cybercrime made up 24 per cent of all economic crime being perpetrated in South Africa. Many local observers claim that cybercrime is a national crisis costing South Africa at the very least 'a billion rand a year' (Hosken, 2013).

Thus far, the term 'cybercrime' has been used several times in this chapter, but it must be noted that this is a generic term covering a wide range of different forms of crime categories. This section has provided a short overview of the global extent of cybercrime, the costs and losses to its victims, and who those victims were. The South African context was briefly touched on to assist in the contextualisation of the term 'cybercrime' by way of the definitions and typologies that will appear in the next section of this chapter. Following that, the chapter will then proceed to look at some case studies.

Later, there will be a section with a specific focus on cyberstalking and victims thereof. In addition, a review of some of the methods and techniques used by cybercriminals to perpetrate the foundational act of fraud will also be given. The chapter will then list some of the South African legislation that can be used in the fight against cybercrime. This will be followed by a section on cybersecurity vulnerabilities and how to deal organisationally with shortcomings in security measures to prevent cyberattacks.

6.3 Definitions/key concepts

6.3.1 Cyber and cyberspace

The term 'cyber' refers to and is taken in the context of this chapter to mean 'virtual computer-generated'. Typically the terms 'digital' and 'online' are also associated with the term 'cyber'.

'Cyberspace' refers to the 'virtual reality' or imagined (notional) space or realm in which electronic information or data exists or is exchanged. Almost anything that relies on software program coding and has a link to a network could be a part of cyberspace. Included then are smartphones, home computers and laptops, tablets and the internet. Ever smaller and more sophisticated devices are also linked in to cyberspace. Examples are security cameras; elevators; scanning machines (such as credit card readers); global positioning systems (GPS) and satellites; jet fighters; global banking networks; commuter trains; and the computers that control power grids, rail transport networks and water systems (O'Harrow, 2012).

6.3.2 Cybercrime

By way of introducing the concept of cybercrime, the minimalist definition is provided here, namely: criminal activity where a computer or computer network is the source, tool, target or place of a crime. In order to further contextualise this chapter, additional broad definitions of some of the constituent and allied components of the term 'cybercrime' are also provided.

6.3.3 Electronic or hi-tech crime

Cybercrime is also known as electronic crime (e-crime) or so-called 'hi-tech' crime. The latter refers specifically to the use of advanced technology and equipment in the perpetration of cybercrime – besides a base computer or personal computer (PC), devices such as telephones, cellphones, smartphones and tablets (for example iPads), cheque-reading machines, credit-card machines and even biometric (fingerprint, iris or facial recognition) reading machines (see Moore, 2011).

6.4 Variations and forms of cybercrime

There is unfortunately currently low, although increasing, public awareness of cybercrime, especially of the different forms and variations it can take. Most ordinary people do not associate something like losing money from a con or scam perpetrated at an automated teller machine (ATM) as a cybercrime; examples of such scams are criminals tricking users into revealing their secret pin number, or switching cards with them after ostensibly offering to help them, or trapping users' cards with an insert in the card slot in an ATM. Allied to this form of cybercrime are non-cybercrime activities such as credit card skimming or sim card swops (on a mobile device, for example a cellphone); both actions involve theft of digital information and then use of the electronic online medium fraudulently to access, withdraw or transfer funds from a banking account or to pay for a purchase using the ATM users' money. The end result of such a con or fraud is that a cybercrime has been perpetrated with the ATM user as the victim.

Simply put, cyber-, compu-, online-, e-, or high-tech crime can be said to occur in borderless space. In other words, it occurs everywhere – all around us, using electronics as the system, radio waves or electrical impulses as the medium, the internet as the communicating channel (that is, online), and computers or computer-based equipment (for example mobile devices such as smartphones, tablets or laptops/notebooks) as the instrument.

The sheer variety of e-crime and continual criminal innovation have led not only to new forms of computer-related crime, but also to new forms of policing. These, in turn, call for the formulation of new countermeasures and preventative strategies to combat it at source. Law enforcement agencies have been forced to rely on alternative methods of catching e-crime perpetrators, since traditional policing methods have proved inadequate, not only in identifying them, but also apprehending them. Accordingly, the difficulties in collecting digital evidence and pinning down an ethernet or cyberspace suspect have led to policing agencies worldwide turning to non-governmental and private sector resources to assist them in this fight against e-crime. Furthermore, to be truly effective in this fight, and since e-crime literally knows no boundaries, the development and instituting of international cross-border cooperation have become imperative.

However, tracing and tracking the digital evidence raises specific forensic problems that challenge criminologists, investigators, prosecutors, and judges alike. One specific challenge is that e-crime occurs largely across borders, which often also raises questions regarding jurisdiction and sovereignty, as well as legal issues. That is, a type of e-crime might not be defined as an offence in certain countries, whereas it might be defined as one in another country, or have stricter sanctions, for example. This problem also extends to such issues as the extradition of a cybercrime suspect – again the cybercrime that is being perpetrated might not be an extraditable offence in one country, whereas it is in the other country asking for such extradition.

> **CRITICAL REFLECTION** From all the definitions and typologies given above, can you think of, and possibly formulate (list), some new techniques, forms, and typologies to describe other new applications of the broad term 'cybercrime'?

6.5 Cybercrime versus a traditional crime

There is broad consensus on what constitutes a crime in the traditional sense – it occurs in real time, determined by the physical circumstances which give rise to it, usually within distinct social and geographical boundaries, and crucially within an observable place, that is, the place where the criminal behaviour takes place is the same place as that in which the impact of the crime is felt. Furthermore, a traditional crime is subject to a body of substantive law created by a legitimate legislature or by common law.

In contrast, cyberspace is a virtual environment in which values are largely attached to ideas, rather than to traditional, physical property. These values are constantly under threat and have to be protected in order to prevent them from being appropriated, damaged or distorted – the idea of 'intellectual property' is central here. It is the changing nature of property that complicates the issue. For instance, the concepts of electronic cash (cybercash) and cybershopping through cyberconsumption networks will supersede conventional money in a future cyberworld. Moreover, as this chapter has already mentioned, such networks have provided new opportunities for theft and fraud. Furthermore, money's transformation into cybercash has given rise to evidential problems in the investigation of theft and fraud.

There has been debate over the terms 'computer-related crime' (compu-crime) and 'cybercrime' (and more recently the term 'online crime' or 'e-crime') for the past 35 years. It would appear that the first attempt at formulating some sort of definitions of these terms was done in a report by the Stanford Research Institute as early as 1973 (Parker, Nycum, & Oüra, 1973). The debate was taken up in two subsequent US Department of Justice reports in 1979 and in 1989 (see Parker, 1979, 1989). Through this debate, generic definitions and typologies for these forms of crime were developed, among others the following: computer-related crime where the computer is regarded as both the subject and object of a crime as well as the instrumentality (as a piece of equipment) (United Nations (UN), 2005).

In the late 1980s a useful reformulation of this conceptual model occurred, namely where computer-related crime is regarded as:

> **Conduct proscribed by legislation and/or jurisprudence that is directed at computing and communications technologies themselves; involves the use of digital technologies in the commission of the offence; or involves the incidental use of computers with respect to the commission of other crimes, and hence the computer as a source of digital evidence (UN, 2005, pp. 3–4).**

For greater detail on the latter approach see Smith, Grabosky, and Urbas (2004).

Discernable from the above is that the computer, or a computer-like device, is central to the commission of cybercrime. Since the early 1980s, in recognition of the threat posed by e-crime, a number of countries have passed laws to deal with it internally, and have also subscribed to international treaties in order to sustain and encourage an international cooperative approach to combating it. (An example is the Council of Europe's Convention on Cybercrime.) These have defined various types of computer-related crime (such as crime against the confidentiality, integrity or availability of computer systems; content-related offences; and offences related to intellectual property) (see Council of Europe, 2001).

Since the early days of computers and the development of the internet there have been growing opportunities for the exploitation of this form of electronic communication for illegal, fraudulent, and criminal gain. In essence, what we are talking about is computer-related crime based on an electronic/digital medium. In other words, the use of computers, the internet (online), and cyberspace for the perpetration of a specific form of crime.

The elements of e-crime are, then, the computer as the physical instrument, the software program as the means, and the internet (the coming together of computer and communication technologies) as the conduit or communication channel; the intent is the fraud perpetrated on a victim (owner of a computer linked to the internet network); and the eventual crime (for example theft of identity leading to theft of money or goods by means of fraud) is the criminal act. All this occurs in the context of cyberspace, which encompasses both the real and virtual worlds.

Essentially, new rules defining the perpetration of a variety of cybercrimes have become necessary, rules concerning evidence, proof of the commission of crime, and collection of so-called virtual - that is, digital - evidence of crime activities on computer hard-drives, servers and networks - all of which complicates the prosecution of cybercriminals.

CHECK POINT

- Monetary losses and other costs of cybercrime are huge and are spread globally.
- The cybercrime foundational act is largely the perpetration of fraud making use of cyberspace as the medium and online (internet) activities as the vehicle.
- Cybercrime is a truly multicategory global crime and is a complex diverse crime difficult to combat and prosecute.
- Nobody working online or using mobile devices is immune from becoming a victim of cybercrime.
- As cyber technologies become more sophisticated and complex, so cybersecurity vulnerabilities incrementally increase.
- As one avenue of cyberattack is closed to cybercriminals, new forms or more powerful lines of attack are developed.
- Cybercrime descriptions and typologies are evolving all the time.
- As more people get connected online and neglect to follow and implement standard online and personal mobile security measures, exploitable opportunities for global cybercriminals will continue to arise.

6.6 Typologies and classification of cybercrime

Some early classifications of cybercrime focused on the individual and have therefore sought to identify types of offenders, for example hackers, players, contemporary white-collar criminals, pornographers, perverts, computer spies, and computer terrorists. Other classifications concentrated on behaviour, for example theft, embezzlement, fraud, vandalism, extortion, blackmail, and holding to ransom. But the main problem with these classifications was that they were drawn up largely before the commercial exploitation of the internet. One of the problems in this exploitation has been the slow response from the computing industry in acknowledging and recognising 'the increasing sophistication of hackers, as modern hackers are more likely to be criminals than the hooligans and hobbyists of the 1990s' (McCormick, 2007, p. 39).

Modern laws relating to cybercrime need to make the distinction between accidental misuse of a computer system, negligent misuse, and intended unauthorised access to a computer (or other storage devices) via network (online) systems. To deal with these interpretational problems a number of broad generic cyber issues have been developed.

6.6.1 Hacking and hackers

Originally, hacking referred to the accessing of a computer by computer experts for the purpose of exploring systems, programs, or networks, and then identifying vulnerabilities and developing ways to correct vulnerabilities and improve systems, programs or networks. In the context of current cybercrime, a so-called 'hacker' is someone who seeks and exploits weaknesses in a computer system or computer network. Hackers may be motivated by a multitude of reasons, such as profit, protest, or challenge (that is, to crack open and gain access to information). There is some definitional controversy over the term 'hacker' – computer programmers themselves prefer to label someone breaking into computers as a 'cracker' although computer security experts, in contrast, prefer to see themselves as 'hackers', and see computer criminals (the so-called 'black hats') more as 'crackers'. It is the crackers who can bring a computer system to a grinding halt, or make copies of sensitive information for use in an unlawful manner. For example, the cracker might copy a file with all a company's customers' credit card information, planning to use it to buy goods on credit.

Accordingly there are a number of different types of hackers, depending on their motivation and occupation. For example, hacktivists are hackers who hack into secure databases to make a social, ideological, religious or political point. In general, most hacktivism involves website defacement or denial-of-service attacks. However, the art of hacking, and the techniques used to access information databases, is the cornerstone of all cybercrime and allied illegal cyber activities (see below for further definitional typologies).

6.6.2 Cyberactivism

Cyberactivism is associated with hacktivist activities (see the conduct and deeds of Wikileaks or a hacker group like Anonymous).[2]

---

2 Wikileaks – the so-called whistleblower or anti-secrecy web site – is largely dependent on information provided by organisation insiders like US Marine Pte Bradley Manning and Edward Snowden (a data and systems analyst contracted to the US National Security Agency (NSA) with security clearance) both of whom, in 2012 and mid-2013, respectively supplied the Wikileaks founder, Julian Assange, with confidential US government information. Manning provided 700 000 government files (Savage, 2013). Snowden provided details regarding the extent of the PRISM e-Surveillance and Monitoring Programme, that is, data mining, of the US NSA (Poplak, 2013). In contrast to Wikileaks, the group known as Anonymous hacks and defaces or destroys (corrupts) information databases of targeted organisations or government departments. These are the so-called 'hacktivists'.

6.6.3 Cybertrespass

Cybertrespass is closely related to the activity known as hacking. Within this continuum there are a range of those who use this for various purposes: social (cyberactivists), political or military (cyberspies), ideological (cyberterrorists), and criminal. Cybertrespass – that is, literally the unauthorised intrusion into cyberspace – as an activity can involve the deliberate planting of computer viruses via software programmes (so-called 'malware'); hacking into databases and stealing sensitive information (information warfare); or disrupting and destroying network systems. In terms of criminal activities the threat of disruption can be used for the purpose of extortion or holding a company to ransom or even selling to a third party the stolen sensitive information.

6.6.4 Cybertheft

The cybercrime of cybertheft consists of two types:

1. the appropriation of intellectual property
2. the theft of information.

Traditionally criminal law's definition of theft is based on physical possession – that is, the moveable corporeal thing (object) must be taken out of the owner's control, and the intent must be permanent removal. The elements of theft alone make it clear that the South African courts will not easily accept the crime 'theft of information' since this so-called 'crime' falls short of the requirements for theft as laid down in South African criminal law. The revision of the Electronic Communications and Transactions Act (25 of 2002), also known as 'ECTA', and the promulgation of the Financial Intelligence Centre Act (38 of 2001), also known as 'FICA', have made it easier in the law to prosecute for 'theft of information'.

6.6.5 Cyberobscenity

Cyberobscenity can be broadly described as pornography over the internet. The problem here is that individual countries have varied definitions of obscenity and pornography and the criminalisation of the harm (impact) arising out of images of pornography. Here the need is to distinguish clearly between illegal acts (for example child pornography; videoing the performing of sex acts with under-the-age-of-consent children) subject to penal sanctions, and non-illegal activities which may harm a child's development (for example a child gaining unauthorised access to a pornographic internet site).

From a criminal justice perspective, it is important to note that although child pornography is condemned by the state, pornography per se is not. The other point of importance here is that it is virtually impossible to prevent the spread of child pornography without international cooperation.

6.6.6 Cyberfraud

Currently cyberfraud is the biggest proportion of all internet crime and mainly involves the appropriation of cybercash. This is centrally related to the use of credit cards and identity (ID) theft. In addition, such cyberfraud often involves the activity of money laundering or the fraudulent electronic transfer of money.

The most common form of cyberfraud, however, remains the fraudulent use of appropriated credit cards to buy goods over the internet from a cybershopping mall. The important fact here is that the offenders do not actually need to have the physical credit card – they only need the relevant details of an individual credit card, for example number, name of credit card holder, expiry date and the three-digit security number on the back of the card.

6.6.7 Cyberstalking

Cyberstalking can take on a variety of forms – a typical example being the sending of unsolicited e-mails to the victim. Another example is perpetrators assuming the identity of their victims and misrepresenting themselves to someone else over the internet. Allied to this are cyberhoaxing and cyberbullying (see Section 6.9 for more detail on cyberstalking).

6.6.8 Cyberhoaxing

Cyberhoaxing typically involves people misrepresenting themselves on the internet. This happens largely on the internet via so-called 'social media' – on sites such as MySpace and Facebook (where the cyberhoaxer communicates with other people on the internet but uses a false persona, or creates a fake MySpace or Facebook page (containing false information). Alternatively, the cyberhoaxer may hack into another person's personal internet page and load false information about that person.

Such cyberhoaxing can have serious consequences. An example is the 2006 case of teenager Megan Meier (the victim) and Lori Drew (a 40-year-old mother whose cyberhoax led to Meier's suicide) (see Minnaar, 2008, for details). But the difficulty is in tracing the hoaxer/hacker and proving that there was malicious intent behind the false (hoaxing) information.

6.6.9 Cyberbullying

In cyberbullying, the cyberbully – often using the cyberhoax to gain the confidence of a cyberfriend/acquaintance – might cyberbully a victim with threats of revealing intimate details, or even, where a cyber-romance has occurred on the internet, threatening that the romance has been conducted under false pretences and will be publicly exposed, or that the romancer must now take the romance further and they must meet or even offer marriage.

Cyberbullying is prevalent amongst adolescents when social media sites and cellphones are used to target children with malicious intent to ruin their reputation. This is often done by posting demeaning, degrading and malicious rumours and/or embarrassing images, which are more often than not untrue. The aim is to shame the child/victim in the eyes of peers by means of social media sites. Cases of adolescent suicides have been reported in the media as a direct result of cyberbullying. These occur as a result of the stress and anxiety such bullying causes for the adolescent.

6.6.10 Cybervigilantism

In cybervigilantism, users might well take the law into their own hands in terms of punishing transgressors (for example hackers, cyberbullies, and cyberhoaxers) by either destroying (hacking into and infecting with a virus) the perceived transgressors' website, webpage, information on a social networking site, or e-mail address (by sending them spam repeatedly to clog up their computers) or, even, launching a sophisticated distributed denial of service (DDoS) cyberattack. Spam is unsolicited electronic junk mail, which is often commercial (for example an advertisement for services or products), delivered by mass e-mailing posting (often repeatedly) on the internet to reach as large a number of recipients as possible.

6.6.11 Cybermanipulation

Cybermanipulation is the popular means of gaining access to, and bypassing, technical systems (upgrades, security kits and high-end encryption) completely. It often means tricking someone into helping an unauthorised person to gain access to information technology (IT) systems. It therefore preys on the weakest link in a security system - the human being. Basically, the perpetrators of cybermanipulation are con artists who exploit human vulnerabilities such as ignorance and naiveté, and possibly an individual's own greed (that is, through bribery and corruption).

Nowadays a common form of such a computer-based attack is the hiding of spyware in an innocent e-mail message or in a pop-up an employee may encounter informing them that they have lost their connection to the server. The user is then advised to type in his or her username and password, and to press enter. This information is then e-mailed automatically to the perpetrator, and the user ends up being unaware that any breach of security has occurred.

6.6.12 Cyberransom

Cyberranson occurs when a hacker holds a company's electronic information database to ransom. That is, the hacker blackmails a company by demanding payment of a sum of money (ransom) and threatening, if this payment is not made, to sell this information to the highest bidder (an industry or competitive rival) or to corrupt the information in its entirety, making future operations of the company difficult or virtually impossible.

In recent times a number of additional typologies have been added to those listed above, namely:

6.6.13 Cybersecurity

Cybersecurity refers, typically, to all organisational actions required to ensure protection from online danger of attacks, threats and risk to the security of information in all its forms (digital electronic and so-called 'hardcopy' or physical), and the security of the computer equipment, systems and networks where information is stored, accessed, processed, and transmitted. Cybersecurity also refers to precautions taken to guard against crime, attack, sabotage, espionage, accidents, and failures.

Cybersecurity also includes countermeasures against cyberattacks of all kinds. Some of these so-called 'defensive' or preventative measures include such techniques and information protection software as:

- intrusion protection systems (IPS), pre-emptive blocks, blacklisting
- hunting within networks (actively searching for insiders and other adversaries or malware)
- passive and active intelligence (including law enforcement) employed to detect cyberthreats
- actions to temporarily isolate a system engaged in hostile cyberactivities.

So-called 'offensive' countermeasures might include electronic jamming or other negation measures intended to disrupt an adversary's cybercapabilities during employment (see DoD, Sa(b)).

6.6.14 Cyberattack and cyberthreats

A cyberattack has been defined as a hostile act using a computer (or computer-like device such as a smartphone, tablet or notebook) via networks or systems. Such an attack is intended to disrupt, deny access to and/or destroy or degrade an adversary's critical cyber systems, assets, or functions. The intended effects of a cyberattack are not necessarily limited to the targeted computer systems or information databases themselves; such attacks may manipulate or destroy information on the target information system itself but also, even, destroy a target's communication and logistic channels.

Some individuals use cyberspace for their own devious actions, targeting unsuspecting individuals for their own enjoyment, nefarious purposes or exploitation, or simply for profit (cybercrime). When government or military establishments are attacked through cybermethods, this is another kind of attack known as cyberwarfare or cyberterrorism.

6.6.15 Cyberwarfare and cyberdefence

In 2010, Clarke defined cyberwarfare as 'actions by a nation-state to penetrate another nation's computers or networks for the purposes of causing damage or disruption' (Clarke, 2010, p. 6).

In 2011 the US Department of Defense (DoD) formally identified cyberspace as a new domain of warfare (DoD, Sa(a)). Cyberwarfare is defined as conflict executed in cyberspace as a military operation, that is, typically conducted by the armed forces of a state in order to deny an opposing force the use of cyberspace systems and weapons in time of war. It includes the concepts cyberattack and cyberdefence. Some cyberwarfare attacks have been perpetrated in cyberspace without the formal declaration of war between two states. One such attack was launched by the United States against Iranian information databases and electronic systems in order to disrupt the latter's nuclear programme. In other words, in cyberwarfare hacking techniques are used to sabotage electronic systems, or to undertake cyberspying/espionage – literally undertaking information warfare.

Cyberdefence, or what is now being termed 'proactive cyberdefence,' means acting in anticipation to oppose an attack against computers and networks. Proactive cyberdefence will most often require additional security from internet service providers (see DoD, Sa(b)).

6.6.16 Cyberterrorism

Eugene Kaspersky, founder of Kaspersky Lab, concludes that 'cyberterrorism' is a more accurate term than 'cyberwarfare,' since with a cyberattack the element of surprise – with its potential for creating fear in the target – is enhanced by the randomness of such cyberattacks. That is, victim targets never really know who the perpetrators are, or when they might strike again – both elements of 'terrorism' per se. Cyberterrorists also make use of the same attack modus operandi to exploit vulnerabilities in cybersecurity in trying to achieve their goals. However, their targets are more likely to be critical infrastructure of all kinds in order to impart as much widespread chaos, terror, and destruction as possible by cyber means (see Stiennon, 2011, and Bell, 2013).

Cyberterrorism – representing as it does the threat of attack on critical infrastructure and strategic installations using electronic means via interconnected computers, with the internet as the medium launching such attacks – has become one of the major security concerns of the digital information age, facing governments, organisations, businesses, companies, and individuals alike. Reliance on digital data and electronic devices for communication - and many other aspects of business, industrial processes, services delivery and government operations - has incrementally increased vulnerabilities, making network systems susceptible as an avenue for terrorist actions.

6.6.17 Cyberespionage

Simply put, cyberespionage is the act or practice of obtaining secrets (sensitive, proprietary or classified information) from individuals, competitors, rivals, groups, governments, and enemies - and also for military, political, or economic advantage - using illegal exploitation methods on the internet, networks, software and/or computers. Classified information that is not handled securely can be intercepted and, even, modified, making espionage possible from places separated by great distance (see Clarke as cited in Farrel, 2010).

Computer hacking represents a modern threat in ongoing industrial espionage. As such, it is presumed to occur widely in the corporate world, with companies and corporations worldwide daily facing numerous cyberattacks. For obvious reasons, such cybercrime is largely under- or unreported.

Cyberwarfare, cyberterrorism and cyberoffensive operations have huge potential to disrupt and cripple whole economies. For instance, impact of an attack on critical infrastructure or strategic installations could be major - these include railways, electricity grids, airlines, nuclear power stations, and, even, large irrigation dams dependent on computer systems for their effective and efficient operations. For instance, a terrorist hacker could manipulate a large dam to release a flood of water downstream and thereby destroy valuable farmland and urban areas alongside the river. Cyberterrorists could also use access to a nation's critical infrastructure to blackmail its government.

CRITICAL REFLECTION

Having read the definitions and list of typologies given here, do you think you can add to this list more definitions and new typologies that can increase our understanding of the complexities around the term 'cybercrime' and its multiple offshoots?

6.7 Know the crime

6.7.1 White-collar crime: the foundational crime

Essentially, cybercrime is an extension of or offshoot of so-called 'white-collar crime'. Within criminology, white-collar crime was first defined by the sociologist Edwin Sutherland in 1939 (see Sutherland, 1949) as a financially motivated non-violent crime committed for illegal monetary gain. Initially the term became synonymous with so-called 'white shirt, tie and suit wearing' perpetrators in the business or corporate world and the government sphere. That is, it referred to 'white-collar' professionals, as opposed to 'blue-collar' (overall-wearing) factory workers or even those typecast as often-violent so-called 'common' or 'street' criminals, as found within syndicates and gangs operating in the world of organised crime. Unfortunately, many conceptual ambiguities have arisen in defining white-collar crime within strict category boundaries, since it is made up of a number of different criminal behaviours and activities. Furthermore, in terms of cybercrime, it must be remembered that nowadays it has elements of the latter crime typologies as well.

The research done on the psychological profile of white-collar offenders (WCOs) is useful and relevant in aiding our understanding of the offender or cybercriminal. Ragatz, Fremouw, and Baker (2012, p. 978) outline several characteristics unique to WCOs as opposed to non-white collar (NWC) offenders. They found that WCOs were more likely to be male, Caucasian, older, graduates of high school and college, and less likely to be unemployed, compared with NWC offenders. They were also less likely to have an arrest history, to be drug users or to abuse alcohol, but were more likely to exhibit above average academic performance, the latter very often putting them in managerial positions. White-collar offenders may also exhibit some psychopathic tendencies, such as self-centredness (which may be recognised as self-confidence) or a lack of specified goals (which might be seen as 'visioning'). Further features of psychopathy which may be found in WCOs include superficial charm, shallow affect, remorselessness, grandiosity, lack of responsibility, impulsivity, and versatility in criminal acts.

For operational and investigation purposes, the FBI of the US Department of Justice defined white-collar crime as follows:

> **Illegal acts which are characterized by deceit, concealment, or violation of trust and which are not dependent upon the application or threat of force or violence. Individuals and organizations commit these acts to obtain money, property, or services, to avoid the payment or loss of money or to secure personal or business advantage (Federal Bureau of Investigation (FBI), 1989, p. 3).**

Essentially, then, the two foundational crimes underpinning the perpetration of white-collar crime are fraud and theft, and the term is now commonly associated with frauds ranging from banking or insurance fraud to money laundering, investment fraud, corruption, bribery and kickbacks in tenders, among others. In fact, the range of frauds that can be perpetrated is as wide as the con-artist cybercriminals' creative and ingenuously devised methods of scamming a victim. Fraud is then broadly defined as the crime of cheating someone, that is, obtaining money or some other benefit by deliberate deception.

Like its offshoot, cybercrime, white-collar crime is not a victimless crime, involving as it does such crimes as commercial fraud, the cheating of consumers (for example false advertising), swindles, the use of insider trading in stock market trading, expense account padding, embezzlement, tax fraud, and other forms of dishonest business schemes (for example so-called 'Ponzi pyramid investment schemes').[3] A single scam can destroy a company, devastate families by wiping out their life savings, or cost investors huge amounts of money. But with the onset of the digital/information age, fraud schemes have become more sophisticated than ever.

3 A Ponzi Scheme is a type of investment fraud in which belief in the success of a non-existent enterprise is fostered by the payment of quick returns to the first investors from money invested by later investors. This gives the appearance that the investments of the initial participants increased dramatically in value over a short time period. It is named after Charles Ponzi (died 1949), who carried out such a fraud (1919–20) by creating what was then known as a 'stockmarket bubble'. Typically such a fraudulent investment scheme promises investors high interest rate returns. A Ponzi scheme works in its initial stages but inevitably collapses as more investors participate; after the initial payment of a high return invested funds run out and later investors lose all their money. A Ponzi scheme is a variation of illegal pyramid sales schemes. In a pyramid sales plan, a person pays a fee to become a distributor. Once people becomes distributors, they receive commissions not only for the products they sell but also for products sold by individuals that they bring into the business. These new distributors are beneath the person who brought them into the pyramid scheme, so they are 'under the pyramid.' In illegal pyramid schemes, only the people at the top of the pyramid make substantial money because they get a commission from the products sold by everyone below them. As more people become distributors, the people lower in the pyramid have less chance to make money (adapted from Ponzi Scheme, n.d.).

6.7.2 E-crime categories and terminology

Cybercrime itself can be categorised into three basic categories, namely:

- white-collar crimes such as fraud/theft (via online phishing scams)
- social fabric crime (for example sexual offences or pornographic exploitation largely using social media platforms)
- the broad category of security state crime (the category of cybercrime perpetrated by governments and their agencies, for example cyberwarfare, cyberespionage, hacker activists, and the like, whose main thrust is via cyberattacks).

Over the last few years a number of new terms have been formulated to describe some of the more common forms of e-crime, particularly ID theft and credit card/bank account fraud. Sections 6.7.2.1 and 6.7.2.2 attempt to define and describe the various activities associated with e-crime (including cybercrimes). The first activity discussed is the physical aspect of obtaining credit card details, which is often the first step in the perpetration of an e-crime.

6.7.2.1 Skimming

In skimming, the details of a credit card encrypted on its magnetic strip are skimmed (duplicated) in a shop or a restaurant, using a small electronic device. This information is sold to a criminal syndicate, and then, by means of a computer, burned onto a blank counterfeit credit card. The syndicate then uses this to embark on a spending spree. In a new twist, skimming devices featuring clandestine video recorders can be attached to ATMs; these recorders record the input of the victim's pin number.

Increasingly, however, a criminal does not need to make a fake card. Thanks to the growth in telephone and internet shopping, criminals need to know only the credit card details. Here a common con is a telephone call in which victims are told the caller is from their bank or credit card company – the caller usually refers to a transaction that has triggered a security flag on the bank's systems.

In broad detail, such a telephone call proceeds as follows. The caller states that the victim's bank/credit card company needs to confirm whether a certain transaction occurred, and explains that if it did not, the victim will be issued with a credit on the account, and a fraud investigation will be launched. The caller advises that if the victim has any questions, he or she should phone the security department at '0800 … '. If the victim calls this number, he or she will be asked to provide a control number (a six-digit code) – which the caller has provided. Then the victim is asked to verify if he or she is still in possession of the credit card, and asked: 'Please turn your card over – you will see a string of numbers. Please read the last three – they are the security numbers.' These last three numbers appear on the back of a credit card; because they are not on the front, they are not recorded when swiped through a machine in a shop. They were introduced by banks as a security measure, and most online retailers now require online shoppers to give them to prove that the shopper is actually in possession of the card. So, by giving all this information either to the caller or when phoning the 'Security Department' telephone number provided, the victim gives the fraudsters all the information they need to go on an online spending spree!

A further innovation has been the use of cellphone cameras to photograph the details or information on both sides of a credit card – these details are sufficient for spending on buying or paying for anything on the internet by cybershopping, that is, credit card cyberfraud. To counter this form of cybercrime banks introduced the so-called 'smart' credit card – that is, with a chip embedded in it. Now, when a credit card transaction is done by machine, the transaction requires the credit card owner to insert his or her secret pin number.

The next step in obtaining information is the electronic approach to a potential victim, in particular those aspects of e-mail spam scams that use the so-called 'phishing' approach.

6.7.2.2 Phishers, phishing, and phish-pharming

The term 'phishing' is derived from 'fishing', that is:

- baiting the hook (the temptation and the believable, convincing approach)
- casting the fishing line (e-mailing the tempting offer)
- seeing what is caught (a gullible victim's identity details).

The technical definition for 'phishing' is that type of computer online identity theft that employs an approach to a potential victim via an e-mail, in order to steal the recipient's personal identity data and financial account(s) credentials. In effect, these e-mails are false (so-called 'spoofed') and designed to lead recipients to counterfeit websites that aim to trick them into divulging financial data such as account usernames and passwords.[4]

In other words, phishing is a method of deceitfully obtaining personal information such as passwords, identity numbers and credit card details, by sending e-mails that look as though they come from trusted sources, such as banks or legitimate companies.

In some phishing attacks the phishing e-mail sent by the so-called 'phishers' (that is, the con artists and cyberfraudsters) requests that users click on a link (a so-called 'hyperlink') in the e-mail which will direct users to a spoofed website.[5] The e-mail will try to convince recipients that the website to which they are being directed is genuine and that, therefore, they should feel safe in responding and providing the requested information. For example, some such approaches hijack (appropriate) brand names of banks, e-retailers and, even, credit card companies to make the request appear to originate from well-known businesses and therefore genuine.

This spoofed website – designed to fool users into thinking that it is legitimate – will look almost exactly like that of a legitimate and well-known financial institution, in the hope that recipients will be tricked into disclosing their personal information in bogus online forms on it. It only takes a few duped individuals to make phishing a profitable business for cybercriminals.

Phishing attacks also make use of a number of different techniques and changing forms of approaches to a victim. Two are the so-called 'phish-pharming' and 'spear-phishing'.

In 'phish pharming', the phishers go 'mass phishing' (that is, 'throw their net as wide as possible') on the internet, using group e-mails randomly sent across the globe. The term 'spear phishing' describes a more direct online variation of a phish-attack: in this case online criminals try to pry passwords and other sensitive information out of companies. This form of attack makes use of bogus e-mails presented as e-mails

4 See the Anti-phishing Working Group (APWG) web site for a more detailed technical definition (www.antiphishing.org) and the South African Banking Risk Information Centre (SABRIC) web site at https://www.sabric.co.za/.

5 'Spoofing' is the term used to describe the setting up of a web site to resemble an official site. The 'spoofed' site will then be used by the fraudsters to harvest confidential and other personal information when people go to it and transact on it. The setting up of such web sites is facilitated by the theft of Digital Certificates (DCs). DCs are a system intended to verify the authenticity of a particular web site – to ensure, in effect, that a web site is genuine/authentic, that is, by verifying a site's identity, and that the connection to the site is encrypted (secure) and difficult for an outsider to monitor. By stealing DCs, hackers can create fake credentials that could allow someone to snoop on internet connections that appear to be secure.

from powerful executives of the targeted organisation or company. Rather than pose as a bank or other online business, spear phishers send an e-mail to employees at a company or government agency, making it appear that the e-mail comes from a powerful person within the organisation. Unlike basic phishing attacks, which are sent out indiscriminately, spear-phishers target only one organisation at a time. Once they trick employees into giving passwords, they can install so-called 'Trojan Horses' (or 'Trojans') or other malicious software programs that ferret out corporate or government secrets (Reuters, 2005).

'Trojans' refer to the Trojan Horse of Greek mythology, according to which attackers hid inside a wooden horse left at the gates of the besieged city of Troy. The wooden horse was taken inside the city, the hidden attackers only emerging late at night to open the gates to the rest of the Greek army (which had sailed away, convincing the Trojans that the siege had been ended). When used in reference to cybercrime, a Trojan (horse) is a computer program concealed on a computer (hard drive) that is meant to disrupt, undermine, subvert or destroy, that is, it contains a hidden function (concealed stratagem) that causes damage to other programs while appearing to perform a valid function.

The box below features a case study of a typical example of a phishing email scam.

CASE STUDY

Below is a recent phishing scam e-mail wherein a South African bank's logo (an exact replica as that on its website) was inserted in the e-mail (the logo and bank name that appeared in the square brackets below have been removed).

Sent: Friday, 26 July 2013 9:40 PM
To: [Recipient's name]
Subject: [SA bank name] banking system interruptions
[SA bank logo]

Due to the growing reports of on-going sim-swap scam whereby your phone number is swapped to get access to your account, [SA Bank] has initiated an online security upgrade procession which you will need to complete by clicking on the link below this message to complete the process.

Failure to do this will lead to the suspension and possible deactivation of your account until we can rightfully verify you as the genuine account owner.

For further checks, we might have a consultant call you for further verifications via phone: click on below to proceed and complete this process and enjoy a safe and secure online banking in future:

FOLLOW INSTRUCTIONS CAREFULLY: PUT IN USER AND PASSWORD, DOUBLE CLICK ON 'LOGIN', WAIT 1 TO 2 MINUTES TO RECEIVE YOUR ONE TIME PASSWORD (OTP VIA YOUR CELLPHONE, FILL IN THE OTP YOU RECEIVE ON THE USER AND PASSWORD FIELD AND CLICK LOGIN AGAIN, CLOSE THE PAGE AFTERWARD. GIVE 24 HOURS FOR YOUR [SA BANK NAME] FIREWALL SECURITY TO BE ACTIVATED ON YOUR ACCOUNT AFTER BEEN ADDED.

Upgrade Here: [this had a website address on which to click]

© Disclaimer | Conditions of access | Privacy and security statement | Site specs | Security centre | PAIA | Fica | NCA | © 2013 [SA bank name] Bank is a licensed financial services provider in terms of the Financial Advisory and Intermediary Services Act and a registered credit provider in terms of the National Credit Act, registration number NCRCP15. – This message has been scanned for viruses and dangerous content by Pinpoint Secure-mail, and is believed to be clean.

It looks official, and it looks professional and formal (especially with the bank's logo inserted in the message), but South African banks routinely warn on their internet banking websites that they will never send such an e-mail soliciting such security steps to be completed online. They also warn that any such information should only be submitted via their official website once the user has logged in with his or her account number, pin number and password. When an attempt was made to block the e-mail address from which this email was sent (inContact@[SA bank acronym name].co.za comms.[SA bank acronym name]mailer.co.za) by sending it to the 'junkmail' option, the e-mail programme returned the message: 'Outlook Web Access was unable to add this e-mail address to the Blocked Senders list because it is not properly formatted'.

The following are examples of similar phishing attacks and the rather innovative subject titles that appear in the e-mails the attackers send – for more detail on these types of phishing scams, see Minnaar (2008):

- Advanced fee (419) scams
- 'Assistance with releasing blocked inheritance'
- 'You have won ...'
- 'Verify bank account details ...'
- 'We tried to reimburse you ...'
- Deposit/refund scam
- Deposit slip scam
- 'Your wife/schoolmate/daughter/neighbour has sent you a birthday/greeting e-card ...'
- 'Check out the pics (photos) I have sent you ... '.

Underlying phishing attacks are a number of computer terms to describe the methods and techniques used in the attack. The next section will discuss these.

6.8 Cybercrime techniques

Essentially, the techniques of cybercrime are dependent upon the following basic steps:

1. theft of information
2. participation by victim (even if unwilling or unknowing)
3. scam approach: mass targeting of likely victims (using internet e-mail spam)
4. foundational action: ID theft (biographical, account details, credit card numbers)
5. use of information to gain access to banking accounts; or
6. payment of fees.

However, these actions are dependent on certain electronic procedures or processes.

6.8.1 Botnets and zombies

The term 'bot' is short for robot. The best definition understandable for non-specialists is that provided by Choo (2007, p. 1): 'Bot programs are codes or programs that operate automatically as agents for a user or another program.'[6] In the early 1990s bot programs were designed to allow internet relay chat (IRC) operators to encode automated responses to their 'chat' activities. As so-called 'chat rooms' gained popularity among internet users, disruptive or inappropriate behaviour started to become a problem. Such misbehaving users were banned from the chat rooms (that is ejected or so-called 'klined'- declined or refused entry). Some of those ejected became disaffected, and as a form of revenge launched attacks by disrupting the IRC service (the DDoS attack) (Choo, 2007, p. 1).[7]

These attacks were done surreptitiously by forwarding targeted victims bot programs (also known as 'malware' - that is, a malicious software program). Such an attack occurs usually via e-mail attachments or peer-to-peer networks, and if the victim visits an infected website.

Bot malware typically takes advantage of system vulnerabilities and software bugs or hacker-installed backdoors that allow a malicious code to be installed on computers without the owners' consent or knowledge. They then load themselves into such computers, often for nefarious purposes. Bots - individual computers infected with bot malware - are then turned into so-called 'zombies.' These can then be used as remote attack tools or to form part of a so-called 'botnet' - a collection of internet-connected programs communicating with other similar programs on captive computers, in order to perform a variety of tasks - under the control of the botnet controller. In other words the zombie computer has a 'sleeper cell' waiting to be activated on the command. If such an attacker can install the malware on a series of computers, a botnet is formed, that is, a network of linked bot computers. In this way a 'bot' computer program allows a net attacker (hacker) to remotely control vulnerable computers. The attacker/controller can establish and form a virtual network of so-called 'zombies' or botnets. Once such botnets have been set up, they are used and manipulated (leveraged) in order to orchestrate a concerted attack against other computing resources (Choo, 2007, p. 1).[8]

Once the malware is installed on a target computer, it is a small step for criminal-minded hackers to manipulate its use for criminal ends.

6.8.2 Crimeware/spyware

The original bot or malware programs were redesigned as either spyware or crimeware, that is, often the two were combined in the theft of information off a computer. Crimeware is software that performs illegal actions unanticipated by a user running the software, and which aims to yield financial benefits to the installer of such software (see www.antiphishing.org). Essentially, this method uses technical subterfuge schemes to plant the crimeware program onto PCs to steal credentials directly. This is where so-called 'spyware' comes into the equation. The spyware typically uses viruses and/or Trojans to install programmes called 'key loggers' on the victim's computer.

6 © Copyright AIC. Reprinted by permission of AIC.
7 © Copyright AIC. Reprinted by permission of AIC.
8 © Copyright AIC. Reprinted by permission of AIC.

Keystroke logging can be done through either hardware or software. Key loggers can be installed simply as running an e-mail attachment that installs the software on a computer. This spyware then uses the installed key logging system to intercept consumers' keystrokes and capture information – this collected information can include online account user names and passwords and other information, including credit card numbers and bank account details (if the victim does internet banking, for instance). The spyware then sends the information back to the phisher and to corrupt local and remote navigational infrastructures to misdirect consumers to counterfeit websites and to authentic websites through phisher-controlled proxies (that is, the zombies).

6.8.3 Ransomware

Hackers use ransomware Trojan horses to encrypt all the information stored on a computer. The hackers then phone the user and demand money for the release of the computer and to free up the information. Such programs (software) are the basis of phishing attacks.

6.8.4 ID theft

Essentially, all the phishing attacks discussed here are aimed at the theft of an individual computer user's identity details, since the possession of someone's identity details is the foundation of the perpetration of various forms of fraud. Such identity theft occurs when someone uses a victim's personal information such as name, credit card number or other identifying information (for example ID number, social security number, driver's licence, address, telephone numbers) without permission to commit fraud or other crimes.

So all phishing attacks are trying to get the victim to divulge such identity information to the phisher so that it can be used for various nefarious, illegal and mostly fraudulent criminal activities.

So in cybercrime terms, identity theft occurs when someone uses personal information such as a name, a credit card number, an account pin number or other identifying information without permission to commit fraud or other crime digital *online*. This is different from traditional hard-copy theft of such things as an ID book, passport, birth certificate, or marriage certificate, or letters and application forms in files.

6.8.5 Vulnerabilities

Other technical and people vulnerabilities (that is, so-called 'insiders'/company employees) are constantly being exploited and used by cybercriminals. It is every organisation's nightmare that a young hacker will infiltrate a computer network from the outside, and crash it or gain access to valuable classified information (for example trade secrets) and publicise it. Although there has been much publicity on hacking destroying computer systems, it is usually not an outside job. Hackers are more commonly known to be an employee, or ex-employee (disgruntled), who has a grudge against the organisation. The computer system is then infiltrated from inside the organisation and then destroyed. Alternatively, valuable information is sold to a syndicate (for criminal purposes), sold to a competitor for possible market advantage (industrial espionage), or used for cyberblackmail/cyberransom.

Hackers log into a computer network, and gain entry to it without having the necessary authority to do so, that is, through cybermanipulation. An example of this is a perpetrator logging into a government network by means of his or her own computer and modem, in order to look at classified documents.

Information security has become an increasingly critical concern for organisations of all kinds. Trends such as mobility, cloud computing, consumerisation and flexi-work mean that more people are accessing enterprise applications and data from more places and in more ways than ever before.

There are also electronic information storage database vulnerabilities linked to mobile devices and to the growing practice of 'bring-your-own-device' (BYOD) to work. Mobile devices (notebooks, smartphones and tablets) are small and valuable. Increasingly, they are becoming a target of theft, not just for the device itself but also for the information stored on it. Keyboards are hard to use or non-existent on phones and tablets. This often results in owners and users auto-saving their passwords for e-mail and virtual private network (VPN) access-passwords. If the device gets into the hands of a cybercriminal it could open up an organisation's or company's information and other resources to anyone who takes possession of the device. For these reasons, the security techniques that work for desktops and PCs are not adequate for mobile devices – a major vulnerability these days in protecting information.

The box below features a case study in which an e-theft of money occurs. This occurred because of such vulnerabilities or technical shortcomings in the target organisation's cybersecurity systems (for example firewalls, level or advanced sophistication of encryption). The case study was compiled from Planting (2012), Chauke (2012), Swart and Afrika (2012), SAPA (2012a; 2012b), and Rasool (2012).

CASE STUDY: R42 million hacked from Postbank South Africa

Between 1 and 3 January 2012 (72-hour heist), approximately R42 million was stolen, by a Nigerian cybercrime syndicate, from the South African Post Office's (SAPO) financial institution, Postbank. The National Intelligence Agency (NIA) and the police launched a high-level probe into the theft. The syndicate (cyber-villains) reportedly opened several Postbank accounts across South Africa in 2011 and during the 2012 New Year holiday period gained access to a Rustenburg-based (in the North West Province) Post Office employee's computer and made deposits from other accounts, into its own (so-called 'mule') accounts. Following that, syndicate members withdrew cash (after their multiple accounts' withdrawal limits were increased) from these accounts at ATMs across Gauteng, Free State and KwaZulu-Natal. The last of these withdrawals was made at 6:11 am on 3 January 2012.

A few days after stealing millions from the Postbank's investments account, three of the syndicate members (believed to be nine in total) were arrested at the Hartbeespoort Dam, west of Pretoria, by Piet Pieterse, head of the SAPS's Cybercrimes Unit. At the time of their arrest the perpetrators were partying in their newly acquired speedboat, in the company of three prostitutes and more than a dozen bottles of expensive cognac. They had also splashed out on luxury cars, expensive clothes, and Cuban cigars. Pieterse's unit and the NIA had enlisted the services of an auditing firm, a forensic risk management company, and self-confessed hacker Alistair Peterson, who was once the most wanted online banking hacker in South Africa, to crack the case.

This incident comes three years after Postbank spent in excess of R15 million to upgrade its fraud-detection service, thus raising serious concerns about the Postbank's internal systems. In 2009, the Postbank said its customers were hard hit by an upsurge in card fraud, via card cloning. In March 2010, SAPO had spent approximately another R250 million on the second phase of its IT upgrade plan. The post office is the body in charge of the government's Trust Centre and authentication service provider under the Electronic Communications and Transactions Act. This means that any government department that performs work using the internet and e-mail services makes use of the post office system. A senior IT and banking security expert stated that the Postbank network and security systems are 'shocking and in desperate need of an overhaul ...'. At the time of the hacking, the Postbank held over R4 billion in deposits, and processed millions of rands in social grants annually. The bank told the press that none of its customers were affected by the hacking. However, we must ask ourselves if IT generally *should* be satisfied with protecting itself with nothing more than a password and a PIN.

The cybercriminals involved in the Postbank case study featured here were caught not by means of a forensic investigation, but because of their own stupidity in splashing out with their ill-gotten money and drawing attention to themselves. The facts of this case point not only to the cyberfraud methods of stealing money electronically, but also to the difficulties in collecting sufficient digital evidence to catch and convict cybercriminals.

Besides public cybercrime of the type featuring in the Postbank case study, fraud is perpetrated inside organisations. In the latter case, the cybercriminal makes use of electronic systems and equipment to steal money through organisational electronic transactions systems. Criminally minded insiders are usually quick to spot and exploit shortcomings or vulnerabilities in systems or procedures, as the case study below shows.

CASE STUDY: Casino scam

In the mid-1990s a number of South African casinos instituted an electronic card system to replace the one in which patrons had to purchase physical gambling chips (each assigned a different monetary value). Before the electronic card system was instituted, patrons would purchase these chips for cash, or via a credit card transaction, at cash–chips teller points situated strategically around the casino. Gambling machines were fed these chips, or the chips were used at the roulette, card or dice tables. At the end of a gambling stint, winnings were exchanged for cash. Casino managements across South Africa, realising that large sums of money were in circulation virtually all the time, with their attendant risks, and wanting to avoid the necessary (and expensive) security measures to secure all this money, decided to institute electronic cash gambling cards.

While the changeover to electronic cash was a slow, evolving process, a system was soon in place whereby patrons could load cash onto electronic cards. These electronic cards could be inserted into certain gambling machines, and money would then automatically be drawn off the card by the machine or at the tables. Winnings could also be paid out at cash machines installed and loaded by the casinos themselves, that is, not bank operated ATMs.

At one casino, the loading of the cards was done by one employer at an electronic loading machine, namely a stand-alone computer. This employee had sole access to the machine. He devised a fraudulent scheme whereby he electronically loaded large sums of money as winnings onto such gambling cards and issued them to accomplices. Over a period of time, the accomplices went directly to the casino's cash dispensing machines and cashed up their apparent winnings.

This insider scam was discovered only after payouts from cash dispensing machine could not be tallied with patrons' winnings at the gambling machines and tables. By then a huge amount of money had already been lost.

What this insider cybercrime points to is the need for both procedural checks and balances to be implemented internally, and what is termed 'double access security'. In other words, just as company cheques have to be countersigned by at least two financial officers in a company, so too should all electronic financial transactions obtain two approvals, that is, by the operator doing the transaction (loading onto a card) and by a supervisor.

CRITICAL REFLECTION

The discussion above suggests the many ways in which cybercriminals try to scam individuals and get access to personal information, or use insider information to hack into databases and use the information there to access bank accounts or to steal money by fraudulent online means. What advice would you give individuals, companies, and organisations to prevent their falling victim to these cyber approaches?

6.9 Unpacking cyberstalking

Basu and Jones (2007, p. 1) explain that cyberstalking, in its simplest form, is the use of the internet or other communication technology to harass or menace someone. While Fraser, Olsen, Lee, Southworth, and Tucker (2010, p. 40) define cyberstalking as stalking through the use of the internet and other technological tools. Cyberstalking usually follows a course of harassing actions that would cause the victim to suffer emotional distress as a result of such behaviour (Whitty & Joinson, 2009, p. 111). Moreover, as clarified by Miller and Morris (2012, p. 83), the threatening nature of cyberstalking makes it more serious than mere harassment, in that cyberstalking can result in serious psychological and sociological consequences for the victim, despite the absence of mutual geographical surroundings.

6.9.1 The nature and modus operandi of cyberstalking

The cyberstalking modus operandi, as well as the impact it has on victims, is of key importance when discussing some of the multifaceted components of cyberstalking.

A cyberstalker uses various methods to stalk, harass, and pursue victims through electronic media. Often the cyberstalker will send repetitive, unwanted messages, as this is cheap and convenient and can be anonymous when the cyberstalker uses unknown accounts and anonymous e-mailers. Accompanying these messages, the cyberstalker makes threats against victims, their families or colleagues. These threats are characterised by abusive and offensive content, and may have pornography attached to them. Cyberstalkers seek to cause continuous distress through a variety of threatening behaviours (Bocij, 2004, p. 12). Additionally, cyberstalkers may attempt to pretend to be their victims through various internet services. For instance, the cyberstalker will enter a chat room, using the victim's identity, and post sexual and degrading invitations to an online audience (Bocij, 2004, p. 14).

Cyberstalkers often act out of revenge and spite, and thus circulate e-mails and notices, or establish websites, containing personal, and often embarrassing, details about their victims. The cyberstalker's intention is to disclose private information about the victim to cause humiliation. A good example of this is the ongoing online international battle between Cynthia Armistead and Richard Hillyard, both of whom have recently updated websites containing degrading and humiliating information about each other (see the respective websites at http://cyberstalked.org/ourstory/affiliations.html and http://www.atlga.com/harassed).

Cyberstalkers may also endeavour to damage a victim's computer system by infecting it with a virus or destructive program. The motive here is to harm or destroy property belonging to the victim. This method of exploitation is practised in order to cause the user distress (Bocij, 2004, p. 14; Mullen, Pathé, & Purcell, 2009, p. 154). Cyberstalkers also engage in identity theft, which takes on many variations and can involve the ordering of goods and services on behalf of the victim or the initiation of contacts under the victim's identity, in order to cause some sort of stress, humiliation or grief to the victim. This behaviour, associated with cyberstalking, is different to the traditional sense of identity theft, as the motives are different. Within the cyberstalking parameters, imposed distress on the victims is intended, whereas traditionally, identity theft is practised for monetary gain (Mullen et al, 2009, p. 154).

6.9.2 The impact of cyberstalking on victims

6.9.2.1 Psychological impact

Cyberstalking often produces psychological effects on the victims (Bocij, 2004, p. 80; Pathé, 2002, p. 51; Drahokoupilová, 2007, p. 152). As distinct from most crimes, cyberstalking involves repetitive and persistent behaviour. The victims of cyberstalking experience numerous forms of harassment, as opposed to a one-off event of misconduct, characterised by unpredictability and threats. Research indicates that stress-related symptoms are more likely to develop when individuals experience inescapability under threat of a prolonged episode, as often transpires in cyberstalking. The stress prompted by cyberstalking results in the victim feeling helpless and powerless (Pathé, 2002, p. 51). Likewise, Bocij reports that victims of cyberstalking often suffer from 'depression, anxiety, guilt, shame, helplessness and post-traumatic stress disorder (PTSD)' (2004, p. 80). Additionally, cyberstalking victims may suffer feelings of loss of control, seclusion, self-blame, hypervigilance, and overactivity. The victims may also experience relentless feelings of intense fear.

6.9.2.2 Sociological impact

Cyberstalking may cause victims to alter their lifestyles in terms of interpersonal, professional, and general social functioning. For instance, victims may:

- change their personal contact information, such as telephone numbers, e-mail addresses or, even, their names
- remove their contact details from public portals
- change their daily routines
- suspend previously enjoyed activities
- find new jobs and schools for their children
- relocate
- end communication with family, friends or colleagues.

Obviously, victims squander a lot of energy, time and money in achieving the above-mentioned changes (Drahokoupilová, 2007, p. 152).

Furthermore, Pathé (2002, p. 52) notes that cyberstalking may bring about avoidance of certain locations, the installation of extra security measures, and restriction of social interaction. Within cases of cyberstalking, victims may also resort to restricted or discontinued access to online activities such as social networks, chat rooms, or e-mail services.

6.9.2.3 Physical impact

Bocij (2004, p. 82) identifies physical effects of cyberstalking, such as sleep disturbances including nightmares, or difficulty in falling asleep or staying awake. In addition, some people may develop issues with intimacy and weight. Pathé (2002, p. 52) point outs physical effects such as 'jumpiness' or panic attacks, poor concentration, weakness, fatigue, nausea and headaches. It is evident that such physical symptoms are likely to interfere in all aspects of a victim's life.

Although the harm experienced by the victims of cyberstalking is often unnoticed or deemed insignificant (Sheridan & Grant, 2007, p. 11), cyberstalking has the potential to manifest itself in a serious psychological, sociological and physical danger (see the case study below). Its nature is made clear and more comprehensible when the intangible and tangible impact on victims of cyberstalking is evaluated .

CASE STUDY: Cyberstalking

This case study graphically illustrates how cyberstalking has the potential to become a serious psychological, sociological and physical danger.

A young female victim met her cyberstalker at university, an interaction characterised by social awkwardness and unshared affections. After numerous romantic gestures, she rejected his attempts at consolidating a relationship. In retaliation, the cyberstalker posted her personal details on the internet. Some of these details included her physical description, contact number, physical address, and details of how to evade her home security system. Additionally, on online portals he posted untrue allegations about rape fantasies regarding the victim. The harassment reached a peak when the cyberstalker started to send her pornography and made threats of gang rape and death.

The victim reported suffering psychological effects as a result of the cyberharassment, such as an intense fear of leaving home, stress, humiliation, and helplessness. Sociologically, the victim faced various disruptions, such as being forced to relocate and losing her job. She was also constantly disrupted and disturbed by the persistence of unknown men contacting her and coming to her home, as directed by the online posts made by the cyberstalker.

Furthermore, the victim says that she suffered from weight loss prompted by the cyberstalking behaviour.

Cyberstalking is a social phenomenon entailing various potential consequences related to social pathology and criminal behaviour. It is a phenomenon that is still relatively unknown in the South African context pertaining to its nature and social dynamics.

Apart from the fact that online stalking thrives on the increasingly innovative application of technology in modern society, which renders cyberstalking difficult to combat, it has multidimensional implications for an individual's social identity. Determining the level of harm suffered by victims is an intricate process, and the true damage is difficult to measure, as it ranges from psychological trauma to physical and emotional reactions.

The profile of the offender is complex in nature as cyberstalkers are a new breed of criminals who are on an intense mission to hunt (stalk and trap) their prey (targeted victims). Victims of cybertechnology deserve to be protected against cyberstalking. Brown (2007, p. 48) points out that, in the past, stalking was associated with behaviour linked to domestic violence, but it is now established as a substantive criminal act in its own right. It took significant legislative demarcation and clarification to enhance the efficacy of this establishment. Relevant South African legislation is the Electronic Communications and Transactions Act (25 of 2002). Coinciding with this is the definition of cybercrime that defines cybercrime as 'any conduct on the Internet or connected with the Internet or Internet usage which constitutes a crime in terms of the South African criminal law, including any conduct punishable in terms of Chapter XIII of Act 25 of 2002' (South Africa, 2006a, pp. 72, 74). Finally, the Protection from Harassment Act (17 of 2011) effectively criminalised the act of cyberstalking (South Africa, 2006b).

CRITICAL REFLECTION Based on the above discussion of cyberstalking, explain why cyberstalking is more than just a social misdemeanour.

6.10 The policing of cybercrime[9]

There is no one piece of legislation solely dedicated to cybercrime. However, one cannot understand any approach to the policing of cybercrime without reference to the current South African legislative framework that is an enabling framework for the investigation of cybercrime. This will be discussed below.

6.10.1 South African legislation pertaining to aspects of cybercrime

6.10.1.1 The South African Constitution

The South African Police Service (SAPS) was established in terms of sections 205 to 208 of the Constitution of South Africa, 1996, and is regulated and structured by the South African Police Service Act (68 of 1995). Before the promulgation in 2002 of the Electronic Communications and Transactions Act (25 of 2002), common law offences and their supporting statutes were used to arrest and prosecute online offenders, for example defamation of character, crimen injuria (also known as cybersmearing), fraud, defeating the ends of justice, contempt of court (publishing of any court proceedings without the court permission), among others.

6.10.1.2 Electronic Communications and Transactions Act (25 of 2002) (ECTA)

In terms of so-called 'statutory offences', the primary piece of reference legislation is the Electronic Communications and Transactions Act (25 of 2002) (ECTA) which was drafted into South African law on 30 August 2002 (South Africa, 2006b). It came about as a mechanism whereby the government could establish a formal structure to define and regulate e-commerce in South Africa. The ECTA has a direct impact on any illegal transgressions associated with electronic communications, data messages, and transactions. It pertains to all forms of communication such as e-mail, the internet or short message services (sms), cellphones, and digital cameras. The act also functions as an informative and enabling resource in which concepts are legally identified and defined in order to resolve any ambiguity relating to e-commerce (The Institute for Risk Management of South Africa (IRMSA), 2005).

9 The assistance of Col. J. Buys, Section Commander, Financial and Cyber Crime Intelligence Centre, Crime Intelligence and Protection Services, SAPS, in formulating and compiling this section is gratefully acknowledged.

This act provides, inter alia, for:

- the facilitation and regulation of electronic communication and transactions
- the creation of certain cyberoffences such as computer-related extortion, fraud, and forgery (sections 85 and 86)
- the appointment of cyber-inspectors. (Cyber-inspectors must be appointed in and by the Department of Communications – this is a big drawback to the actual policing of cybercrime, since they are not police officers, nor do they have the powers of arrest or crime investigation skills.)

Chapter 13 of the act, and in particular sections 85 to 89, seeks to make the first statutory provisions or cybercrime in South African jurisprudence. The act seeks to introduce statutory criminal offences (cybercrime) relating to information systems and it includes:

- unauthorised access to data
- interception of or interference with data
- computer-related extortion
- fraud
- forgery.

Cybercrime is defined in terms of item 4 of the *Guidelines for Recognition of Industry Representative Bodies of Information System Service Providers*, as: '[A]ny conduct on the Internet or connected with the Internet or Internet usage which constitutes a crime in terms of the South African criminal law, including any conduct punishable in terms of Chapter XIII of Act 25 of 2002' (South Africa, 2006a, pp. 72, 74).

With regard to cybercrime, the act attempts to pioneer statutory criminal offences relating to the following key issues:

- It addresses unauthorised access to data, such as hacking and trading passwords to commit an offence.
- Interception (tapping into data flows) and interference with data (launching virus attacks) are now seen as illegal.
- It challenges computer-related extortion, such as fraud and forgery, in order to tackle the unlawful financial gain of offenders through the use of technology.

In addition, the act states that any person assisting another in the performance of any of the above-mentioned crimes will be guilty as an accessory. The penalties involved in such transgressions range from a fine to imprisonment for a period not exceeding six months (South Africa, 2006b, p. 72).

6.10.1.3 Prevention of Organised Crime Act (121 of 1998) (POCA)

The Prevention of Organised Crime Act (121 of 1998) (POCA) was promulgated essentially to introduce measures to combat organised crime, money laundering, and criminal gangs. The POCA also provides for the criminal and civil forfeiture of any deemed proceeds of criminal activity. The National Prosecuting Authority (NPA) established the Asset Forfeiture Unit (AFU) in May 1999 as a specialised unit to ensure the implementation of the forfeiture provisions in the POCA.

6.10.1.4 Prevention and Combating of Corrupt Activities Act (12 of 2004) (PCCA)

The Prevention and Combating of Corrupt Activities Act (12 of 2004) (PCCA) provides the legal definition of corruption and creates a variety of offences pertaining to corruption. This act follows the trend in international legislation, specifically by unbundling the term 'corruption'. Hence, numerous specific corrupt acts and practices are legally defined. The act provides for offences in respect of corrupt activities. It constructs a general offence of corruption, which can be committed by anyone, whether in the public service or in the private sector. It then goes on to describe specific types of corrupt activities. Put simply, corruption occurs when a person offers someone in a position of power something, in order that he or she uses his or her power, illegally, to the advantage of the offering person. Consequently, a minimum of two people are required for the crime to take place, and both parties will be guilty of corruption.

In addition, the act allows for people found guilty of certain offences (such as those related to tenders) to be blacklisted, and it requires senior officials to report corrupt activities. Underlying acts of corruption are fraud and bribery, which can easily be perpetrated online in attempts to get access to networks via insiders of an organisation. This act is therefore one of the pieces of legislation crucial to extending legal fights against cybercriminals (see South Africa, 2004).

6.10.1.5 Counterfeit Goods Act (37 of 1997)

The Counterfeit Goods Act (37 of 1997) protects the intellectual or copyright holders against acts of counterfeiting and piracy, especially nowadays online piracy ranging from illegal music to video copying.

6.10.1.6 Financial Intelligence Centre Act (38 of 1998) (FICA)

The principle objective of the Financial Intelligence Centre Act (38 of 1998) (FICA) is to assist in the identification of money laundering and terrorist financing, particularly via online banking services.

6.10.1.7 Criminal Procedure Act (51 of 1997) (CPA)

Section 256 of the Criminal Procedure Act (51 of 1997) (CPA) states that if evidence in the criminal proceedings does not prove the commission of the offence, but can prove that the accused attempted to commit that offence, or any other offence of which an accused may be convicted on the offence charge, the accused can be found guilty of attempt to commit that offence or an attempt to commit any other offence.

Section 252A of the CPA allows traps and undercover operations in the combating of organised crime (and also cybercrime, for example by the use of so-called 'honey-pot stratagems' for entrapment online of cybercriminals).

Sections 20–22, 25, and 205 of the CPA allow the police, by virtue of a search warrant, to seize anything, take evidence, and summon witnesses as to any alleged offence.

6.10.1.8 Regulation of Interception of Communication and Provision of Communication-Related Information Act (70 of 2002)

The Regulation of Interception of Communication and Provision of Communication-Related Information Act (70 of 2002) provides, inter alia, for the prohibition of the manufacturing, assembly, possession, selling, purchase or advertising of certain equipment (for example computer software such as malware, key loggers, and skimming devices) (see sections 45(1) and 49(1)).

6.10.1.9 The Protection for Constitutional Democracy Against Terrorist and Related Activities Act (33 of 2004) (PCDATARA)

The Protection for Constitutional Democracy Against Terrorist and Related Activities Act (33 of 2004) (PCDATARA) provides for a number of offences related to terrorist activities, inter alia the financing thereof, and in the context of cybercrime and cyberterrorism this includes money laundering.

6.10.1.10 Films and Publications Act (65 of 1996)

This refers to online child pornography.

6.10.1.11 Protection from Harassment Act (17 of 2011)

Although the legislation was seven years in the making, it was tabled in Parliament in February 2010, approved in August 2011, and published in the *Government Gazette* on 5 December 2011. The Protection from Harassment Act (17 of 2011) was purposively designed to address harassment and stalking incidents in which the assailant and victim do not have a domestic relationship. This includes stalkers who are neighbours, friends or, even, strangers. It was drafted by the South African Law Reform Commission to bring it in line with existing norms. In terms of section 1 of the act, 'harassment' means

> **directly or indirectly engaging in conduct that the respondent knows or ought to know-**
> ***(a)*** **causes harm or inspires the reasonable belief that harm may be caused to the complainant or a related person by unreasonably-**
> **(i) following, watching, pursuing or accosting of the complainant or a related person, or loitering outside of or near the building or place where the complainant or a related person resides, works, carries on business, studies or happens to be;**
> **(ii) engaging in verbal, electronic or any other communication aimed at the complainant or a related person, by any means, whether or not conversation ensues; or**
> **(iii) sending, delivering or causing the delivery of letters, telegrams, packages, facsimiles, electronic mail or other objects to the complainant or a related person or leaving them where they will be found by, given to, or brought to the attention of, the complainant or a related person;**
> ***(b)*** **amounts to sexual harassment of the complainant or a related person (South Africa, 2011, p. 4).**

In terms of the same section, 'harm' is defined as any 'mental, psychological, physical or economic harm' (South Africa, 2011, p. 4). This act specifically recognised that previous South African legislation regarding stalking did not make provision for cyberstalking, resulting in the act of cyberstalking going largely without censure or sanction. Accordingly, the act included cyberstalking as a criminal offence, making it easier to prosecute. Courts now have the authority to consider whether reporting or posting damaging content online can be constituted as harassment.

6.10.2 Investigation of cybercrime

The combating of cybercrime within South Africa is, according to the Constitution, the responsibility of SAPS. However, other institutions/departments also have a role to play, namely the Department of Communication (cyber-inspectors) and the NPA's AFU.

Within SAPS, the Directorate of Priority Crime, the Detective Service, and Crime Intelligence and Protection Services are involved in the combating of cybercrime.

When cybercrimes are investigated, the same investigation methodology must be applied as that used when any other crime is investigated, for example obtaining statements from the victim(s), the registering of the case, crime scene management, obtaining evidence (usually digital), interviewing of witnesses, and arrest of suspects.

The gathering of digital evidence forms a major part in the investigation of cybercrimes. If the gathering and continuity thereof are done incorrectly, the evidence could be found inadmissible in a court of law. Attempts to investigate cybercrimes often fail because of mistakes made at this stage. Essentially, digital evidence is ignored, destroyed, compromised or inappropriately handled.

CRITICAL REFLECTION

From the above-mentioned pieces of legislation, what legal approach would you implement in a prosecutorial plan to convict a cybercriminal. In other words, how would you piece together cyberevidence in order to ensure that cybercriminals are caught and do not slip through the net.

6.11 Preventing and combating cybercrime

6.11.1 Insider prevention

A key aspect of computer-related crime is malicious tampering with computer data by disgruntled or dishonest employees. A virus can be entered manually onto a company's system and, for instance, spread through a retail chain's group of stores across the country, thereby damaging the company's computer network. In one such case in 1999, an employee at a large retail chain in South Africa inserted a virus which caused a massive computer crash, and sales had to be entered manually (Workplace Staff, 2006).[10]

Other attacks on a company's information systems could include deletion of company address books or client lists, or the deliberate deletion or destruction of other information. These can have far-reaching economic consequences for any company. Whole databases containing sensitive customer information are also stolen and sometimes offered for sale to a competitor, or thieves set up business for themselves, using this information to get their business off the ground.

However, because there is virtually no foolproof way of stopping determined employees who want to do harm to their employer, it is essential that a range of IT systems be put in place to track the electronic movement of each and every employee. This includes having access to employees' e-mail and keeping a watchful eye on their activities on the internet (Workplace Staff, 2006).

How are these cybercrime practices combated? First, companies can install their own spyware on all computers on the company network, that is, they can track the keystrokes of all employees' and any activity via company networks, for example source of viruses generated via company e-mail. Second, companies can employ so-called 'cybersleuths' who undertake periodic forensic investigations in the company for which they work. Once a

10 A forensic investigation found a trail that led back to the employee, who was subsequently found guilty on charges of malicious damage to property, since at the time there were no laws in South Africa that specifically gave protection to data or related to computer-specific crimes. This situation has subsequently been remedied with two pieces of legislation, namely the Regulation of Interception of Communications and Provision of Communication-related Information Act (70 of 2002) and the Electronic Communications and Transactions Act (25 of 2002). Both make it possible for employers to keep a much closer look at what their employees are up to, including the tracking of employees' internet and e-mail activities as well as enabling employers to put written policies in place governing the handling and protection of electronic data (Workplace Staff, 2006).

cybersleuth has detected some cyberfraud or other cybercrime, a company should then immediately call in experts. Such experts should know exactly how to download digital evidence from a computer, laptop or server, both correctly (technically) and within the parameters of the law requirements (legally) so that such digital evidence can be used in court to prosecute cybercriminals. So-called 'cyberforensics' investigative methods are used to build a cybercase against a cybercriminal.

An additional security measure companies can use is the hardening of network and information security systems with the securing of networks and individual computers by means of sophisticated firewalls and antivirus software. Furthermore, security can be increased by frequent (compulsory) changing of passwords by employees and IT administrators and allowing access to sensitive information only to selected individuals who have been background checked and integrity checked.

A further security measure is the formulation of an effective company whistle-blowing policy, which needs to be in place (implemented, rather than just being a policy in a manual) so that honest employees can blow the whistle on their crooked colleagues.

However, awareness is the biggest weapon against cybercriminals who try to obtain banking, other financial or ID details by e-mail or, more recently, via cellphone. One would not give one's ATM pin number to a stranger, so there is no reason for individuals to share private details with an unknown source on the internet or cellphone. The same principle applies to all e-mails: one should deal only with credible and known sources. If any e-mail is received from a retailer of whom one has never heard or from whom one has never agreed to receive mail, the mail should be deleted immediately. One should never click on any links in the e-mail message, and should always be suspicious of e-mails with puzzling origins.

6.11.2 Combating cyberattacks via cybersecurity

The concepts of 'cybersecurity' and 'proactive cyberdefence' have already been discussed in section 6.6.13.

In terms of DDoS attacks, according to the US Department of Defense Cyber Command Unit, at least 85 per cent of targeted cyberattacks could be prevented by organisations' implementation of three simple strategies:

1. Employment of so-called 'application whitelisting' – the opposite of blacklisting: This is done by the creation of a list of approved programs for running on all networked devices. This will prevent malicious software, malware, and other non-approved programs from running on their network systems.
2. Regular network installation of so-called 'patches' to all applications: These patches are designed to fix programs or update a computer system or software to prevent bugs and viruses by patching applications, operating systems, and web browsers. Patches are routinely provided by software developers for the secure running of their licensed programs.
3. Minimisation of the number of users with administrative login privileges and implementation of strict accountabilities at each access level (Leathley, 2013).

However, it is not as simple as that. Instead of relying on existing firewalls (which cannot resist a powerful DDoS), individual organisations or companies need to purchase dedicated DDoS mitigation appliances and deploy them in their IT/data centre. These are specialised hardware devices that are connected in front of their normal servers and routers, and are specifically built to detect and filter any malicious traffic and to detect and deflect cyberattacks like DDoS.

The next level up of cybersecurity is that provided by – and the responsibility of – internet service providers (ISPs). Some organisations and businesses use their ISP (that is, the same network provider as that from which they get their bandwidth) to provide network security against DDoS attacks. These ISPs usually have access to much more bandwidth than the organisation itself, and therefore could deal with or deflect the big attack volumes of internet traffic.

The final level of cybersecurity is that provided by cloud services providers. These are the experts at providing network protection from the so-called 'cloud' against DDoS cyberattacks. This means they have developed massive amounts of network bandwidth and DDoS mitigation capacity at multiple sites all over the internet. This huge network/ bandwidth capacity can take in any type of network traffic (whether use is made of multiple ISPs, own data centre, any number of cloud information storage service providers, and the like). Such cloud security providers typically so-called 'scrub' the internet traffic for a client and send the so-called 'clean' traffic back towards an organisation's information hub or data centre.

Cloud mitigation service providers have become the logical choice for organisations for their DDoS protection needs. They are the most cost-effective and scalable solution to keep up with the rapid advances in DDoS attacker tools and techniques (Leach, 2013, p. 3).

The use above of the term 'mitigation' should be noted; one can never prevent a cyberattack, but can only 'mitigate' (lessen) its impact. One of the ways to do that is constantly to be alert and utilise intrusion detection software. This software program will alert the security centre that a cyberattack (network intrusion) is underway. The scale of impact is lessened, therefore, by the speed of the response or counterattack measures taken. This speed factor again requires expensive services such as 24-hour so-called 'live' or 'real time' monitoring. Often, to break up or deflect a cyberattack, a network security provider can instruct an organisation immediately to shut down its server.

The bottom line is that any network cybersecurity system is only as good as its weakest link. Simple passwords for a PC or mobile device for gaining access to an organisation's network, LAN or intranet are simply no longer sufficient. There is a need for the implementation and use of additional cybersecurity measures, for example biometrics software on a computing device. Mobile devices (and, of course, human beings on the inside of organisations) remain the most vulnerable routes for hacker intrusions.

6.12 The use of grounded theory in understanding and analysing cybercrime

In criminal justice research, we need to generate new theories to meet the sociological demands of the twenty-first century. The grounded theory design is concerned exclusively with the generation of new theories, rather than the testing of theory. This requires the researcher to collect and analyse data to generate a practical theory (Calman, Sa). Because cybercrime is a fairly new crime phenomenon and growing in complexity daily, existing criminological theories are very difficult to apply to the wide range of criminal activities which can be classified as cybercrime. As a result of cybercrime's complexity and wide range of criminal activities, a researcher would in most cases have to apply a grounded theory approach when researching and collecting data on any given aspect of cybercrime.

The aim of grounded theory is to generate or discover a theory, which is done by systematically gathering data obtained from social research and avoiding theoretical preconceptions. Grounded theory is ideal for exploring the behaviour of individuals or groups where there has been little exploration of contextual factors that affect individuals' lives. It is a new way of investigating the social world. It is qualitative in nature, as the researchers identify an area of interest and immerse themselves in the data to try and understand what the participants see as being significant and important.

Patton states that 'one of the strengths of the grounded theory is the inductive, naturalistic inquiry strategy of approaching a setting without any predetermined assumptions' (2002, p. 129). Grounded theory design is aimed at developing an often situation-specific emergent theory founded upon the interpretation and analysis of the actual research findings. In other words, as a research design, grounded theory seeks to generate a theory from (that is grounded in) the empirical data through ongoing interpretation and analysis of that data.

There are a number of features that all grounded theories have. These are:

- simultaneous collection and analysis of data
- creation of analytic codes and categories developed from data and not by pre-existing conceptualisations
- discovery of basic social processes in the data
- inductive construction of abstract categories
- theoretical sampling to refine categories
- writing of analytical memos as the stage between coding and writing
- integration of categories into a theoretical framework.

The existing literature and theory, as well as the prior knowledge and experience of the researcher, can also be used to inform the development of categories. However, the categories should not be forced to fit the literature and should not be used to create categories. Literature can be used as data and constantly compared with emerging categories to be integrated in the theory (Calman, Sa). The existing body of literature and especially the definitions of various types of cybercrime would therefore serve as a good source of information/foundation on which to build a grounded theory for the understanding of a specific cybercrime phenomenon.

According to Glasier (2001, p. 176),'We do not know what we are looking for when we start ... we simply cannot say prior to the collection and analysis of data what our study will look like.' Glasier's view is that the researcher must allow the theory to emerge from the data rather than utilising specific pre-set categories. According to so-called 'emergent procedure', the researcher enters the field with only a broad topic of interest in mind, without prior reading or understanding of literature in the area of study, or preconceived research questions. The researcher could, for example, immerse him- or herself in various chat rooms in order to gain enough data to identify patterns or trends which emerge from the conversations that take place on these platforms. Researchers cannot enter this type of research with preconceived ideas of how these conversations should take place in order to suit the research aims.

CRITICAL REFLECTION

A researcher should approach the field (for example a chat room, Facebook page or Twitter) with an open mind, and not have preconceived ideas of how the information gathered should be formulated. There is tremendous freedom in researching cybercrime from a grounded theory perspective, which can give rise to rich and meaningful data that would not be possible within other more constrained theoretical paradigms. What do you think?

6.13 Criminological application: policing and prevention

According to Herbig and Hesselink (2009, p. 441), criminologists have traditionally viewed and applied the profession as a mechanism to improve the understanding, control, prevention, and reduction of crime and criminal behaviour. Recent developments in the discipline have facilitated this task and assisted in the expansion of the criminological field. Herbig and Hesselink (2009) state that contemporary criminological focus is rapidly evolving in response to societal and other needs in a multidisciplinary context. Criminology is not just a discipline based on theories and theoretical issues, but rather an integrated, multidisciplinary field that marries academic and contemporary social concerns about crime.

Although criminologists do not play a direct role in the apprehension of cybercriminals, as an expert in the theory of crime and the criminal mind, a criminologist can play a vital role by:

- documenting the definitional and theoretical aspects of the crime phenomenon
- advising the police and support agencies regarding the above
- researching new developments and modus operandi in cybercrime
- collaborating and assisting with crime prevention strategies and police intelligence gathering, resulting from expertise gained through research
- acting as expert witness in court proceedings to assist in the understanding of the crime phenomenon being prosecuted, for example cyberstalking
- collaborating with industry experts in building up a body of knowledge to assist law enforcement officials in the apprehension of cybercriminals
- evaluating the effectiveness of current strategies being utilised in the investigation of cybercrime cases
- advising on any policy changes regarding legislation in respect of cybercrime prevention and policing.

Although the criminologist's potential contribution has been highlighted, it is clear that many challenges remain to incorporate such expertise effectively in a practical manner. Herbig and Hesselink (2009, p. 466) emphasise that it is important to note that criminology and criminologists are not attempting to dominate the field of crime research and/or application, but rather seek to contribute as much as possible in crime eradication for the benefit of all.

Therefore, any aspiring criminologist wanting to make a contribution to the combating of cybercrime should make every effort to get to know the crime and understand it in all its facets and varieties. Once specialised in this examination by way of research activities, a criminologist with cybercrime specialist knowledge can be called on by the police to come to court and provide expert testimony as a recognised expert witness.

Criminologists can also be involved in the publicising of this form and type of crime, especially by highlighting the existing systemic vulnerabilities in computer systems and networks, but also within organisations themselves in terms of the principles of cybersecurity and information protection.

6.14 Conclusion

The conceptualisation of cybercrime emerged from a combination of the inception of the internet and the consistent expansion of new technology. Cybercrime has thus resulted in the challenge of addressing old and new crimes facilitated by the use of new technology

(Lucks, 2004). As clarified by Schell and Martin (2004), cybercrime is a crime allied to technology, computers and the internet that causes harm to property and/or persons. The nature of cybercrime therefore creates opportunities for the relatively effortless commission of covert illicit online activities. For any agency wanting to deal not only with cybercrime, but also with cyberwarfare, cyberespionage, and cyberterrorism, it is important for executives, managers, police, and security personnel to have a basic grasp and understanding of one of the most intricate, multifaceted and complex constructions developed by humans, namely cyberspace.

The accessibility of the digital world and its speed, facilitated as it is through the ease and high levels of connectivity, while creating many benefits, if not properly controlled, enable individuals and organisations - easily and with little expense - to eavesdrop on or interfere with operations from remote locations for any purpose, be it financial fraud, information theft or terrorist sabotage. Moreover, the heavy reliance of modern infrastructure systems on information technology makes critical assets highly vulnerable to cyberattacks.

The international challenge for many governments, organisations, and businesses has been to provide adequate preventative and protective cybersecurity measures for all kinds of information and services. Some of the proposed measures infringe on other rights, such as privacy, freedom of expression, consumer rights and commercial rights. Further problems have arisen around international prosecutions and obtaining adequate evidence of the commission of a cybercrime in order to enable the prosecution and conviction of cybercriminals. Nevertheless, the digital environment has no international boundaries, and increasingly governments are looking to a coordinated international approach to the regulation, control, combating and prosecution of cybercriminals. However, the needed measures are all in the realm of cybersecurity, and the very essence of cyberspace is its unfettered and open nature, which, essentially, is uncontrollable.

But with the exponential expansion of cyberspace with increased broadband capabilities (rate of data transference with ever more powerful communication technologies) and improved Wi-Fi connectivity, the proliferation of mobile and handheld devices and the practice of BYOD to work has also increased vulnerabilities of information databases and methods of storage (for example in the so-called 'cloud').

In a context of increasingly sophisticated attacks from gangs of cybercriminals and foreign governments probing systems for sensitive data, threats frequently go undetected for days, weeks and, even, months. It is not just financial data that is being stolen. Terrorists and rogue governments may steal confidential data, including intelligence information, that can expose a country and its citizens to potential harm.

Unfortunately, the traditional fortress approach no longer suffices. Firewalls, intrusion detection systems, and other security devices can stop the average hacker, but new threats use stealth techniques that these defences cannot detect on their own.

Over the last few years, these security risks have grown exponentially. Hackers, attackers, and cyberthieves have enlisted far more sophisticated attack methods to put computers and entire networks at risk. Security threats are growing and evolving. As a consequence, organisations and individuals have had to adopt more stringent preventative and protection cybersecurity measures, mostly revolving around so-called 'defence-in-depth' cybersecurity measures.

With the inclusion of highly mobile workforces and network efficiency, worker productivity has improved, while also causing the cyberspace networks to become increasingly more complex and more vulnerable. Hackers and cybercriminals are exploiting new attack vectors using more powerful, sophisticated, and automated techniques.

As cyberthreats intensify and workers bring more mobile devices to work, cybercriminals have viewed the latter as having huge profit potential. As a result they have increasingly aimed to gain access to users' confidential personal and financial information via hacking and mass cyberattacks on a range of databases, using mobile devices as the conduit for such cyberattacks. Hence cybercrime, in its evolution, has become literally the new crime frontier, requiring ever more integrated and coordinated responses from governments, organisations, and individuals alike.

Critical thinking questions

1. Given the complexities of the internet and the difficulties of implementing absolute cybersecurity to prevent all cybercrimes, how would you go about drafting a holistic cybercrime combating measure for implementation in an organisation/company/business?
2. One of the problems that has arisen in successfully prosecuting and convicting cybercriminals has been the technical difficulties in collecting court-accepted digital evidence. Do you think it is necessary for criminologists also to have a competent understanding of technical IT issues regarding electronic databases?
3. Crucial to the protection of all digital information are the principles of information security combining both physical and electronic protection measures. How would you go about drawing up an integrated Information Protection Security Plan incorporating both aspects?
4. Have you, a family member or close friend ever been a victim of a cybercrime? If so, try to describe: what you, the family member or close friend experienced; what you could have done to prevent it from occurring; and what you would change in the future to prevent it. Did you report the crime to the police?
5. Crucial to combating all forms of cybercrime is public awareness of the dangers of cybercriminals gaining access to personal, and in particular, financial information. How would you go about making yourself more aware of the inherent dangers in all cybercrime and cyberattack approaches?
6. How could law enforcement officials use the principles of grounded theory in the policing and/or prevention of cybercrime? Look at the examples given in Section 6.12 and make some suggestions of your own.

References

Armistead, C. L. *Cyberstalked: Our story*. (Sa). Retrieved July 23, 2013, from http://www.cyberstalked.org/ourstory/.

Anti-phishing Working Group (APWG). *Phishing activity trends report, August 2006*. Retrieved October 6, 2006, from www.antiphising.org/reports/apwg_report_august_2006.pdf.

Basu, S., & Jones, R. (2007). Regulating cyberstalking. *Journal of Information, Law and Technology, 2*, 1–30. Retrieved from http://www2.warwick.ac.uk/fac/soc/law/elj/jilt/2007_2/basu_jones/basu_jones.pdf

Bell, L. (2013, April 23). Cyber terrorists are only a matter of time, warns Eugene Kaspersky: will adopt state sponsored type attacks to target infrastructure like telecoms. *The Enquirer*. Retrieved July 25, 2013, from http://www.theinquirer.net/inquirer/news/2263460/

cyber-terrorists-are-only-a-matter-of-time-warns-eugene-kaspersky.

Bocij, P. (2004). *Cyberstalking: harassment in the internet age and how to protect your family.* Wesport: Praeger.

Brown, S. L. (2007). *Counseling victims of violence: a handbook for helping professionals.* Alameda: Hunter House.

Calman, L. Sa. *What is Grounded Theory?* School of Nursing, Midwifery & Social Work, University of Manchester. Retrieved November 5, 2013, from http://www.methods.manchester.ac.uk/events/whatis/gt.pdf.

Chauke, A. (2012, February 10). Exclusive: Inside the R42m heist. *The Times.* Retrieved July 25, 2013, from http://www.timeslive.co.za/local/2012/02/10/exclusive-inside-the-r42m-heist.

Choo, K-K. R. (2007). Zombies and botnets. *Trends & issues in crime and criminal justice.* No. 333. March. Canberra: Australian Institute for Criminology (AIC).

Clarke, R. A. (2010). *Cyber war: the next threat to national security and what to do about it.* New York: HarperCollins.

Council of Europe. (2001). *Convention on cybercrime.* European Treaty Series, 185, Budapest, Hungary, 23 November.

Department of Defense (DoD). Sa(a). *The cyberdomain: security and operations.* Washington: The US Department of Defense. Retrieved July 27, 2013, from http://www.defense.gov/home/features/2013/0713_cyberdomain/.

Department of Defense (DoD). Sa(b). *Department of Defense Dictionary of Military and Associated Terms,* JP 1-02. Washington: The US Department of Defense. Retrieved July 27, 2013, from www.dtic.mil/doctrine/new_pubs/jp1_02.pdf.

Drahokoupilová, J. (2007). Cyberstalking. *Journal of Law & Technology,* 145–155. (Masaryk University, Prague). Retrieved June 1, 2012, from http://heinonline.org/HOL/Page?handle=hein.journals/mujlt1&div=36&g_sent=1&collection=journals.

Farrel, L. (2010, September 24). Clarke: more defense needed in cyberspace. *The Capital Gazette.* Retrieved July 25, 2013, from http://www.capitalgazette.com/news/clarke-more-defense-needed-in-cyberspace/article_45a2ac40-396c-573e-b331-f269f0816841.html.

Federal Bureau of Investigation (FBI). (1989). *White-collar crime: a report to the public.* Washington, DC: US Department of Justice.

Fraser, C., Olsen, E., Lee, K., Southworth, C., & Tucker, S. (2010). The new age of stalking: technological implications for stalking. *Juvenile and Family Court Journal, 61*(4), 39–55.

Glasier, B. (2001). *The Grounded Theory perspective: conceptualisation contracted with description.* Mill Valley: Sociology Press.

Grabosky, P. N. (1999). *Crime in cyberspace.* Paper presented to the 12th International Criminology Congress: Crime & Justice in a Changing World: Asian and Global Perspectives, Seoul, Korea, 24–28 August 1998. Updated version prepared for presentation at the Symposium on Information Crime, convened by the Research & Studies Centre, Dubai Police Headquarters, Dubai, 26–27 January.

Herbig, F. J. W., & Hesselink, A. E. (2009). The role and function of Criminologists within the criminal justice and private sector. *Journal of Psychology in Africa, 19*(3), 441–446.

Hosken, G. (2014, February 19). World fraud champs. *The Times.* Retrieved February 20, 2014, from http://www.timeslive.co.za/thetimes/2014/02/19/world-fraud-champs.

Leach, S. (2013). Approaches to DDoS protection: an overview on keeping your networks protected. *Between the dots: verisign industry insights,* 12 June.

Leathley, S. (2013). Fighting back against cyber crime. *Risk Management,* August. Retrieved August 13, 2013, from http://www.riskmanagementmagazine.com.au/article/fighting-back-against-cyber-crime-178046.aspx.

Lucks, B. D., (2004). *Cyberstalking: identifying and examining electronic crime in cyberspace* (Unpublished DPhil thesis). Alliant International University, California, USA.

McCormick, J. (2007). A common-sense approach to computer security. *Baseline, 75*, September, 39.

Miller, B. N., & Morris, R. G. (2012). Cyber-related violence. In M. DeLisi & P. J. Conis (Eds.). *Violent offenders: theory, research, policy and practice* (2nd ed.). London: Jones & Bartlett Learning.

Minnaar, A. (2008). 'You've received a greeting e-card from ...': The changing face of cybercrime e-mail spam scams. *Acta Criminologica: South African Journal of Criminology*, CRIMSA 2007 Conference Special Edition No. 2, 2008, 92–116.

Moore, R. (2011). *Cybercrime: investigating high technology computer crime* (2nd ed.). Burlington, MA: Elsevier/Anderson Publishing.

Mullen, P. E., Pathé, M., & Purcell, R. (2009). *Stalkers and their victims* (2nd ed.). London: Cambridge University Press.

O'Harrow, R. (2012, 2 June). Zero Day: The Threat in Cyberspace – digital universe riddled with holes. *The Washington Post* (Special Report). Retrieved June 5, 2012, from http://www.washingtonpost.com/investigations/understanding-cyberspace-is-key-to-defending-against-digital-attacks/2012/06/02/gJQAsIr19U_story.html

Parker, D. B. (1979). *Computer crime: criminal justice research manual*. Washington, DC: United States Department of Justice.

Parker, D. B. (1989). *Computer crime: criminal justice research manual*. Washington, DC: United States Department of Justice.

Parker, D. B., Nycum, S., & Oüra, S. S. (1973). *Computer abuse*. Menlo Park, CA: Stanford Research Institute.

Pathé, M. (2002). *Surviving stalking*. London: Cambridge University Press.

Patton, M. Q. (2002). *Qualitative research and evaluation methods* (3rd ed.). Thousand Oaks, CA: Sage Publications.

Planting, S. (2012). How R42m was stolen from Postbank. *Moneyweb*. Retrieved July 25, 2013, from http://www.moneyweb.co.za/moneyweb-special-investigations/how-r42m-was-stolen-from-postbank.

Poplak, R. (2013, June 12). Edward Snowden Prism and the privacy we never had. *Mail & Guardian*. Retrieved June 14, 2013, from http://mg.co.za/article/2013-06-12-edward-snowden-prism-and-the-privacy-we-never-had.

Ponzi Scheme. (n.d.) Retrieved from http://legal-dictionary.thefreedictionary.com/Ponzi+Scheme.

Ragatz, L.L., Fremouw, W., & Baker, E. (2012). *Criminal justice and behaviour: the psychological profile of white-collar offenders: demographics, criminal thinking, psychopathic traits and psychopathology*. Sage publications: Retrieved from http://cjb.sagepub.com/content/39/7/978.

Rasool, F. (2012, February 7). Three arrested for Postbank heist. *ITWeb*. Retrieved July 24, 2013, from http://www.itweb.co.za/index.php?option=com_content&view=article&id=51313.

Reuters. (2005, August 18). Scammers pose as execs to 'spear-phish.' *Independent Online (IOL)*. Retrieved September 7, 2005, from www.iol.co.za/general/news/newsprint.php?art_id=qw1124343009552B232&sf.

SAPA (2012a, January 15). Millions stolen in Postbank hacking. *News24*. Retrieved July 24, 2013, from http://www.fin24.com/Companies/Financial-Services/Millions-stolen-in-Postbank-hacking-20120115.

SAPA (2012b, March 20). Man sentenced for Postbank cyber heist. *News24*. Retrieved July 24, 2013, from http://www.news24.com/SouthAfrica/News/Man-sentenced-for-Post-Bank-cyber-heist-20120320.

SAPA (2013). Business should focus on cyber crime. *Moneyweb*. Retrieved September 17, 2013, from http://www.moneyweb.co.za/moneyweb-south-africa/business-should-focus-on-cyber-crime.

Savage, C. (2013, August 15). Manning, facing prison for leaks, apologizes at court-martial trial. *New York Times*. Retrieved 18 August, 2013, from http://www.nytimes.com/2013/08/15/us/manning-apologizes-for-leaks-my-actions-hurt-people.html?nl=todaysheadlines&emc=edit_th_20130815&_r=0.

Schell, B. H., & Martin, C. (2004). *Cybercrime: a reference book*. California: ABC-Clio.

Sheridan, L. P., & Grant, T. (2007). Is cyberstalking different? *Psychology, Crime & Law, 13*(6), 627–640.

Smith, R. G., Grabosky, P. N., & Urbas, G. F. (2004). *Cyber criminals on trial*. Cambridge: Cambridge University Press.

South Africa. (2004). The Prevention of Corruption Act 12 of 2004. *Government Gazette, 466* (No. 26311), 28 April. Pretoria: Government Printer.

South Africa. (2006a). Guidelines for recognition of industry representative bodies of information system service providers. *Government Gazette* (No. 29474). Pretoria: Government Printer.

South Africa. (2006b). Electronic Communications and Transactions Act 25 of 2002 (ECTA). *Government Gazette* (No. 23708). Pretoria: Government Printer.

South Africa. (2011). The Protection from Harassment Act 17 of 2011. *Government Gazette* (No. 34818). Pretoria: Government Printer.

Stiennon, R. (2011). Kaspersky and cyber terrorism. *Forbes Magazine*. Retrieved July 15, 2013, from http://www.forbes.com/sites/richardstiennon/2011/11/02/kaspersky-and-cyber-terrorism/.

Sutherland, E. H. (1949). *White collar crime*. New York: Dryden Press.

Swart, W., & Afrika, W. (2012, January 15). It was a happy New Year's Day for gang who pulled off... R42m Postbank heist. *The Times*. Retrieved July 25, from http://www.timeslive.co.za/local/2012/01/15/it-was-a-happy-new-year-s-day-for-gang-who-pulled-off...r42m-postbank-heist.

Symantec. (2011). *Norton cybercrime report: South Africa*. Retrieved December 12, 2013, from http://za.norton.com/cybercrimereport/promo.

Symantec. (2012). *Norton cybercrime report: September*. Retrieved December 12, 2013, from http://www.norton.com/2012cybercrimereport.

Symantec. (2013). *Norton Report: October*. Retrieved December 12, 2013, from go.symantec.com/norton-report-2013.

The Institute for Risk Management South Africa (IRMSA). (2005). *Guide to the ECT Act 2005*. Retrieved March 7, 2012, from http://www.irmsa.org.za.

US Department of Homeland Defense/SRI International Identity Theft Technology Council/Anti-Phishing Working Group. (2006). *The crimeware landscape: Malware, phishing, identity theft and beyond. A Joint Report of the US Department of Homeland Defense, SRI International Identity Theft Technology Council and the Anti-Phishing Working Group*. Retrieved October 6, 2006, from http://www.antiphishing.org/reports/APWG_CrimewareReport.pdf.

United Nations (UN). (2005, April). *Workshop 6: Measures to combat computer-related crime*. Background paper, 11th United Nations Congress on Crime Prevention and Criminal Justice: Effective measures to combat transnational organized crime, Bangkok, Thailand. A/Conf.203/14.

Verizon Risk Team (2012). *2012 Data Breach Investigations Report*. Retrieved September 17, 2013 from http://www.verizonenterprise.com/resources/reports/rp_data-breach-investigations-report-2012-ebk_en_xg.pdf?r=4 .

Verizon Risk Team (2013). *2013 Data Breach Investigations Report*. Retrieved September 17, 2013, from http://www.verizonenterprise.com/resources/reports/rp_data-breach-investigations-report-2013_en_xg.pdf.

Whitty, M. T., & Joinson, A. N. (2009). *Truth, lies and trust on the internet*. New York: Routledge.

Workplace Staff. (2006, August 28). Compu-crime costs SA economy R40bn. *Independent Online*. Retrieved October 6, 2006, from www.iol.co.za.

Chapter 7

Restorative justice in practice

M Schoeman

7.1 Introduction

In South Africa native African traditions, customs, and laws grounded in the ubuntu philosophy traditionally served as the foundations for control and justice in African societies. With colonisation these traditional justice practices were replaced with westernised judicial ideologies (Schoeman, 2013). Over the past decade a new way of thinking about how we should view and respond to crime and delinquency has been gaining momentum, not only internationally, but also in South Africa. This paradigm shift, favouring a more restorative approach in comparison to the prevailing retributive justice approach, has a significant influence on criminal justice policy and practice. Like the transition from apartheid to democracy that took place in South Africa in the early 1990s, the transition from a retributive to a restorative paradigm in justice is characterised by reconciliation rather than revenge (Skelton, 2002).

Restorative justice revolves around the idea that crime is primarily a conflict between individuals and is not only a delinquent act, but also involves harm to people and human relationships. Consequently it is proposed that the primary aim of the justice process should be to reconcile parties while addressing the harm caused by the offence. This approach introduces new role players to the justice process and necessitates the active involvement of the offender, victim and community in this process.

This chapter will give a broad outline of the principles of restorative justice and explore the theoretical basis of restorative justice. It will, furthermore, examine the differences between restorative justice and other prevailing retributive conceptions of justice. The similarities between restorative justice and traditional African justice will be explored. Lastly, contemporary restorative justice practices will be discussed and the role of practitioners within a South African context highlighted.

7.2 Definitions and key concepts

No universally accepted definition exists to define restorative justice. This is primarily because restorative justice is not a one-dimensional construct, but rather refers to a set of principles, aims, practices and processes associated with the adjudication of justice within a restorative paradigm. Zehr postulates that, as such, 'Restorative Justice is not a map but the principles of restorative justice can be seen as a compass pointing a direction' (Zehr & Gohar, 2003, p. 9).

The restorative justice compass points us towards the way to deal holistically with crime and the harm it causes. Restorative justice offers guidelines on how to resolve both the conflict and the harm caused by crime. Furthermore, it focuses on addressing the underlying causes of criminal behaviour (Marshall, 1995). Zehr (2002) defines restorative justice as a process that involves, as far as possible, all parties who have a stake in a specific offense, with the purpose of collectively identifying and addressing harms, needs, and obligations caused by the criminal act, in order to heal and put things as right as possible. Restorative justice thus not only focuses on the crime that has been committed, but also recognises crime as a social problem with distinct societal causes and solutions. Central to restorative justice is recognition of the systemic harmful impact of crime on the broader community in addition to the primary victim of a crime. Restorative justice therefore aims to restore the well-being of victims, offenders and communities damaged by crime, and to prevent further offending (Liebman, 2007). The concepts that underpin restorative justice will be explored in more detail in the next section.

The practices associated with restorative justice include mediation, conferencing and sentencing circles (Shapland et al., 2007).

7.2.1 Mediation

Mediation is the process whereby various parties come together in an attempt to seek a mutually acceptable and beneficial resolution to a shared grievance. Examples of mediation are victim–offender mediation and community mediation. Victim–offender mediation, which will be discussed in more detail later in this chapter, is viewed as one of the oldest restorative justice practices (Umbreit, Bradshaw, & Coates, 1999). It is also entrenched in traditional African justice practices.

7.2.2 Conferencing

A similar process as in mediation is followed in conferencing, with the exception that conferencing includes other relevant parties and is not focused only on the offender and aggrieved party (Schoeman, 2012a). Conferencing is a restorative justice approach used in planning and decisionmaking in cases involving young offenders. Conferencing traditionally involves the offender's family network, representatives from the criminal justice system and other organisations, such as non-governmental organisations (NGOs) involved in the care and rehabilitation process. The purposes of these conferences are to explore potential methods to make amends for harm caused, to educate offenders about the harm their behaviour has caused, and to devise a service plan to support the offender and his or her family (Umbreit & Armour, 2011). An example of conferencing is family group conferencing. Conferencing can be compared to the traditional African dispute resolution process known as a *lekgotla*. A *lekgotla* is characterised by lengthy discussions in which each speaker is generally provided with an equal chance to speak up until an agreement, consensus or group cohesion is reached.

7.2.3 Sentencing circles

A sentencing circle, also called a peacemaking circle or talking circle, is a sanctioning and healing practice which originated from the American Indians in the United States of America and aboriginal peoples in Canada. It is a holistic approach designed to address the criminal behaviours of offenders as well as the needs of crime victims, their families, and communities in general (Bazemor & Umbreit, 2001). The circle traditionally includes the crime victim, offender, family and friends of the parties, representatives from the criminal justice system (including police officers, lawyers, and judges), and interested community residents. The members of the circle take turns discussing the criminal event, with the purpose of trying to search for an understanding of what happened. After the discussion, members of the circle arrive at a consensus for a sentencing plan inclusive of steps needed to assist in the healing of all affected parties. Actions to prevent similar future crimes are also identified as part of the sentencing plan (Bazemor & Umbreit, 2001).

Similarities exist between sentencing circles and traditional justice practices in Africa whereby the crime victim and offender had to appear before the tribal chief and Council of

Elders. The victim and offenders were represented by elders from their clan, and both parties were given the opportunity to state their case. Once both cases had been heard, the elders deliberated to decide on the best resolution to the conflict. The purpose of this gathering was similar to that of sentencing circles, namely to address both the harm caused by the crime and the needs of the victim, and to promote reconciliation within the community (Kinyanjui, 2009).

7.3 The theoretical foundations of restorative justice

As was the case in defining restorative justice, the task of identifying a single theory on restorative justice is ambiguous. This is primarily because restorative justice is grounded in theory, practice, and research which change over time, each informing the other (Umbreit, Coates, & Vos, 2007). Restorative justice theory is therefore incomplete, as its creation is an ongoing effort. In this regard Umbreit et al. (2007) highlight the important role restorative justice dialogue plays in the formation of restorative justice theory. It is furthermore important to recognise the role of Africa's traditional practices in the modelling of our perceptions about restorative justice theory and practice.

The roots of restorative justice in indigenous philosophy and practice are widely acknowledged. It is even claimed that the values and practices of restorative justice can be traced back to traditions of justice in ancient Greek and Roman civilisations (Braithwaite, 2002). In Africa, the restorative tradition is deeply rooted in the ubuntu philosophy, and therefore a significant correlation exists between restorative justice practices and those in African traditional justice. The similarities between indigenous African justice practices and restorative justice will be discussed in more detail later in this chapter.

Marshall (1995) is of the opinion that restorative justice theory evolved from restorative justice dialogue amongst practitioners who questioned the justice system's foundation. As a result, increasing pressure from judicial, academic and government structures, as well as from practitioners, resulted in efforts to justify, and theoretically ground, restorative practices. Gavrielides, in an attempt to map the theoretical position of restorative justice, identified three layers of theories in, as he put it, the 'world of theories' (2005, p. 87).[1] Schematically, he envisions the world of theories as seen in Figure 7.1.

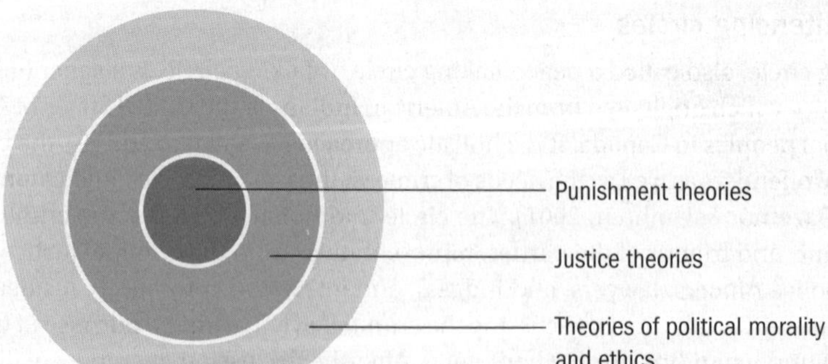

Figure 7.1 The world of theories (adapted from Gavrielides, 2005, p. 87)[2]

1 Copyright © 2005 John Wiley and Sons.
2 Copyright © 2005 John Wiley and Sons.

The outer circle which encloses the other circles includes broad philosophical assumptions associated with political morality and ethics, and includes theories associated with philosophies of humanism, liberalism, utilitarianism and so forth. The second circle includes theories for the justice system that deal with the justice system in its totality, inclusive of issues deriving from all stages of the justice process (Gavrielides, 2005). The third and innermost circle deals with discipline specific theories, in this instance theories about criminal justice, such as theories covering the justification of punishment. An example is the just desert theory (Gavrielides, 2005).

Gavrielides (2005) concludes that restorative justice falls within the second circle of justice theories because it provides a framework for the evaluation and construction of the justice system in its totality. Restorative justice is therefore of relevance in the different sectors making up the justice system, such as the police, the courts, the judiciary and the correctional system. Furthermore, restorative justice can address issues that might arise during the justice process, such as restitution, victim support and crime prevention.

With regard to discipline specific theories found in the innermost circle, Braithwaite (2004) identified the following theories relevant to restorative justice practices: reintegrative shaming, unacknowledged shame, procedural justice, and defiance theories.

7.3.1 Reintegrative shaming theory

Shaming in a criminal justice context is generally associated with stigmatisation. Consequently, it results in the offender being treated disrespectfully and labelled as a bad person. This is counterproductive as stigmatisation has been found to make crime worse. In restorative justice, the emphasis is on reintegrative shaming, which proposes that offenders should be treated with respect and empathically, thus acknowledging offenders as inherently good people who have done something bad. Shame is furthermore linked to the offender's reaction: offenders acknowledge the community's disapproval of their behaviour and thus the wrongfulness the deed (Cullen, Wright, & Blevins, 2008).

The rationale of the theory is based on moral reasoning similar to that found in the interaction between families in the socialisation of children. During the socialisation of a child, parents generally inform the child about behaviours deemed acceptable or unacceptable in the interaction with others in society. This is generally done in a non-judgemental manner and with empathy. Such moral reasoning shapes children's value systems and promotes prosocial behaviour (Braithwaite, 2004). Hence, the reintegrative shaming theory also illustrates why restorative justice processes have the potential to prevent crime more effectively than retributive practices do.

Research has found a significant correlation between delinquency and both a lenient parenting style (which fails to confront and disapprove of children's misconduct) and a punitively authoritarian parenting style (which features overly restrictive and punitive parents). In contrast, delinquency has been found to be less likely when parents confront wrongdoing with moral reasoning. In this regard, Braithwaite postulates that the justice system 'will do better when it facilitates moral reasoning by families over what to do about a crime as an alternative to punishment by the state' (2004, p. 47).

The core premises of the reintegrative shaming theory are as follows:

- Tolerance of crime makes things worse and increases the likelihood of criminal behaviour.
- Stigmatisation, disrespectful outcasting and shaming of offenders increases the likelihood of reoffending.

- Reintegrative shaming associated with disapproval of antisocial and criminal actions, within a continuum of respect for the offender, decreases the likelihood of criminal behaviour, and more so if the disapproval of criminal behaviour includes rituals of forgiveness as can be found in restorative justice practices (Braithwaite, 2004).

In this regard, it has been found that societies that fail to communicate that crime is shameful – in other words not acceptable and harmful to others – will have a higher crime rate than societies that do communicate this (Cullen et al., 2008).

Braithwaite (in Tibbetts & Hemmens, 2010) argues that shaming is reintegrative if it reinforces an offender's membership in a community of law-abiding citizens and prevents the offender from adopting a delinquent lifestyle. Thus, even though disapproval is communicated during reintegrative shaming, this is done within a process that promotes respect for both the offender and the other stakeholders in the process.

An example of reintegrative shaming is evident in the procedures followed during the South African Truth and Reconciliation Commission (TRC). The purpose of the commission was to help South Africans deal with the conflict and human rights abuses during apartheid. During the commission hearings, people who committed human rights violations could apply for amnesty against prosecution for their actions. To qualify for the amnesty, they had to give a full disclosure of all relevant facts regarding their activities, thus acknowledging their wrongdoing. The narratives from the victims of such human rights violations, in turn, served to communicate society's disapproval of their behaviour.

Research has found that general shaming by, for example, police officials, the media or general public is not as effective as disapproval from a person's immediate support system. Hence, reintegrative shaming has been found to be most effective if people who have a significant emotional connection with the offender form part of the restorative justice processes (Braithwaite, 2004). This emphasises the important role primary stakeholders, namely persons who are directly associated with the crime, and secondary stakeholders, such as people who are vicariously influenced by the crime, play in the restorative justice process.

7.3.2 Theory of unacknowledged shame

This theory focuses on the impact unacknowledged shame can have on criminal behaviour, and emphasises the effect (disruptive impact) of unacknowledged shame on offenders. The theory postulates that offenders need a way to deal with feelings of shame that arise from criminal offending, because if offenders do not address them these feelings can manifest in feelings of anger and resentment. Consequently, a denial of these feelings of shame can result in what Scheff and Retzinger (in Braithwaite, 2004) refer to as shame-rage. According to them, if shame is not confronted, and the emotional harm it causes not addressed, it will become chronic and complicated, resulting in feelings of rage which can produce a perpetual shame-rage spiral.

Retzinger and Scheff (in Braithwaite, 2004) acknowledge the potential of restorative justice practices to heal the damage done by crime, through the communication and subsequent acknowledgement of shame. They postulate that when hurt is communicated and shame acknowledged by those who caused it, respect is naturally shown to the victim. The respect is reciprocated when the victims in turn communicate the hurt they have suffered.

Zehr (1995) postulates that 'disrespect begets disrespect'. Criminal behaviour is probably one of the actions that most clearly communicate disrespect. In this regard Zehr (2002) highlights the victim's need for vindication. This need for vindication is associated with the interactive relationship between honour and humiliation that is communicated during the interaction between victim and offender. The criminal justice system in general does not acknowledge the need for reciprocity, as the focus in criminal proceedings is primarily on establishing guilt and the sentencing of the guilty party. However, in restorative justice, constructive conflict occurs when victims and perpetrators have the opportunity to talk about their experiences during the criminal act. This interaction creates the opportunity to acknowledge and deal with emotions, such as shame and rage.

In order to address unacknowledged shame, it is important to accentuate the positive and confront the negative. Such practices are found in restorative justice where the interaction of the stakeholders serves to take advantage of the positive aspects, such as restitution and reconciliation, while minimising the negative effect, namely stigmatisation and punishment. By dealing with conflict in such a constructive manner, a sense of community is developed and strengthened (Braithwaite, 2004). The strengthening of social cohesion has the potential to prevent crime and reoffending, as will be discussed in more detail below.

A victim–offender mediation session, as discussed in more detail later on in this chapter, is an example of a context in which restorative justice procedures grant offenders the opportunity to interact with victims. The purpose of such interaction is for offenders to accept accountability for the harm caused by their actions, while the victim is granted the opportunity to share the impact the crime had on their lives. This in turn strengthens the perpetrator's bond with society and promotes prosocial law-abiding behaviour.

7.3.3 Procedural justice theory

The procedural justice theory is concerned with the fairness and transparency of the justice process, for example during courtroom proceedings. It proposes that fair procedure will be perceived as being legitimate and result in equitable outcomes where the offender will be more likely to comply with directives. In contrast, people who have first-hand or vicarious experience of what they perceive as being unfair or unjust interactions with the legal system tend to view the system as less legitimate; they are less likely to comply and cooperate with sanctioning agents, such as criminal justice officials and the community in general (Reisig & Mesko, 2009).

This theory also focuses on the correlation between shaming and respect. The rationale is that even though disapproval is communicated during reintegrative shaming, this is done within a process that promotes respect for both the offender and the other stakeholders in the process. According to Braithwaite (2004), during adjudication respect is demonstrated through fairness, attentive listening and empowering the stakeholders, while refraining from bias on the grounds of factors such as age, gender or race. In this regard, restorative justice practices by nature of the process are fairer, due to the stakeholders who control and participate in the process. Research has indicated that in cases in which judicial processes are perceived to be fairer, such as in restorative justice, compliance with the law improves (Braithwaite, 2004).

Again referring to the example of the Truth and Reconciliation Commission in South Africa, its public hearings created not only a platform for offenders to acknowledge the human rights crimes they committed, but also for primary and secondary victims, such as family members, to question the perpetrators. The transparency of the procedures contributed to their being perceived as fair and just.

7.3.4 Defiance theory

Sherman (in Braithwaite, 2004) incorporated the propositions from the reintegrative shaming, unacknowledged shame and procedural justice theories to develop the integrated theory of defiance. Broadly, he explored the potential reaction to, and impact of, sanctions on the offender's social functioning. In this context sanctions refers to methods of punishment for crimes committed. Sherman developed the following three propositions:

1. Sanctions provoke future *defiance* of the law: Sherman proposes that offenders view sanctions as a persistent and repeated violation against them. This results in offenders feeling isolated from the sanctioning community, which reinforces the already weakened bond offenders tend to have with sanctioning agents. Because offenders deny their shame, thus failing to acknowledge the harm caused by the crime, they develop a sense of pride in their isolation. As a result, the sanctions serve to strengthen their perceived isolation, which is, as was discussed previously, associated with criminal behaviour.
2. Sanctions produce future *deterrence* of law-breaking: In this instance sanctions result in the offender desisting from criminal behaviour. Offenders experience the sanctioning conduct as a legitimate reaction to their criminal behaviour; they thereby accept responsibility for the harm caused by the crime. Consequently offenders have a strong bond with the sanctioning agent and community, and accept their shame and live in harmony with the community.
3. Sanctions become *irrelevant* to future law-breaking: Sanctions have no effect on offenders' behaviour to the extent that the factors that either encourage or deter defiance are fairly evenly counterbalanced (Sherman in Braithwaite, 2004). In this instance, the fear of sanctioning conduct, the reaction of shame, and the perception of whether the sanction was fair or not have no impact on the offender's decision to persist in or desist from criminal behaviour.

In analysing the three propositions, Sherman concluded that restorative justice is more likely to meet the conditions of the second proposition, namely that restorative justice as a sanction deters future criminal behaviour. Restorative justice guides offenders to accept the responsibility and shame associated with their offending behaviour. It is also generally perceived to be fair and just, as recognition is given to all the stakeholders. This perception is supported by research which has found that restorative justice practices are more likely than other practices to empower offenders, thereby strengthening the bond between the offender, the sanctioning agency and the community (Braithwaite, 2004). There is a clear similarity between the second proposition of this theory and the principles of traditional African justice as discussed later in this chapter.

In summary, from the four theories discussed above, it can be deduced that restorative justice offers a holistic and fair approach to adjudication by recognising the significance and rights of all stakeholders. Restorative justice's emphasis on restoration and reintegration strengthens the bonds between the offenders and society in general. It is interesting to note that similar principles are evident in traditional African justice practices. The four theories furthermore provide theoretical grounds to validate restorative justice's position as a justice theory.

7.4 The philosophical foundations of restorative justice

Continuing from the exploration above of the position of restorative justice in the world of theory, the question of which philosophy supports restorative justice remains to be clarified. Even though there is still some debate as to which philosophy can be associated with restorative justice, it is universally accepted that restorative justice is underpinned by a restorative paradigm. A paradigm, according to Zehr (1990), is 'particular ways of constructing reality'. In other words, a paradigm is the way an individual shapes, defines and understands his or her life world. Restorative justice provides an alternative paradigm to understanding our reaction to crime and wrongdoing (Zehr & Gohar, 2003).

As was mentioned previously, restorative justice focuses on the needs and roles of people who have been involved in, or affected by, crime. Its emphasis is on repairing the harm done to people and relationships, rather than on the punishment of offenders. Furthermore, it strives to heal and empower those who have been harmed as a result of crime.

In restorative justice, crime is viewed as a violation of people and interpersonal relationships. Restorative justice processes and programmes therefore focus on restoration of relationships and reconciliation of parties, while addressing the harm caused by the crime. This requires all parties to be actively involved in the reconciliation process. According to McCold and Wachtel (2003), parties involved in the restorative process are divided into two groups, namely primary stakeholders and secondary stakeholders. Primary stakeholders are the role players directly affected by the offence; they include the victim, the offender and individuals who have a significant emotional connection with either the victim or offender. These individuals constitute the victims' and offenders' communities of care and include the victim or offenders' parents, spouses, siblings and friends. Because the harm done and needs created are specific to the particular offence, the restorative responses require active participation of all parties to achieve healing and reconciliation.

The secondary stakeholders include the people who are affected by the offence and experience the harm done vicariously. This group can include individuals from formal or informal systems in society, such as governmental, educational, religious, business or social structures, as well as community members (McCold & Wachtel, 2003). The function of these role players is to support the restorative processes in general. In restorative justice, the community is motivated to participate, and take ownership of the justice process. Community members are encouraged to take responsibility for the welfare of their members, including victims and offenders, in order to enhance social cohesion. According to McCold and Wachtel (2003) the degree to which the victim, offender and community are involved in meaningful emotional interaction, exchange and decisionmaking will influence the degree to which an intervention can be termed completely restorative.

Restorative justice initiatives, according to Zehr and Mika (1998), involve both systemwide interventions and individual programmes. As was mentioned previously, it is important to keep in mind the fact that the interventions focus more on the harms of wrongdoing than on the rules broken when a crime is committed. The interventions thus show equal concern and commitment for victims and offenders, and involve both parties in the justice process. In this regard, the restorative justice process emphasises the restoration of victims by empowering them and responding to their needs holistically. It also supports offenders while encouraging them to understand the impact and harm caused by the crime. Furthermore, it guides offenders to accept responsibility for their actions while assisting them to carry out their obligations to right the wrongs. Restorative justice recognises that these obligations may be difficult for offenders, but they are not intended as punishment and therefore need to be achievable.

CHECK POINT

- Restorative justice theory evolved from restorative justice dialogue amongst practitioners who questioned the justice system's foundation.
- A significant correlation exists between restorative justice practices and those in African traditional justice, because restorative justice is deeply rooted in the ubuntu philosophy.
- Restorative justice is relevant in the different sectors making up the justice system, such as the police, courts, judiciary, and correctional system. Furthermore, it is capable of addressing issues that might arise during the justice process, such as restitution, victim support, and crime prevention.
- From the theoretical analysis discussed above, it can be deduced that restorative justice offers a holistic and fair approach to adjudication, because it recognises the significance and rights of all stakeholders.
- It can therefore be concluded that restorative justice provides an alternative paradigm to understanding how people view and react to crime and wrongdoing.

7.5 Restorative justice in South Africa

The justice system used in South Africa nowadays is predominantly based on Western judicial ideologies. Traditionally, native African traditions, customs, and laws grounded in the ubuntu philosophy served as the foundations for control and justice in African societies (Schoeman, 2013). This changed with the colonisation of sub-Saharan Africa with the introduction of Western-based criminal justice systems. These replaced the traditional restorative practices with a Western individualistic and retributively oriented justice system (Omale, 2006). Currently, restorative justice in South Africa is predominantly used in child justice and domestic disputes and is aimed at reactively addressing the harms caused by crime. It is rarely used pre-emptively for crime prevention or as a mechanism for alternative community-based conflict resolution. Government's support for restorative justice initiatives is also mostly limited to its application in the criminal justice system, while community-based interventions are driven by NGOs and church-based organisations in civil society. These initiatives are funding driven and rarely sustainable (Schoeman, 2012a).

Johnstone (2004) argues that in order to obtain a comprehensive understanding of restorative justice, it is necessary to explore its roots in traditional and contemporary indigenous communities, such as those found in Africa. It is thus important to acknowledge that South Africa's restorative tradition is deeply rooted in the ubuntu philosophy. The clear similarities that can be identified between the philosophy, values and practices of restorative justice and ubuntu have already been mentioned in this chapter. Exploring these resemblances makes it clear that both restorative justice and ubuntu promote a normative system that recognises the interconnectedness between the individual and community, thereby attempting to achieve a more community-centred approach in adjudication and conflict resolution. Both African indigenous justice and restorative justice practices are community based and human centred, and each employs restorative and transformative principles in conflict resolution (Schoeman, 2013). Antithetical to a westernised ideology in which the judicial processes serve to advance the interest of individuals or factional groups, traditional justice practices promote social cohesion and are inclusive rather than selective in meeting the needs of all stakeholders (Sullivan & Tiff, 2004). Maintaining positive relations within a community is therefore viewed as a collective responsibility, and a dispute between community members is perceived not merely as a matter of curiosity with regard to the affairs of one's neighbour, but as conflict belonging to the entire community (Murithi, 2006). Harm caused by criminal behaviour can therefore not be considered fully resolved until the peace, the relationships and the social harmony damaged by the crime are restored. This perception of crime as social harm plays an important role in the generation of societal cohesion (Okafo, 2006). Community participation serves to acknowledge the close-knit relationship between members in a society, and promotes ownership of the judicial process. Restorative and ubuntu justice are therefore interactive and democratic processes which make use of mediation to provide opportunities for dialogue between the victim, offender and other affected parties in the community (Elechi, 2004). According to Ovens and Prinsloo (2010), such dialogue is more than a linguistic exchange; it acknowledges the human rights and dignity of all individuals in society.

Dignity and respect are viewed as central values in both ubuntu and restorative justice. Both restorative and ubuntu justice ensure that the adjudication process takes place in an environment which supports values such as respect, honesty, humility, mutual care, accountability and trust, and encourages humanitarian behaviour towards others (Dyck, 2004). The terms 'offenders' and 'victims' are also modern legal terms and were referred to as the 'wrongdoers' and 'the parties wronged' in traditional communities (Kinyanjui, 2009).

Both justice systems, furthermore, acknowledge the offender's need for support, guidance and healing. As was mentioned earlier, offenders are not shunned, but are instead guided to understand the impact of their wrongdoing and accept responsibility for their actions. The purpose of this is to promote healing through reconciliation, rather than just to punish (Schoeman, 2013).

Restorative justice, like ubuntu, is a creative process that is flexible in its approach to finding the best solution in addressing crime or the resolution of a dispute. Restorative justice and ubuntu justice view and deal with crime in a fundamentally different way from most conventional justice systems. For example, crime is viewed in both restorative and ubuntu justice as a violation of people's rights and interpersonal relationships, rather than as a legalistic dispute between an individual and the state (Zehr, 1990). Gavrielides (2005) postulates that restorative justice replaces conventional criminal justice processes with a new philosophy, moving away from retributive justice's focus on the violation of the law towards focusing on the violation of people and relationships. In a restorative paradigm, victims and offenders are offered an opportunity to explore the actual effect of the harm done and find a solution that fits the unique circumstances associated with the conflict. Because the emphasis is on individual victims and offenders, and each case is viewed as unique, both traditional ubuntu justice and restorative justice processes, unlike the judicial law, are not controlled by the rule of *stare decisis*, or the law of precedent. They are therefore not bound by legalistic regulations, such as the necessity to consider the outcomes of any previous court cases (Skelton, 2007).

Even though a post-colonial westernised legal system is still dominant in South Africa, ubuntu remains a recognised philosophy that is entrenched in current sociocultural practices and legislation. Metz (2012) is of the opinion that ubuntu is not only applicable to the normative-theoretical understanding of morality in Africa, but also recognises the importance of individual liberty in a diverse African society, hence creates a promising foundation for human rights. This is evident in the African Charter on Human and Peoples' Rights, which promotes human rights that protect national communal rights, rather than individual rights. The intention of the African Charter is to recreate the bonds of the pre-colonial era among individuals and between individuals and the state (Mutua, 1995). The Constitution of the Republic of South Africa 1996 and South African Traditional Courts Bill 2008 are further examples of legislation that aim to affirm ubuntuism and strive to reintroduce customary law and practices in adjudication.

By exploring the similarities between restorative justice and the ubuntu philosophy, we acknowledge that the ubuntu and restorative justice paradigms are philosophically in agreement in their endeavours to bring about restoration and healing in the resolution of conflicts inclusive of criminal actions. Skelton (2007) argues that a willingness to learn from indigenous justice systems is based on the recognition that such systems have something to teach. Not recognising this knowledge by relying solely on westernised legal policy denies the potential of justice to become more than a judicial process - a reconciliatory process.

CRITICAL REFLECTION

Is there a place for traditional justice in a modern judicial system?

The South African society is characterised by ethnic diversity and other overlapping affinity groups that are broader than mere race and ethnicity. Cultural values and practices are also influenced by urbanisation, level of education and acceptance of postmodern notions (Schoeman, 2012b). Furthermore, African culture has transitioned from a traditional and culture-based society to a more modern humanity. According to Ovens and Prinsloo (2010), the incorporation of Western effects and cultural practices has influenced individuals' identification with their own ethnicity. It is thus a challenge to find a universally acceptable criminal justice system. Even though there is interest in finding an alternative to the current retributive justice system, and restorative justice and traditional justice practices are becoming more prominent, the question remains as to whether these will be an acceptable alternative for the retributive paradigm within a pluralistic society such as South Africa.

A further question that arises when we explore the role of traditional justice is whether people living in South Africa still adhere to ubuntu or, at least, endeavour to do so? Van der Merwe (in Ovens & Prinsloo, 2010) is of the opinion that, due to the ubuntu philosophy, an attitude of solidarity and a commitment to peaceful coexistence is emerging amongst ordinary South Africans, in spite of their differences. Cornell (2008) concurs, stating that in striving to achieve solidarity, the saying *a botho bag ago a nne botho seshabeng* - which literally means 'let your welfare be the welfare of the nation' - is still relevant as it challenges South Africa to be an self-improving nation in which an individual's well-being or welfare is developed and enhanced by seeking the well-being of the larger community. Do you agree with these authors? In your opinion, is the ubuntu philosophy still relevant in modern day criminal justice?

7.6 Restorative versus retributive justice

Before exploring the differences between a restorative and a retributive paradigm in justice, we need to ask whether a new approach in the prevailing justice system is needed. In answering this question, the first logical step is to look at the nature and extent of crime in

South Africa. During 2011/2012 approximately 2.18 million crime cases were registered in South Africa, of which the majority were serious crimes: 28.6 per cent were contact crimes (which include assault with grievous bodily harm, common assault, aggravated robbery, sexual offences, common robbery, murder and attempted murder), and 24.6 per cent were other serious crimes, such as commercial crime and theft (South Africa (SA), South African Police Service (SAPS), 2012, p. 1). According to the annual report of the Judicial Inspectorate for Correctional Services for 2011/2012, an average of 112 536 inmates were incarcerated; 54 per cent of the offenders were held for aggressive crimes, 23 per cent for economic crimes, 16 per cent for sexual offences, 2 per cent narcotics crimes and 5 per cent for other crimes. With an overcrowding rate of 39.95 per cent (SA Judicial Inspectorate for Correctional Services, 2012). The average cost of incarceration is an estimated R123.37 per day per offender (SA Department of Correctional Services, 2013). In 2013, according to S'bu Ndebele, then Minister of Correctional Services, South Africa had the highest incarceration rate in Africa and the ninth highest rate worldwide (SAPA, 2013).

Batley (2005) is of the opinion that the criminal justice system will not be able to decrease these numbers if it continues to focus on a purely retributive approach to crime. Essentially, a retributive approach contributes to the prevailing problem of overcrowding and reoffending, because the primary focus of the current criminal justice system is to increase arrests, prosecutions and the sentencing of offenders. It can therefore be hypothesised that, due to the nature of its purpose, the retributive system is flawed, because its efficiency is measured by increased arrests and prosecutions as well as harsher sentences. In this regard, research has shown that a retributive approach has little success in actually decreasing the number of offenders or preventing crime and reoffending. Furthermore, a retributive approach does not acknowledge the needs of the victims; it also does not nurture a culture that values morality and encourages offenders to take responsibility for their behaviour (Batley, 2005). It is therefore clear that a retributive criminal justice system neither meets the needs of those harmed by crime nor succeeds in addressing the high rates of crime. These factors, and the socio-economic costs of crime, necessitate the exploration of a restorative judicial paradigm.

Zehr (2002) is of the opinion that conventional criminal justice systems focus on three questions in adjudication, namely:

- What laws have been broken?
- Who did it?
- What should the punishment be?

However, from a restorative justice perspective, an entirely different set of questions are asked, namely:

- Who has been hurt?
- What are their needs?
- Whose obligation is it to right the wrongs?

It is clear that the objectives of restorative justice differ unequivocally from those of the retributive paradigm generally followed in South Africa's formal justice system. A punitive approach used in a retributive justice paradigm is characterised by high control of and low support for the stakeholders during the justice process. Both offenders and victims tend to be stigmatised and harmed by negative labels (McCold & Wachtel, 2003). Contrary to popular belief, restorative justice - analogous to a retributive paradigm - also has high control during the judicial process, but, in contrast, it also features high support for stakeholders. In restorative justice, the confrontation of offenders with their wrongdoing and communication of disapproval of the crime occurs in a non-judgemental environment, with dignity, respect and recognition of the intrinsic worth of the offender. This means that, according to McCold and Wachtel (2003), the 'essence of restorative justice is collaborative problem-solving'. It can therefore be reasoned that restorative justice changed how crime is defined, from being acts that contravene a country's laws to acts which cause harm to society (Kinyanjui, 2009; Zehr, 1990). Where the formal retributive justice system emphasises the meting out of just deserts punishment, in restorative justice the restoration of harm done is central (Zehr & Gohar, 2003, p. 22).

Restorative justice is quintessentially victim centred. In a retributive system – such as South Africa's current formal criminal justice system – victims are viewed as secondary actors receiving limited recognition and playing only an insignificant role during the judicial process. This is so because the focus in court cases is on the prosecution of the offender, thus being offender centred rather than victim centred. As a result, victims' primary responsibility in the judicial process is limited to acting as witnesses, thereby assisting the criminal justice system in the prosecution of offenders (Walklate, 2007). Furthermore, the retributive system does not pay attention to the effect of the crime on the victim and/or community, other than taking it into consideration during the sentencing of the offender. In comparison, the restorative justice paradigm considers the impact of the crime on all the stakeholders. It also focuses on crime prevention by identifying the factors contributing to offending, reoffending and recidivism. Restorative practices provide an opportunity for the primary stakeholders to come together to share their feelings, describe how they were affected and develop a plan to repair the harm done. Part of this process is to devise an action plan to prevent a reoccurrence thereof. The restorative approach is thus reintegrative, allowing the offender to make amends and shed the offender label (McCold & Wachtel, 2003).

Restorative justice also changes the levels of accountability. In retributive justice, the criminal justice system takes responsibility for the judicial process, while, as was stated earlier, restorative justice encourages the community to participate and take ownership of the justice process. This therefore introduces new actors to the adjudication process, as it requires community members to participate actively in seeking restoration for the victim, the community, and the offender. Communities are furthermore required to play an active role in crime prevention through participation in the development of culturally and community sensitive intervention strategies (Swanson-Jacobs, 2007). The utilisation of restorative justice thus requires not only a radical paradigm shift in the way criminal justice practitioners think about and understand justice, but also a similar change in perceptions from members of society. It will be necessary for members of society to become involved in the administration of justice before a transition from a retributive to a restorative justice paradigm can take place.

CRITICAL REFLECTION

Is South Africa prepared to move away from a retributive to a restorative paradigm?

As a result of South Africa's legacy of crime and violence, South African citizens are exposed – if not at first hand, then vicariously – to the trauma caused by crime. Studies have found a direct correlation between this tertiary traumatisation and the development of post-traumatic stress syndrome (PTSS) (Bezuidenhout, 2008; Burton, 2007). In reaction to the high rate of crime, a perception that the criminal justice system in South Africa is ineffective has developed, resulting in growing support for community justice associated with vigilante activities (Pelser, Louw & Ntuli, 2000). A pertinent question that needs to be asked in this regard is whether South Africa's citizens are willing to adopt a restorative approach to justice, thus moving away from a retributive frame of thinking to a restorative paradigm. What do you think?

7.7 Restorative justice in practice

As has been stated, restorative justice is inclusive as it has the interest of all stakeholders at heart. McCold and Wachtel (2003) thus recognise that stakeholder groups have broken restorative justice down into the types and degrees of restorative justice practices (see Table 7.1).

Table 7.1 Types and degrees of restorative justice (adapted from McCold & Wachtel, 2003, p. 3)[3]

	Offender	Victim	Community
Fully restorative	Peace circles Family group conferencing Community conferencing	Peace circles Family group conferencing Community conferencing	Peace circles Family group conferencing Community conferencing
Mostly restorative	Victim-offender mediation Victim restitution Victimless conferences Therapeutic communities	Victim-offender mediation Victim restitution Victim support circles	Victim support circles Victimless conferencing Therapeutic communities
Partly restorative	Community service Programmes aimed at creating empathy	Victim services Victim empowerment	Offender family support services

In Table 7.1 the three stakeholders and types of restorative interventions are depicted. The degree to which all three stakeholders are involved in meaningful interaction and decisionmaking determines the degree to which the intervention can be termed as restorative. In the case of interventions classified as fully restorative, all three stakeholders actively participate in the restorative process. An initiative is classified as partly restorative if only one of the stakeholders - such as in victim services - is involved. In victim-offender mediation - where only two of the stakeholder groups, namely the offender and victim - are involved, the intervention is classified as mostly restorative (McCold & Wachtel, 2003).

Restorative justice services involving the three key stakeholder groups will be discussed below.

7.7.1 Working with offenders

The restorative justice philosophy has not had a large-scale impact on prison policy and practice and is not utilised optimally in correctional centres (Dhami, Mantle, & Fox, 2009). Restorative justice programmes in South African correctional centres are predominantly

3 The contributions of McCold, P., and Wachtel, T. are gratefully acknowledged.

classified as partly restorative, as they do not include all stakeholders in the interventions, tending instead to be didactic or to focus on the development of empathy through reflexivity. Offenders who have been sentenced to correctional supervision may also be expected to do community service, which is a form of restitution.

The most groundbreaking development in this field is the incorporation of restorative justice principles in child justice. The Child Justice Act (75 of 2008) created the foundation for a separate juvenile justice system for children in conflict with the law. Restorative justice played a significant role in the development the act and the child justice system in general. Thus a restorative approach was found to be a better alternative for the rehabilitation and development of young offenders, compared to the retributive paradigm previously used in child justice.

The act, which embraces restorative justice concepts and principles, provides a juvenile justice system that reinforces both children's rights and children's respect for the rights of others (Skelton & Tshehla, 2008). In the act the need to be proactive in crime prevention is recognised. This places increased emphasis on the importance of effective rehabilitation and reintegration of children in order to minimise reoffending. Furthermore, the act balances the interests of children and community with due regard to the rights of victims (Badenhorst, 2011). Diversion – the process of directing children under the age of 18 who have committed offences and have admitted their guilt away from formal criminal justice – is central to the act. Diversion programmes focus on rehabilitation and restoration and aim to reintegrate children in conflict with the law back into their communities (Steyn, 2005).

In accordance with the act, diversion should be considered as the first option in all cases dealing with youths in conflict with the law. The incarceration of young offenders should be considered only as a last resort and only if the child offender poses a threat for other youths in places of safety or the wider community (Berg, 2013). Diversion is developed to assist the diverted children to foster insight into the impact and consequences of the crime they committed, enabling them to accept responsibility and make amends. This correlates with restorative justice practices, whereby offenders are also held accountable for their actions and have to accept responsibility for the harms, needs, and obligations caused by the criminal act (Batley, 2005). According to Sloth-Nielson and Galinetti (2011), the four key elements of restorative justice are:

1. encounter
2. reparation
3. reintegration
4. participation.

In child justice, the aim of these elements is to restore the harm done by the crime through the rehabilitation and reintegration of the diverted child. A further aim is to prevent reoffending by focusing on initiating a positive change in behaviour, rather than on punishment (Berg, 2013; Zehr & Gohar, 2003).

Diversion can include formal programmes, such as a life skills programme, vocational skills training, community service, victim-offender mediation or family group conferencing. In addition, depending on the type and severity of the offence, diversion orders – such as a police caution, the writing of an apology letter, participation in an alternative dispute resolution forum or being placed under supervision – can also form part of the diversion intervention (Wood, 2003).

A study conducted by Berg (2013), which explored the degree to which child diversion programmes and non-governmental providers in the Western Cape comply with the minimum programme outcome standards as stipulated in the act, found that the majority of NGO service providers complied with the minimum standards for diversion. Challenges associated with the implementation of diversion programmes included staff shortages, inappropriate programme recommendations, inadequately trained officials, and a decrease in funding. Further challenges were also identified: the evaluation of programme effectiveness, the accessibility to programmes, and the lack of formalised participant follow-ups to evaluate the long-term impact of the interventions.

7.7.1.1 Family group conferencing

A family group conference is a restorative justice process wherein stakeholders affected by the crime come together to formulate a strategy on how to right the wrong caused by a criminal act. Typically, the conference will take place between a victim and offender, along with a facilitator and people significant to both parties, such as parents, spouses or members of the community. The purpose of a family group conference is to assist these parties to engage in an open and honest dialogue about the crime and the impact it had on the victim and society (Zehr, 2004).

According to Umbreit and Fercello (2000), a family group conference session commences with the facilitator setting down ground rules to facilitate dialogue, in order to protect the rights of all stakeholders who participate in the conference. The victim and the offender are asked to describe the events surrounding the crime and the impact it had on their lives. After both parties have shared their stories, the other participants are given an opportunity to speak and to also share how the crime affected them. Next, the facilitator invites the parties to discuss alternative possibilities for restitution, which could include an apology, financial or other forms of compensation, and/or community service. An important component of family group conferencing is that the victim and the offender must agree to the restitution before it is finalised. Dialogue and negotiation are central to this process, with the primary emphasis being on healing and restitution and not only on establishing blame for past behaviour (Schoeman, 2012a).

The role of the facilitator is to prepare the parties for the family group conferencing process and to create a safe environment that stimulates open and honest discussion. The facilitator is also responsible for directing the process and ensuring that each participant's human rights are respected (Umbreit & Fercello, 2000).

According to Huntsman (2006), family group conferences have successfully been used in child justice as well as cases where domestic violence and/or substance abuse are present. Cases unsuitable for family group conferencing are those in which one of the participants - such as the victim or offender - has serious mental health issues, there is serious and unresolved interpersonal or interfamilial conflict which might harm one of the parities, or the offender has no significant support system.

7.7.2 Working with victims of crime

During legal actions, victims of crime are represented by the state, which often results in the victim becoming the forgotten party in the justice process (Schoeman, 2012a). This is so primarily because the current legal system leaves little room for victim participation. According to Laxminarayan (2010), this is of concern as ideally participation in a court case should have a positive outcome for the victim. However, in many instances this does not happen, as exposure to the court procedures could actually infringe even further the rights of victims and result in revictimisation. Sadly, it is often professionals and paraprofessionals - such as police officers, health professionals and legal practitioners - working in the criminal justice system who are responsible for this revictimisation (Hill, 2009).

South Africa has an extensive legislative framework and policies to protect the rights of crime victims during their dealings with the criminal justice sector. In this regard, the *Service Charter for Victims of Crime* (the *Victim's Charter*) outlines the services to victims as well as victims rights. The *Minimum Standards on Services for Victims of Crime* (*Minimum Standards*) is an information document that ensures that the rights of victims are adhered to. Both these documents are part of South Africa's Victim Empowerment Programme (VEP), which is in line with the National Crime Prevention Strategy's vision of a victim-centred criminal justice system.

The important role victims play in the justice process was recognised only with the establishment of the TRC in 1995, when the psychosocial impact of crime on victims was recognised (Nomoyi & Pretorius, 2001).

Victim empowerment is a philosophy of care and assistance aimed at facilitating a crime victim's access to a range of services. It strives to reduce secondary victimisation by providing information on matters such as the status of the investigation, the functioning of the court system, and the rights of victims. Furthermore, through educational campaigns it aims to prevent repeat victimisation. Victim empowerment is also motivated by the realisation that crime victims need, in addition to victim support services, recognition and to play a more central part in the criminal justice process (SA Department of Social Development (DSD), 2009). Hence, victim empowerment is based on restorative justice principles and aims to promote a victim-centred approach to criminal justice. In this regard, supporters of restorative justice point to research proving that a restorative approach has been successful in reducing crime, satisfying victim needs and restoring the culture of ubuntu (Skelton & Tshehla, 2008). Furthermore, research has indicated that a victim-centred approach results in a reduction of victimisation, while simultaneously improving service standards in the justice system (SA DSD, 2009).

Restorative justice makes use of dialogue, mediation and problem solving techniques to meet the individual needs of victims. It offers an alternative to traditional offender-driven approaches, which primarily focus on the crime committed and the reaction to the crime (Armour, 2008). Hence, as active participants in the judicial process, victims are also given an opportunity to make their voices heard.

As was discussed previously, the core value of restorative justice is to balance the needs of the offender, the victim and the community. Although restorative justice interventions are diverse, the direct participation by victims and offenders is central to all of them (Hargovan, 2007). In South Africa the most frequently used restorative justice programmes in which victims participate are victim–offender mediation and family group conferencing.

7.7.2.1 Victim–offender mediation

Victim–offender mediation is a process that provides interested victims of crime with the opportunity to meet – in a safe and structured setting – the offender who transgressed against them. Humanistic mediation is central to victim–offender mediation, due to the process being dialogue driven rather than outcomes driven. It is grounded in a paradigm of healing and peacemaking rather than problem-solving and conflict resolution. In other words, the emphasis is on the sharing of experiences and emotions about the crime within a non-judgemental environment, with the aim of addressing the harms done, in order to achieve reconciliation (Umbreit, Bradshaw, & Coates, 1999).

The purpose of the meeting is for victims and offenders to share their stories about the criminal event. As a result, the offenders are held accountable for their behaviour while providing an opportunity for victims to make their voices heard. Victims have the opportunity to let the offender know how the crime affected them, as well as to receive answers to questions they may have. Offenders, in turn, are able to take responsibility for their behaviour and have the opportunity to become aware of, and learn from, the full impact of their actions. The victim can also become directly involved in developing a restitution plan for the offender, thus advising the criminal justice officials, and offender, on how to make amends to the victim (Umbreit, 2008). In essence, victim–offender mediation humanises the criminal justice experience for both victim and offender (Umbreit et al., 1999). The offender might be the one to request a victim–offender mediation session in order to make amends with the victim. Such requests should be handled with care, and victims should be given the choice as to whether they would like to participate.

According to Umbreit (2008), the restitution agreement resulting from the victim–offender mediation sessions is of secondary importance to the dialogue between the parties that addresses the emotional and informational needs of victims. The dialogues have been found to be central to the victims' healing process. The offender could, in turn, also benefit from the development of victim empathy, which can lead to a decline in further criminal behaviour.

The role of the facilitator is to prepare both parties for participation in the victim–offender mediation process and to facilitate the session. The preparation involves meeting face to face with the offender and victim prior to mediation. In terms of the victim, it is important for the facilitator to be understanding of the victimisation phases resulting from dealing with the grief and loss due to the crime victimisation. Facilitators should also be knowledgeable about symptoms related to post-traumatic stress and its impact on the psychosocial functioning of crime victims. In dealing with the offender, the facilitator should be mindful of personal prejudices and remain non-judgemental in all instances, notwithstanding the nature and seriousness of the crime. Furthermore, the facilitator should be knowledgeable about the criminal justice and corrections system in order to gain access to the offender (Umbreit et al., 1999).

Victim–offender mediation is generally used for economic and less serious crimes, but it has recently also been used with victims and perpetrators of violent crimes (Schoeman, 2012a). A pilot project conducted by the Departments of Corrections in Texas, Ohio, Pennsylvania, and several other states in the United States of America has proved that victim–offender mediation can also have a positive impact on the lives of both the victims and offenders involved in violent crimes such as homicide, rape, and other cases involving extreme violence (Umbreit, Vos, Coates, & Brown, 2003). It should be noted that more intensive preparation of both parties should take place in such cases, and that this should occur over an extended period of time prior to the mediation session.

7.7.2.2 Victim impact statements

From a restorative justice perspective, victim impact statements are recognised as a method whereby victims' right to participate in court procedures is being acknowledged (Chambliss, 2011). Victim impact statements are written and/or oral statements that describe the impact of a crime on the victim and people who have a significant connection with the victim (Schoeman, 2013). They are different from the general testimony during the court proceedings, as they allow victims to personalise the crime and to shed light on the multidimensional impact of a crime on the victim's physical, social, economic and psychological functioning (Clark, Davis, & Booyens, 2003). They give victims the opportunity to make their voices heard in an offender-centred criminal justice system (Tolhurst, 2008).

Victim impact statements are thus a method whereby the values of restorative justice are incorporated in the judicial process.

A victim impact statement may be made by any person against whom an offence has been committed, such as the victim and/or other people who suffered harm as a result of the offence, or secondary stakeholders, for example family members of the victim or other people who have a significant relationship with the victim.

Victim impact statements are generally presented during sentencing deliberations after an offender has been found guilty of a crime, but they can also be submitted during the bail hearing or parole board hearings of the offender who transgressed against the victim. In the *National Policy Guidelines for Empowerment* (SA DSD, 2009) it is suggested that a victim impact statement should include a description of the harm done - for example of the physical or mental injury, emotional suffering, economic loss the victim suffered - and/or facts pertaining to how the victim's human rights were impaired. In addition, victims can include a description of any other consequence resulting from their victimisation.

It is the victims' choice if they wish to read the victim impact statement to the court. If the victim chooses not to do so, the prosecutor can present the victim impact statement. It is not necessary for victims to appear before the court if the contents of a victim impact statement are not disputed, but they may be called to testify if the contents of the statement are disputed (SA DSD, 2009).

Even though victim impact statements are generally written, they are not always confined to written documents. Very young children can be encouraged to draw a picture, tell a story or write a poem to explain how they feel and how the crime affected them (Clark, Davis, & Booyens, 2003). In addition, a parent, guardian or practitioner - such as a criminologist or social worker - can also represent the child victim. In this regard, information about how the crime influenced the child's behaviour, interaction with other people, scholastic performance and so forth can be included in the statement.

Roberts (2003) is of the opinion that a victim impact statement creates the opportunity for communication between a victim and the offender. Furthermore, it adds to victim satisfaction and has been found to aid psychological healing. Practitioners in criminal justice - such as those in the criminological field - can play an active role in educating crime victims and other stakeholders about the process associated with the submission of a victim impact statement, as well as guide them in writing such statements.

CASE STUDY

Victim impact statements are written and/or oral statements that describe the impact of a crime on the victim and the people who are in contact with the victim. The following is an example of a written victim impact statement that was presented during pre-sentencing arguments.

Example of a victim impact statement

On January 27, 2011, life as I knew it was changed forever. I was attacked by two older kids from my school. They thought it was funny to bump me around and kick and hit me. They held me down, so I didn't have much chance. Not that I could fight them off because they are much bigger than I am. When I started to cry they struck me with a bottle on my head and I blacked out. They left me lying there.

After the attack I spend two weeks in hospital with head injuries and broken ribs. My liver was also damaged and I had an operation to fix it. My mother is unemployed and do not have money to pay for the glasses I need after the attack. I cannot go outside on my own or to school because I have trouble seeing. The doctor told my mother that I will have to go to a special school for blind people.

The actions of Peter Botha and Gift Moloi have greatly affect my life. I am unable to sleep since the attack. I no longer trust people like I did before. They have no respect for my life.

They were previously in trouble with the police for hurting other people but do not stop. I loved to go to school and wanted to go to university but they took my dream away. Every morning I wake up and feel as if I have no reason to live anymore.

I would like to see them going to prison so that they can feel how it feels when someone takes away your freedom and your dreams. They should also pay for the medical care I still need as a result of the injuries. They need to pay for what they have done but it doesn't change the fact that no matter what their sentence is it will not change what they made me.

Richard Plaatjies

7.7.3 Crime prevention

Owing to the high rate of crime in South Africa, people living in the country are exposed to crime – if not directly or indirectly, then vicariously through the media. Thus it can be hypothesised that South African citizens are all tertiary victims of crime. Research shows that a significant number of South Africans are desensitised and perceive crime as a normal part of daily life, while others are more sensitive to the exposure and may even experience trauma-related symptoms due to their indirect exposure to crime (Burton, 2007). In severe cases, the psychological effects of such exposure may result in tertiary victims suffering from PTSS, which can include paranoia or psychosomatic symptoms such as hypervigilance or depression, as well as substance abuse (Bezuidenhout, 2008). This may result in feelings of powerlessness, anger and rage as well as vigilante behaviour, during which citizens take the law in their own hands.

South Africa's youth are particularly vulnerable to tertiary victimisation. They are constantly confronted with serious crime incidents, and their conceptual and emotional inability to understand and deal with the information results in feelings of insecurity and a sense of powerlessness in controlling their environment (Burton, 2007). These feelings, as well as the normalisation of criminal behaviour, can result in acting out behaviour, delinquency and their becoming involved in criminal activities (Bezuidenhout, 2008; Burton, 2007; Stravrou, 1993).

As was stated previously, restorative justice is predominantly used in South Africa reactively in response to crime. For this reason, Schoeman (2012b) is of the opinion that restorative justice values offer the ideal platform for the teaching of prosocial cultural values and a restorative method of conflict resolution. According to Johnstone (2012), an alternative way of constructing restorative justice is as a loosely linked assortment of beliefs, practices, values and ways of life, which can be broken down into a set of teaching on how individuals should conduct themselves in the world. This also includes values on how people should see and relate to others and deal with challenges and conflicts they encounter.

The use of restorative justice principles for proactive crime prevention and restoration mechanisms stems from the belief that norms and values in a society are influenced by attitudes and values to which a community adheres and by the attitudes and behaviours deemed acceptable or unacceptable in a specific society. These behaviour patterns are generally entrenched in culture-, gender- and/or community-based values and beliefs. For example, in violent societies, the social hierarchy within the system often supports the formation of groups which sustain a culture of violence, for example in gang and crime-ridden areas (Schoeman, 2012b). Furthermore, it has been found that antisocial attitudes of influential figures – such as community or traditional leaders, parents and peers – may contribute to a culture of delinquency, thus reinforcing delinquency or a culture of violence (Swart & Bredekamp, 2009).

In order to change the behaviour of individuals, it is necessary also to change the culture (values, norms, and beliefs) of society in general. This requires reforming the existing dysfunctional value system and replacing it with prosocial alternatives. As was mentioned previously, there are recognisable similarities between restorative justice values and norms and those found in the ubuntu philosophy. The interconnectedness of restorative justice values and an ubuntu worldview could therefore offer the ideal medium for starting a revival process. From this perspective, the purpose of restorative justice teachings will be to develop a restorative frame of thinking within communities, one that is in line with the restorative values of respect, honesty, humility, mutual care, accountability, and trust (Pranis, 2007).

Utilisation of restorative justice teachings in social transformation and crime prevention is a holistic approach and can be successful only if both top-down and bottom-up approaches are followed. In other words, the teaching and implementation of a restorative value system should focus on both the formal and informal leadership of a community, as well as the community members. Murithi (2006) postulates that the perpetual cycle of violence and crime can be broken only if people change the way in which they perceive themselves and their responsibilities to others, as well as to society in general.

Holtmann (2011) is of the opinion that a reactive response to crime and violence in society does little to improve the quality of life of a country's citizens, thus it is necessary to identify proactive solutions to social problems. She goes on to argue that even though everything that happens in society is not about crime, conflict and violence, certain aspects – such as people's social welfare – will also improve if communities adopt a restorative and prosocial value system.

Providers of victim empowerment services can make a valuable contribution to crime prevention in this regard by educating and empowering not only primary and secondary victims, but also potential victims of crime. Utilising restorative justice principles in crime prevention will thus address the potential harm of crime victimisation in communities. Interventions to educate potential victims also empower communities; such interventions could include training in restorative conflict resolution at schools.

7.7.3.1 Community mediation

Community mediation is a restorative justice process that provides a constructive process whereby differences between individuals, groups or organisations in a community can be resolved (Miller, Hess, & Orthmann, 2011). The purpose of community mediation is to bring together various parties, for instance community and gang members, in an attempt to seek a resolution which is acceptable to all the parties. It is also a method of addressing prevailing problems and concerns in a community, such as substance abuse or domestic violence. Like other restorative justice processes, community mediation seeks to make good harm that has been done and to find a mutually agreed upon solution to a social problem. Thus the mediation process facilitates the negotiations and leads community parties to explore their culpability in the conflict or social ill, in order to reach consensus and come to a peaceful resolution (Miller et al., 2011). The role of the practitioner is to facilitate the mediation process and to assist the parties to define and clarify issues associated with the conflict or concern, to reduce obstacles for communication, and to explore possible solutions in order to find a mutually satisfactory resolution. It should be noted that in community resolution, as with all restorative processes, it is not the role or responsibility of the facilitator to find a solution to disputes, as the power and responsibility to find an acceptable resolution lies with the parties themselves. The facilitator's role is to enable and empower participants to take ownership of and responsibility for the resolution of the dispute (Miller et al., 2011).

Even though this approach is only partly restorative, it can be effectively used to address causative factors associated with criminal behaviour and crime victimisation. For example, community mediation can be used to achieve peaceful resolution during conflict between South African citizens and foreigners, in cases of xenophobic attacks.

CASE STUDY

The following case study is an example of how programmes based on restorative justice principles can be used in crime prevention. In this instance, violent behaviour was identified as a risk factor associated with crime causation in the targeted population. The Face It programme was used to make the learners aware of their aggressive behaviour and to teach them alternative methods of conflict resolution.

Prevention of youth violence: what is learned can be unlearned

Eron postulates that 'what is learned can be unlearned and new ways of behaving can be adopted' (in Heleta, 2007, p. 11). A study conducted by Schoeman (2011) examined whether youth programmes based on restorative justice principles can be used to change violent cognitions and behaviour patterns associated with violence and crime. The sample consisted of 278 secondary school children between the ages of 13 and 20 years from 7 schools in the Johannesburg and surrounding areas. These schools were identified by the City of Johannesburg in areas where problems are experienced with youth violence and delinquency. The Face It programme, which is based on restorative principles, was presented to the sample group by Khulisa Social Solutions, an NGO working with at risk youth. The purpose of the programme is to develop knowledge about the risk and causative factors, as well as the social dynamics, associated with aggression and violent behaviour. Participants were introduced to more effective alternative non-violent methods of dealing with conflicts and life challenges, as well as assisted in developing relevant life skills. The programme demonstrates how violence (physical, emotional, and verbal) is ingrained in culture and belief systems, and how it emerges in daily interactions. Though the programme, participants were introduced to practical ways of minimising violent behaviour and empowered to restore interpersonal and other relationships (Schoeman, 2011).

Evaluation research making use of a pre-test–post-test design was followed. The pre-test was conducted before the programme commenced to establish a baseline; this was followed by a post-test after each of the 10 programme sessions. The programme's effectiveness was measured by determining if prosocial modification of participants' cognitive comprehension, attitude and behaviours concerning violence took place. Data collection occurred by means of a questionnaire (Schoeman, 2011).

Findings from the research confirmed that the Face It programme is effective as an early prevention programme to address violence and violent behaviour amongst youths. The programme was found to be effective because it facilitated the learning of prosocial methods of dealing with aggression and conflict. Didactic and experiential learning elements were used to replace violent cognitions and attitudes with prosocial alternatives, thus empowering the respondent with the knowledge of how to make non-violent decisions. Even though this programme is an example of only one instance in which an intervention was used for the proactive prevention of violent behaviour, valuable lessons can be learned from it. The study confirms that proactive interventions could be utilised effectively for crime prevention to address aggressive attitudes and behaviour acquired through a process of social learning (Schoeman, 2011).

Conclusion

Crime victimisation is generally a traumatic and often life-altering experience in victims' lives. It also has a destructive impact on communities in general. Research has indicated that a retributive approach to crime does not acknowledge the harm done to individuals and communities, and has highlighted the need for a more restorative approach in adjudication.

From the discussion in this chapter it should be clear both that restorative justice offers a multidimensional approach to dealing with harm caused by criminal behaviour, and that it focuses on addressing the underlying causes of criminal behaviour. Because restorative justice views crime as a violation of people and interpersonal relationships, and not only as a legal dispute with the state, it opens up opportunities for reconciliation. As a result, offenders are not shunned; they are, instead, guided to understand the impact of their behaviour and to accept responsibility for their actions. As a result, restorative justice promotes healing and reconciliation, rather than aiming simply to punish. By recognising the uniqueness of each case, restorative justice offers an opportunity to explore the actual effect of the harm done and find a solution that fits the unique circumstances associated with the conflict.

Even though restorative justice is currently predominantly utilised in child justice, its potential value for offenders and victims was highlighted in this chapter. The value of restorative justice in crime prevention was also discussed. It is the responsibility of all service providers and practitioners in the criminal justice system to familiarise themselves with restorative justice principles and practices. It is also important that they undergo specialised training in order to ensure effective services.

Critical thinking questions

1. Do you think crime should be viewed as a conflict between individuals or as a delinquent act in which state laws are transgressed?
2. Could restorative justice be used as an alternative to the retributive paradigm currently utilised in the South African judicial system?
3. Which stumbling blocks in your community could prevent the implementation of restorative justice?
4. What risks could result in the revictimisation of victims during a victim-offender conferencing session?
5. How can restorative justice be used proactively to prevent crime is South Africa?

References

Armour, M. P. (2008). Restorative justice. In C. M. Renzetti & J. L. Edleson (Eds.), *Encyclopedia of interpersonal violence*. Thousand Oaks, CA: Sage Publications.

Badenhorst, C. (2011). *Overview of the implementation of the Child Justice Act, 2008 (Act 75 of 2008): good intentions, questionable outcomes* (Occasional Paper No. 10). Pinelands: Open Society Foundation for South Africa.

Batley, M. (2005). Restorative justice in the South African context. In T. Maepa. *Beyond retribution: prospects for restorative justice in South Africa*. (Monograph No. 111). Institute for Security Studies.

Bazemor, G., & Umbreit, M. (2001). A comparison of four restorative conferencing models. *Juvenile Justice Bulletin*, February, 1–19.

Berg, S. (2013). *Child diversion minimum programme outcomes standards compliance in the Western Cape: an explorative study*. (MA dissertation, University of South Africa, Pretoria).

Bezuidenhout, C. (2008). *The psychological impact of crime on the South African society*. Paper presented at the 3rd International Conference on Interdisciplinary Social Sciences, Tuscany, Italy.

Braithwaite, J. (2002). Setting standards for restorative justice. *British Journal of Criminology, 42*, 563–577.

Braithwaite, J. (2004). *Restorative justice theories and worries*. Retrieved July 9, 2013, from http://www.unafei.or.jp/english/pdf/RS_No63/No63_10VE_Braithwaite2.pdf.

Burton, P. (2007). *Someone stole my smile: an exploration into the causes of youth violence in South Africa* (Monograph series No. 3). Centre for Justice and Crime Prevention. Cape Town: ISS.

Chambliss, W. J. (Ed.) (2011). *Courts, law and justice*. Thousand Oaks, CA: Sage Publications.

Clark, D., Davis, L., & Booyens, K. (2003). A silver era for victims of crime: reassessing the role of victim impact statements can play in improving victim involvement in Criminal Justice procedures. *Acta Criminologica, 16*(2), 43–56.

Cornell, D. (2008). *uBuntu, pluralism and the responsibility of legal academics to the new South Africa*. Retrieved November 6, 2012 from http://www.uct.ac.za/downloads/uct.ac.za/news/lectures/inaugurals/Drucilla_Cornell.pdf.

Cullen, F. T., Wright, J. P., & Blevins, K. R. (Eds.) (2008). *Taking stock: the status of criminological theory*. New Brunswick: Tenasaction Publishers.

Dhami, M. K., Mantle, G., & Fox, D. (2009). Restorative justice in prisons. *Contemporary Justice Review, 12*, 433–448.

Dyck, D. (2004). Are we – practitioner, advocates – practicing what we preach?. In H. Zehr & B. Troews (Eds.). *Critical issues in restorative justice*. New York: Criminal Justice Press.

Elechi, O. O. (2004). *Human rights and the African indigenous justice system*. Retrieved November 6, 2012, from www.restorativejustice.org/articlesdb/articles/5450.

Gavrielides, T. (2005). Some meta-theoretical questions for restorative justice. *Ratio Juris, 18*(1), 84–106.

Hargovan, H. (2007). Restorative justice approaches to justice: 'compulsory compassion' or victim empowerment? *Acta Criminologica: Southern African Journal of Criminology, 20*(3), 113–123.

Heleta, S. (2007). *Human aggression: pre-disposed or learned?* Retrieved July 2, 2013, from http://www.scribd.com/doc/63716676/Human-Aggression-Pre-Disposed-or-Learned-by-Savo-Heleta.

Hill, J. (2009). *Working with victims of crime: a manual applying research to clinical practice*. Canada: Department of Justice.

Holtmann, B. (2011). *What it looks like when it is fixed: a case study in developing a systemic model to transform a fragile social system*. Johannesburg: Ultra:Litho.

Huntsman, L. (2006). *Family Group Conferencing in a child welfare context*. Centre for Parenting & Research. Research, Funding & Business Analysis Division. Retrieved April 26, 2013, from http://www.community.nsw.gov.au/docswr/_assets/main/documents/research_family_conferencing.pdf.

Johnstone, G. (2004). How and in what terms should restorative justice be conceived? In H. Zehr & B. Troews (Eds.) *Critical issues in restorative justice*. New York: Criminal Justice Press.

Johnstone, G. (2012, June). *The teachings of restorative justice*. Paper presented at the 1st international symposium on the Philosophy of Restorative Justice and Human Rights, Skopelos Island, Greece.

Kinyanjui, S. (2009). Restorative justice in traditional pre-colonial criminal justice systems in Kenya. *Tribal Law Journal, 10*, 1–16.

Laxminarayan, M. (2010). Measuring crime victims' pathways to justice: developing indicators for costs and quality of access to justice. *Acta Criminologica, 23*(1), 61–83.

Liebman, M. (2007). *Restorative justice: how it works*. London: Jessica Kingsley Publishers.

Marshall, T. (1995) Restorative justice on trial in Britain. *Mediation Quarterly, 12*, 217–231.

McCold, P., & Wachtel, T. (2003, August). *In Pursuit of paradigm: a theory of restorative justice*. Paper presented at the 13th World Congress of Criminology, Rio de Janeiro, Brazil.

Metz, T. (2012). Ethics in Africa and in Aristotle: some points of contrast. *Phronimon, 13*(2), 99–117.

Miller, L. H., Hess, K. M., & Orthmann, C. H. (2011). *Community policing: partnerships for problem solving*. New York: Delmar, Cengage learning.

Murithi, T. (2006). Practical peacemaking wisdom from Africa: reflections on ubuntu. *The Journal of Pan African Studies, 1*(4), June, 25–34.

Mutua, M. W. (1995). The Banjul Charter and the African fingerprint: an evaluation of the language of rights and duties. *Virginia Journal of International Law, 35*(2), 339–340.

Nomoyi, C., & Pretorius, R. (2001). Impact of the dynamics of the Reparations and Rehabilitation Committee of the Truth and Reconciliation Commission on female victims. *Acta Criminologica: Southern African Journal of Criminology, 14*(1): 1–10.

Okafo, N. (2006). Relevance of African traditional jurisprudence on control, justice, and law: a critique of the Igbo Experience. *African Journal of Criminology & Justice Studies: AJCJS, 2*(1), 37–62.

Omale, D. J. (2006). Justice in history: an examination of 'African restorative traditions' and the emerging 'restorative justice' paradigm. *African Journal of Criminology and Justice Studies, 2*(2): 33–63.

Ovens, M., & Prinsloo, J. (2010). The significance of 'Africanness' for the development of contemporary criminological propositions: a multidisciplinary approach. *Phronimon, 11*(2), 19–33.

Pelser, E., Louw, A., & Ntuli, S. (2000). *Poor safety: crime and policing in South Africa's rural areas* (Monograph no. 47). Pretoria: Institute for Security Studies.

Pranis, K. (2007). Restorative values. In G. Johnstone & D. W. Van Ness (Eds.). *Handbook of restorative justice*. Portland, OR: Willan Publishings.

Reisig, M. D., & Mesko, G. (2009). Procedural justice, legitimacy, and prisoner misconduct. *Psychology, Crime & Law, 15*(1), 41–59.

Roberts, J. V. (2003). Victim impact statements and the sentencing process: enhancing communication in the courtroom. *Criminal Law Quarterly, 47*(3): 365–396.

SAPA. (2013, March 3). Ndebele: SA has highest prison population in Africa. *Mail & Guardian*. Retrieved from http://mg.co.za/article/2013-02-11-south-africa-has-highest-prison-population-in-africa-says-ndebele.

Schoeman, M. (2011). Prevention of youth violence: what is learned can be unlearned. *Child Abuse Research: A South African Journal, 11*(2), 9– 20.

Schoeman, M. (2012a). Working with victims of crime. In L. Holtzhausen & C. Nieuwenhuizen (Eds.). *Criminal justice social work: a South African practice framework.* Cape Town: Juta & Co.

Schoeman, M. (2012b). A philosophical view of social transformation through restorative justice teachings: a case study of traditional leaders in Ixopo, South Africa. *Phronimon, 13*(2): 19–38.

Schoeman, M. (2013). The African concept of Ubuntu and restorative justice. In T. Gavrielides & V. Vartinopoulou (Eds.). *Reconstructing restorative justice philosophy.* London: Ashgate.

Shapland, J., Atkinson, A., Atkinson, H., Chapman, B., Dignan, J., Howes, M. ... Sorsby, A. (2007) *Restorative justice: the views of victims and offenders. The third report from the evaluation of the three schemes.* Sheffield: Centre for Criminological Research.

Skelton, A. (2002). Restorative justice as a framework for justice reform: a South African perspective. *British Journal of Criminology, 42*, 495–513.

Skelton, A. (2007). *Reforming the juvenile justice system in South Africa: policy, law reform and parallel developments* (136th International Training Course visiting experts' papers, resource material Series No. 75). Centre for Child Law, Faculty of Law, University of Pretoria, South Africa.

Skelton, A., & Tshehla, B. (2008). *Child justice in South Africa* (Monologue No. 150, September). Pretoria: Institute for Security Studies.

Sloth-Nielsen, J., & Gallinetti, J. (2011). 'Just say sorry?' Ubuntu, Africanisation and the child justice system in the Child Justice Act 75 of 2008. *PER, 14*(4), 63–90.

South Africa (Republic) (SA). Department of Correctional Services. (2013). *Department of correctional services incarceration levels 2013/02.* (2013). Retrieved March 19, 2013, from http://www.dcs.gov.za/AboutUs/StatisticalInformation.aspx

South Africa (Republic) (SA). Department of Social Development (DSD). (2009). *National policy guidelines for victim empowerment.* Pretoria. Retrieved July 2, 2013, from http://www.pmg.org.za/policy-documents/2009/07/12/national-policy-guidelines-for-victim-empowerment.

South Africa (Republic) (SA). Judicial Inspectorate for Correctional Services. (2011). *Annual report 2011/2012: treatment of inmate and conditions in correctional centres.*

South Africa (Republic) (SA). South African Police Service. (2012). *Crime statistics overview RSA 2011/2012.* Pretoria.

Steyn, F. (2005). *Review of South African innovations in diversion and reintegration of youth at risk.* Cape Town: Open Society Foundation of South Africa.

Stravrou, V. (1993). Psychological effects of criminal. *The Child Care Worker, 11*(7), 3–5.

Sullivan, D., & Tiff, L. (2004). What are the implications of restorative justice for society and our lives. In H. Zehr & B. Troews (Eds.), *Critical issues in restorative justice.* New York: Criminal Justice Press.

Swanson-Jacobs, J. (2007). *Launch of Minimum Norms and Standards booklet on diversion.* Pretoria: Department of Social Development. Retrieved March 19, 2013, from http://www.polity.org.za/article/sa-swansonjacobs-launch-of-minimum-norms-and-standards-booklet-on-diversion-13072007-2007-07-13.

Swart, E., & Bredekamp, J. (2009). Non-physical bullying: exploring the perspective of Grade 5 girls. *South African Journal of Education, 29*(3), 405–425.

Tibbets, S. G., & Hemmens, C. (2010). *Criminological theory: a text/reader.* Thousand Oaks, CA: Sage Publications.

Tolhurst, K. A. (2008). Victim impact statements. In C. M. Renzetti & J. L. Edleson (Eds.). *Encyclopedia of interpersonal violence.* Thousand Oaks, CA: Sage Publications.

Umbreit, M. S. (2008). Victim offender mediation and dialogue. In C. M. Renzetti & J. L. Edleson (Eds.). *Encyclopedia of interpersonal violence.* Thousand Oaks, CA: Sage Publications.

Umbreit, M. S., Bradshaw, W., & Coates, R. B. (1999). Victims of severe violence meet the offender: restorative Justice through dialogue. *International Review of Victimology*, 6, 321–343.

Umbreit, M. S., Vos, B., Coates, R. B., & Brown, K. (2003). *Facing violence: the path of restorative justice & dialogue*. Monsey, NY: Criminal Justice Press.

Umbreit, M., & Amour, M. P. (2011). *Restorative justice dialogue: an essential guide for research and practice*. New York: Springer Publishing Company.

Umbreit, M., & Fercello, C. (2000). Practicing restorative justice: family group conferencing and crime in suburban metro area. *Cura Reporter, 30*(2), 15–18.

Umbreit, M., Coates, R. B., & Vos, B. (2007). Restorative justice dialogue: a multi-dimensional, evidence-based practice theory. *Contemporary Justice Review, 10*(1), 23–41.

Walklate, S. (2007). *Handbook of victims and victimology*. Cullompton: Willan.

Wood, C. (2003). *Diversion in South Africa: a review of policy and practice, 1990-2003* (Paper No. 79, October). Institute for Security Studies.

Zehr, H. (1990). *Changing lenses*. Scottsdale, PA: Herald.

Zehr, H. (1995). *Changing lenses* (Rev. ed.). Scottsdale, PA: Herald.

Zehr, H. (2002). *The little book of restorative justice*. Intercourse: Good Books Publishers.

Zehr, H. (2004). Commentary: restorative justice: beyond victim-offender mediation. *Conflict Resolution Quarterly, 22*(1), 305–315.

Zehr, H., & Gohar, A. (2003). *Little book of restorative justice*. Intercourse: Good Books Publishers.

Zehr, H., & Mika, H. (1998). Fundamental concepts of restorative justice. *Contemporary Justice Review, 1*, 47–55.

Chapter 8

Forensic and correctional criminology

A Hesselink

8.1 Introduction

At its roots, criminology is a scientific research-driven discipline. In South Africa, this discipline has progressed from clerical research and analyses to a recognised practised science that has much to offer. This is reiterated by Artz and Moult (2012), who proclaim that there are numerous intersections, unexplored terrains, and possibilities of research (and practice) in criminology, with ample opportunities that still need to be explored – thus, there are many prospects for further interdisciplinary partnerships within the various orbs in the South African society.

Artz and Moult profess that there is significant work that needs to be done in gauging the 'state of Criminology in South Africa, and the potential of a discipline that is inherently interdisciplinary' (2012, p. 2). These authors argue that criminology is splintered by its own varied institutional engagements and lack of (theoretical) solidity and that we must 'work within' to position ourselves institutionally, ideologically, and theoretically to expand the options of criminological work (Artz & Moult, 2012, p. 2).

This chapter will outline forensic criminology and correctional criminology as practised in South Africa. Distinction will be made between traditional criminology and conventional criminology, and an attempt made to unpack what is understood by some criminologists regarding the question 'what is a *criminologist* in South Africa?'. Two case studies will provide the reader with a more practical understanding of selected criminological practices in South Africa.

8.2 Definitions/key concepts

Four central definitions will be outlined to provide the reader with a background on the differences of these concepts.

8.2.1 Traditional criminology

Criminology per se is an interrelated science that incorporates views from sociology, psychology, psychiatry, biology, geography, statistics, social work, public administration, anthropology, politics, and the law (Artz & Moult, 2012; Bezuidenhout, 2011; Hesselink-Louw, 2004).

Traditional criminology is referred to by Artz and Moult as a 'wandering Criminology, travelling comfortably along its path ... with mainstream criminological theories of crime, crime ideologies, crime control and prevention ... when it suddenly encounters an intersection' (2012, p. 1). In essence, this means that criminology busied itself with research, the analysis of policies and administrative issues, and the examination of existing theories, until core intersections (unfamiliar features) were encountered.

Such topographies entailed roving issues of gender (that is, female criminality and gender crime issues), courts (that is, presentence evaluation reports), policing, victimology (that is, victim impact reports), corrections (that is, offender assessments), and youth misbehaviour and crime that demanded theoretical and practical (practice) reorientation (Artz & Moult, 2012).

8.2.2 Conventional criminology

Conventional criminology is more practically oriented. Professional criminologists assist with inputs, opinions, reports, and professional contributions in practice. Criminologists in their professional capacity are also in the employ of the criminal justice and private sectors in South Africa. Thus, conventional criminology links theory to practice in specialised fields such as correctional criminology, EpiCrim (a combination of foci pertaining to criminology, gender issues, violence, medical issues and the law), and victimology (Artz & Moult, 2012; Hesselink & Herbig, 2010).

8.2.3 Correctional criminology

Hesselink-Louw (2004) describes correctional knowledge with a criminological-correctional focus as the core function of correctional criminology. Correctional knowledge includes practical experience in working with offenders through the compilation of criminological offender needs and risk assessments. A criminological-correctional focus refers to the content application and interpretation of offender needs and risk assessments, together with sound empirical research findings and criminological theories to analyse, assess, and explain the behaviour in question (Hesselink & Herbig, 2010; Hesselink-Louw, 2004).

8.2.4 Forensic criminology

Forensic criminology fills the dire need to assist with objective, sound, informed scientific information or opinions regarding offending behaviour, applied especially in South African courts, the South African Police Service (SAPS) and Corrections. The core function remains assessment of behaviour from a criminological perspective.

A forensic criminologist is an expert witness in court who compiles a presentence evaluation report outlining all factors that could play a role in the criminal event. Important aspects may include:

- causes
- motives
- personal history of the person
- social and environmental influences
- precipitating factors
- a scientific explanation of the behaviour in question
- mitigating and aggravating factors
- sentencing guidance to the court (Bezuidenhout, 2011).

Other categories of forensic criminology include criminological victim impact statements and polygraph examinations (Bezuidenhout, 2011).

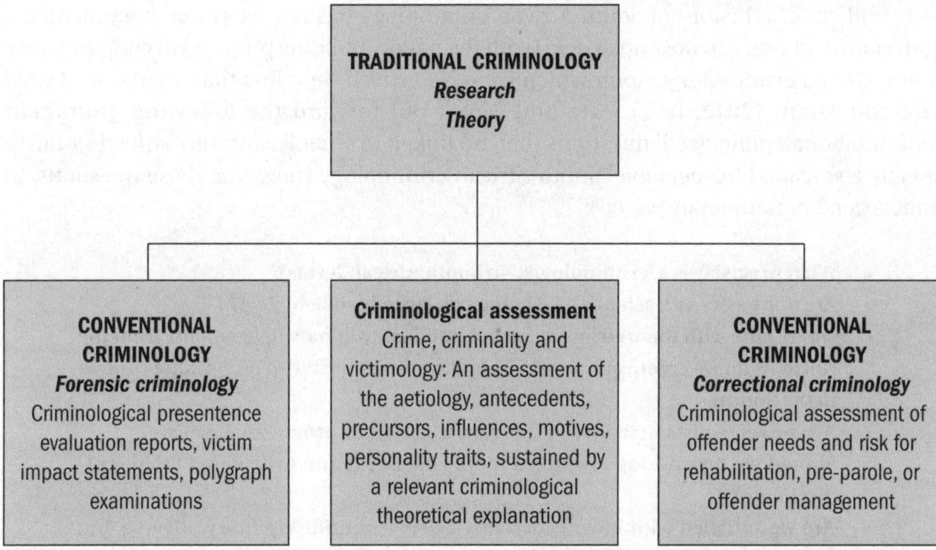

Figure 8.1 *Criminology: Research, theory, assessment, and practice (interpreted from Herbig & Hesselink, 2009; Hesselink-Louw & Joubert, 2003)*

Figure 8.1 depicts the development of traditional criminology to conventional criminology. Criminological theories are derived from empirical research findings that have been tested and retested over long periods of time to identify and explain specific crime causation factors, personality traits, motives, triggers, influences, contributory factors, and high-risk situations pertaining to crime, criminality, and victimology. Often, these research findings are conducted from a multidisciplinary perspective. A theoretical foundation is the core of criminology and of any criminological analysis or assessment (Herbig & Hesselink, 2009).

In South Africa, conventional criminology progressed from traditional criminology, and it entails, amongst others, the fields of forensic criminology and correctional criminology. The common functions and/or denominators of these two practices are:

1. a criminological assessment that is based on
2. a sound theoretical explanation, with
3. foci on the core assessment criteria (that is, causes, motives, contributory factors, modus operandi, and influences) that is vested within the discipline of criminology.

Therefore, relevant and recent research findings, criminological theory, and assessment form the basis of forensic (and conventional) criminology (Herbig & Hesselink, 2009).

8.3 History of criminology and its application in South Africa

South African criminology is said to hold an idiosyncratic history of political, ideological, and methodological internal strife about the origins and purpose of criminology. The existence of a fractured and divided criminology in South Africa is proffered by Artz and Moult (2012). These researchers claim that the history and parameters of South African criminology are contested, and that criminology is fraught with its own internal tensions and conflicts. The history of South African criminology has not been well documented – from apartheid years, to post-apartheid (with the nation-building projects) to contemporary South African criminology, upon which we have arrived 'in a less than methodical way' Artz and Moult (2012, p. 2). Artz and Moult put forward the following prominent confrontational 'politicised' questions that are linked to what is currently strived towards, namely a so-called 'respectable' South African criminology (however, these questions, to some extent, remain unanswered):

- **What precisely is a 'criminologist' in South African terms?**
- **Are our basics as a science psychological, legal or sociological?**
- **Do we side with theoretical structures and institutional engagements from the North or do we create our own Criminology – responsive to our unique context in the South?**
- **Are we reformists, scientists, explorers, theorists or progressive realists?**
- **Should we be working towards a more consistent and articulated (coherent) discipline?**
- **Are we satisfied with how it currently exists – multidisciplinary, diverse, but fractured – does it really matter?**
- **Where are our united and vigorous contributions in informing contemporary public debates on crime and criminal justice reform with our science?**
- **Who is 'in' and who is 'out' in Criminology in South Africa, and what does it mean to be 'in' or 'out' in our discipline?**
- **How does the South African criminological society enhance the exchange of debatable and contrary ideas, theories and methods?**
- **What about all the 'missed opportunities' in unfamiliar fields (i.e. the military and education sectors) of Criminology? (Artz & Moult, 2012, pp. 2–3, 5).**

8.4 Assessment as the core focus and function

The criminologist's core focus remains assessment of antisocial and criminal behaviour. This assessment is based on recent research findings and sound criminological theories that steer the assessment process. It is through this process that the criminologist determines relevant factors that explain criminal behaviour. The research findings and criminological theories highlight scientific-established:

- causes
- motives
- modi operandi
- triggers
- contributory factors and influences (biological childhood, social, environmental)
- personal, familial, and social background
- personality traits
- attitudes
- associations
- needs
- risk
- responsivity

- antecedents of the crime
- high-risk situations.

A relevant theoretical explanation is then proffered to explain this uniquely assessed behaviour (Herbig & Hesselink, 2009; Hesselink-Louw, 2004).

The basis of any offender assessment relies on the needs, risks, and responsivity (treatment response) principles that are practised worldwide. Andrews, Bonta, and Wormith (2011) point out that for effective analysis, correctional treatment, and rehabilitation, the risk–need–responsivity (RNR) model is the leading model for offender assessment and treatment. Andrews et al. (2011) argue the following three basic principles that are involved in the RNR model:

- The risk principle should match the level of programme intensity to offender's risk level, and intensive levels of treatment should be reserved for high-risk offenders, and lower intervention for low-risk offenders.
- The need principle targets criminogenic needs linked to the offender's criminal behaviour.
- The responsivity principle contests the style and mode of intervention to the offender's learning style and ability.

Any interventions based on the RNR principles are said to produce major reductions in recidivism (Andrews et al., 2011).

Needs and risk assessments rely on both static (unchangeable) and dynamic (changeable) factors. Examples of static factors are age, gender, criminal record, and childhood trauma and abuse. Dynamic factors include substance abuse, unemployment, and a low self-esteem. Needs assessment is a goal towards rehabilitation and normally guides therapists and correctional personnel in offender-specific rehabilitation efforts. Hesselink-Louw (2004) describes needs assessment as the identification, analysis, and evaluation of individualised offender needs for therapy and/or rehabilitation. Examples of such needs include:

- cognitive deficits
- education
- problem-solving skills
- substance abuse
- associations
- attitude.

Risk assessment refers to the evaluation, analysis, and pinpointing of behaviour that, if not adequately addressed, may result in reoffending and/or future dangerousness. Often, needs and risks overlap. For instance, some of the examples utilised above with the needs assessment may also be present with risk assessment, namely substance abuse, a low self-esteem, and associations. Other risks include:

- a history of violent and aggressive behaviour
- a criminal record
- criminal diversity
- child-victims
- antisocial personality or psychopathy (Campbell, French, & Gendreau, 2009; Hesselink-Louw, 2004; Lowenkamp, Lovins, & Latessa, 2009).

CHECK POINT

- Research findings are the core focus of criminological assessments because criminological theories and new crime trends (and behavioural aspects) are derived from empirical research findings.
- Recent and relevant research findings broaden the criminologist's understanding of the behaviour in question, and assist in the development of new theories and/or the testing of existing criminological theories.
- All criminological assessments should be conducted on a scientific basis. That is, the assessments should be founded on research findings and criminological theories. This foundation assists the criminologist to evaluate, determine, identify, examine, explain and assess the following: causes, contributory factors, influences, motives, modi operandi, personality traits, triggers, high-risk situations, and risks that are associated with crime, criminality, and victimology.
- Once the criminologist has assessed the behaviour in question, an applicable criminological theory (or a multidisciplinary theory that is related to the field of criminology) should be utilised to explain the crime, criminality, and victimology concerning the offender and the criminal event.

8.5 Established research indicators for offender needs, risk, and responsivity endeavours

Schwalbe, Macy, Day, and Fraser (2008) indicate numerous factors that play a role in (juvenile, youth, and adult) offending behaviour, such as the following:

- poor parental supervision
- problematic school attendance
- attendance at an alternative school
- school dropout
- problematic family relationships
- substance abuse
- peer delinquency
- school (learning and authority) problems
- truancy
- poor parental rule enforcement
- gang-involved peers association
- impulsivity
- no expression of remorse
- hostility toward others
- animal cruelty
- family criminality.

All these factors are, according to Schwalbe et al. (2008), robust predictors of recidivism. Regarding animal cruelty, Hensley, Tallichet, and Dutkiewicz (2012) mention a definite relationship between childhood animal cruelty and later adult violence (toward humans) and personal aggression. Research conducted by Hannon and DeFina (2012) explains that parental incarceration accelerates the relationship between adult imprisonment and subsequent juvenile arrest. Parental incarceration proves to have a dire effect on the following:

- poverty
- resource deprivation
- loss of family income
- loss of social networks
- family disruption
- temper tantrums in children as young as three
- anxiety, depression and physical aggression in older boys.

According to Hannon and DeFina (2012), between 13 per cent and 29 per cent of all serious juvenile delinquency (studied in their sample) could be linked to parental incarceration.

Olver, Stockdale, and Wormith (2009) found that the following are linked to the onset of criminality:

- antisocial attitudes
- antisocial associates
- antisocial personality
- a history of antisocial behaviour, leisure, and recreation.

These authors also hold that factors such as the following are important covariates associated with the origin of criminal behaviour:

- family and marital substance abuse
- employment problems
- education problems.

The following are other factors also mentioned by Olver et al. (2009):

- a criminal history, leisure and recreation activities
- deceitfulness
- manipulation
- callousness
- lack of remorse
- shallow emotions
- failure to accept responsibility
- irresponsibility
- stimulation seeking
- lack of short-term and long-term goals
- criminal versatility
- lack of support
- anger management problems
- negative attitudes
- low empathy skills associated with criminality.

In conjunction to this, Campbell et al. (2009) and MacDonald, Haviland, and Morral (2009) indicate that interpersonal conflict, accommodation problems (once released), a problematic self-esteem, and poor self-control are significant predictors for recidivism. They also mention low parental attachments, an early onset of violence and aggression, involvement in physical fights during childhood, and (further) institutional violence as key role players in future and further offending patterns.

Brezina and Topalli (2012, pp. 1042–1043) perceive self-efficacy as an important factor that shapes criminal thinking patterns, attitude, and ability. Self-efficacy is the belief one fosters to perform a task successfully. These researchers mention that self-efficacy to perform aggression (that is, the belief that it would be 'easy' to shove other kids out of the way) is strongly associated with aggressive behaviour in children – thus, such beliefs may promote crime and violence. One's own efficacy (or personal confidence) is linked to the level of determination and the lengths to which one will persist regardless of obstacles and failures. Efficacy beliefs also guide the meanings that offenders attach to punishment experiences, which are often changed into 'perceived opportunities to learn, improve, and become more effective at crime' (Brezani & Topalli, 2012, p. 1058).[1] Mental illness and related problems have also been found to be positively linked with violence, criminal behaviour, and reoffending (Mandracchia & Morgan, 2012).

Wareham and Boots (2012) researched individual-level predictors associated with violence. They state that there is a link to violence and the following factors:

- prior violence
- deviant peers
- mental health problems
- poor family relations
- neighbourhood decline (safety)
- peer rejection
- conflict.

Ward, Day, Bevc, Sun, and Rosenthal (2010) studied a sample of 378 adult male offenders' childhood, adolescent, and youth backgrounds. They found the following factors to be strong predictors of criminal behaviour:

- psychosocial problems
- substance use and abuse
- low level of social support
- maladaptive coping
- family separation
- marital conflict
- loss of a parent
- poor peer relations
- a broken home
- family transition
- familial abuse
- compromised economic circumstances
- changes in parental figures
- poor family management practices
- a positive familial attitude toward crime.

Van der Laan, Blom, and Kleemans (2009, pp. 428–435) distinguish between long-term risk factors and short-term risk factors associated with juvenile, adolescent, and youth violence and criminality. Table 8.1 depicts these risk factors.

Table 8.1 Long-term and short-term risk factors associated with juvenile, adolescent, and youth violence and criminality (Van der Laan, Blom, and Kleemans, 2009, pp. 428–435)[2]

Long-term risk factors	Short-term risk factors
Impulsivity Lack of social skills Inadequate parental supervision Poor school performance Limited prosocial behaviour High emotional problems High hyperactivity and attention problems Limited emotional support Weak school attachment	Little/no risk of being caught No tangible guardians Co-offenders Having used substances prior to the offence

Research worldwide seems to reiterate the relationship between alcohol use and abuse and involvement in physical violence (Maldonado-Molina, Reingle, & Jennings, 2011). Alcohol is a key instigator to causes of death; and alcohol use and abuse forecasts involvement in violence and criminal behaviour. Early users of alcohol (juveniles, adolescents, and youth) are thus more likely than non-alcohol users to be delinquent and use other drugs during adulthood (Maldonado-Molina et al., 2011). Other research (Browning & Erickson, 2009) has found that alcohol is the most frequently used substance among high-school students with the strongest link with violence. In turn, violent victimisation was found to be related to poor performance in school.

CRITICAL REFLECTION

South Africa has one of the world's highest death tolls due to road incidents that are associated with the use and abuse of alcohol, in terms of not only drunk driving, but also alcohol-related death incidents on the road. One such an incident was that of Sibusiso Langa, an engineer who killed (drove over) five joggers in October 2011 and injured another jogger while driving under the influence of alcohol (Versluis, 2013).

Access South African governmental reports, and/or search the internet for the most recent information on the road death toll that can be ascribed to alcohol abuse in South Africa. Additionally, uncover another media case similar to Sibusiso Langa's mentioned above.

8.6 Correctional criminology

Criminologists have much to offer to the South African Department of Correctional Services (DCS) and should be central to any offender assessment and rehabilitation ventures. Criminologists are skilled in aspects relating to the following:

- crime
- offending behaviour
- causes, motives, and triggers of criminality
- high-risk situations

2 Copyright © 2009 SAGE Publications. Reprinted by permission of SAGE Publications.

- sound scientific theories to explain the behaviour in question (Herbig & Hesselink, 2012; Hesselink-Louw, 2004).

Correctional criminology focuses mainly on expert criminological needs assessments and risk assessments of offenders. Here, criminologists ascertain unique offender needs and risks criteria derived from:

- the offender's crime (causes, motives, triggers, and high-risk situations)
- offending patterns (that is, history of violent and aggressive behaviour and a criminal record) and
- personality traits (that is, proviolent and/or procriminal attitudes)

for:

- treatment (correctional therapy)
- programme allocation
- offender management purposes
- preparole assistance (risk indication for future dangerousness and/or reoffending) (Hesselink & Herbig, 2010; Hesselink-Louw, 2004).

Many criminologists in South Africa practise correctional criminology (Hesselink, in Holtzhausen, 2012). Professional criminological work is rendered in preparole criminological assessments for the DCS (in Gauteng and the Western Cape), criminological assessments are conducted on awaiting trial and sentenced juveniles, expert assistance is given regarding rape in correctional centres, and assistance is provided in programme delivery for juvenile offenders. Other criminologists focus on female offenders with the aim of assessing female offenders from a gender-sensitive, cultural (Africanised), and criminological perspective. Other criminologists also offer experienced criminological skills in offender needs and risk assessments for the DCS and/or Lawyers for Human Rights (LHR).

All aforementioned criminological assessments are based on a sound understanding and utilisation of relevant criminological theories, in order to assist, understand, identify, evaluate, and explain crime and criminality from a criminological perspective. This remains criminologists' unique scientific contribution in their criminological analyses.

8.7 Criminological theory and practice

Criminological theory is an important assessment and analysis tool that underpins a criminological report – whether for court (forensic) or for correctional criminological assessments. Criminologists assess criminal behaviour in the light of selected, applicable, and relevant theories in order to explain criminal behaviour. However, criminologists should not overwhelm the court or the reader with copious theories; they should, rather, select the most suitable theory to expound the criminality to the reader (Hesselink-Louw, 2004; Hesselink, in Holtzhausen, 2012). For instance, in some cases, violent behaviour can be adequately explained by the general strain theory (GST). This theory focuses on research findings pertaining to risk and protective factors for violent behaviour. The following can be explained by strains such as abuse and absenteeism of a parental figure that were endured by the offender:

- disruptive behaviours (for example conflict, anger and aggression)
- personal experiences (for example child abuse and direct exposure to violence)
- certain personality traits (for example being deceitful and cunning behaviour)

- certain pathways (for example minor misdemeanours, such a stealing money from a parent's purse, that progress to shoplifting) (Muntingh & Gould, 2010; Siegel, 2010).

Another example of a theoretical explanation applicable to violent offending is the social learning theory. This theory explains criminality as a result of early, meaningful, and persistent exposure to negative, antisocial, and/or criminal role models. The unbecoming and criminal behaviour is learned (and subsequently imitated) from significant others such as parents, siblings, community role models, and peers. The social learning theory takes into account learned behaviour through differential association, personal observations, personal experiences, and the level of tolerance of the person who is learning the criminal or antisocial behaviour (Chan, Heide, & Beauregard, 2011).

Criminological theories are also important in explaining victimisation in victim impact statements. For example, in cases of domestic violence and family violence, victimisation can be explained by the control balance theory. This theory outlines the imbalance of control applied and received. A young man who grew up in a household characterised by a violent and abusive father might divert to the killing of his father in order to express his helplessness, hopelessness, trauma, and lack of power and control endured over years of physical and emotional abuse. The act of killing restores the control-balance which the young man experienced and received in surplus from his abusive father (Nobles & Fox, 2013).

The following case study illustrates the foci of a criminological assessment for preparole purposes, and it exposes the reader to certain dynamics associated with the practice of criminological assessments.

CASE STUDY: Criminological preparole report indicators

James is a 32-year-old, white male offender (first offender), who received a life sentence for murder and attempted murder. He is a devoted Christian, and he describes his sexuality as being heterosexually oriented. James is one of three siblings. He has two stepbrothers – his biological parents were divorced when he was five years old.

Crime analysis

At the age of 20, James was found guilty of the murder of his father (then aged 42 years). He 'contracted' three other co-accused to kill his father for R140 000. James was also found guilty of attempted murder of his stepmother, who survived the attack.

James says that one evening he mentioned to a friend and co-worker that he wanted to kill his parents because of his dire home circumstances. The friend then offered assistance to kill his parents. The discussions got 'intense and deep and I even drew a map of the house, points of entry and exits.' During the night of the crimes, the offender did not lock the garage door (as he used to do, and as arranged with his co-accused); the offender went out for the evening and when he returned hours later his father had been killed and his stepmother was still alive.

At the time of his murder, the victim (James's father) owned a complex with a bakery, a take-away restaurant, and chalets (attached to the centre) – thus, he was a very wealthy businessman. The offender says he 'thought the business insurance would pay out'. James's co-accused used a butcher's knife to murder his father (whose throat was cut, and who received three stab wounds to his chest and two stab wounds on his arms). James himself was never at the murder scene, and he did not participate in the killing of his father, or the attempted murder of his stepmother. James's stepmother endured two stab wounds to her chest and back.

Prior to these crimes, James was 'fired as a bartender' because he 'stole R80 out of the till'. He also took money from his stepmother and father at times, without asking permission to do so.

Childhood years

James cites his stepmother as the reason for his parents' divorce; apparently his father had an affair with his stepmother while still married to his mother. Even though James's mother received custody of James, he went to live with his father and stepmother because, according to him, his mother was just 'too wild, she partied too much, ... drinking, ... unemployed at times, emotionally unstable, very judgemental, cannot reason with her, and many relationships'. James clearly did not have a positive bond or relationship with his biological mother, as he states that she 'did not even attend my court case on the last day – she did not care.' The offender could not recall her age or birth date, or whether she had completed Grade 12 or not.

James's deceased father completed Grade 11 and obtained various Estate Agent and Insurance diplomas. Neither James's father nor biological mother engaged in criminality, and they did not have criminal records. James's father had no history of substance abuse, although his biological mother abused alcohol regularly.

James states that he has no recollection of his biological parents 'being together'; furthermore, he reports that whenever he visited his mother, she bad-mouthed his father, calling him names such as 'a traitor' and 'rubbish'. He did not get along with his stepmother because he blamed her for the break-up of his parents' marriage. James experienced mixed feelings towards his stepmother. On the one hand, he resented her for abusing him, but, on the other, he acknowledged that his stepmother 'did a lot for me, she cared for me, trying to do the best for me, she even enrolled me at Grey College, ... fussing over me.' This created deep cynicism about his stepmother. He really did not like her as a person, and he struggled to cope with the idea that she was his stepmother.

James remembers severe hostility and conflict at home – directed at him and his father. He recalls enduring constant physical and emotional abuse from his stepmother, especially when his father was not around. He says his stepmother used to 'slap, hit and punch my father too; he did nothing – I think he was used to it.' According to James, his stepmother used to take her frustrations out on him – 'shouting at me, slapping, throwing, and tugging me around the house – she even threw a knife at me once – it got stuck on the kitchen door.' He mentions that before his stepbrothers were born, his father 'stood up' for him, taking his side, and comforting him at night, but this changed after his stepbrothers were born. During this time, James wrote many letters to his biological mother, pleading with her 'to come and take me away, to rescue me', but his stepmother confiscated all the letters and told him that his biological mother was not interested in him any more. This angered him more and left him devastated. James said he always had a hidden hope that his mother 'will come and take me away – rescue me from my stepmother'. The offender maintains that whenever he inquired about his mother, his stepmother would get 'very mad and abuse me ... shouting that I am ungrateful, worthless, and then she would beat me up.' She used to belittle him often, and he says he thinks his stepmother 'wanted to erase all memories of his mother'.

According to the offender, there were times when his father threatened to divorce his stepmother (he overheard him shouting this to her during arguments), but he thinks his father 'never had the guts to do it'. He notes that his father told him once that he thought it would be better for him if he lived with his uncle (due to all the conflict and violence at home), but this never happened. According to the offender, his father had extramarital affairs while married to his stepmother, and, prior to his death, an affair with an Indian woman.

James only once stood up to his stepmother – that was when he was 17 or 18 years old, when he came home drunk after partying with his friends in the afternoon. His stepmother 'went ballistic', and he restrained her when she wanted to slap him; however, he claims that he never lifted a hand against her.

Even though James did not receive support from his father and biological mother, his father's brother (his uncle) supported him (and believed in him) throughout his life – since his parents' divorce, while he was living with his father and stepmother, during his arrest, and during his current imprisonment. His uncle was aware of all the abuse and arguments between James and his stepmother, as he testified about this in court. James recollects visiting his uncle often for weekends while living with his father and stepmother, and during such visits his uncle would arrange contact for James with his mother (without his father and stepmother's knowledge). He remembers two occasions when he was about seven or eight years old. The first memory was at a service station, where there was a Wimpy restaurant, and his mother bought him ice cream, spoke to him, and touched him. The second incident was when his mother took him to CNA to buy a model aeroplane. The only time his mother ever visited him at home was one afternoon after school, when his stepmother allowed her into the house; she visited for a while and she 'promised to stay in contact ... which she did not do.' Later, he believed his mother to be dead, because he never heard of her again, until his arrest, when she came to see him (once) while he was awaiting trial (which lasted for a year and seven months).

At the age of six to seven years, James tried to run away from home – he stayed for two nights at the house of friends who took him home again. This behaviour was repeated during Grade 6, when he cycled away from home – apparently his father caught up with him some 40 kilometres out of town, and took him back home.

School years

The offender mentions that he was a 'prefect' (a school leader) during his primary school years. When asked about his primary school years, the offender said he used to stutter a lot and he was 'a very nervous boy'.

James recalls forging a cheque from his father during grade eight or nine – he was caught and received a severe hiding from his father. He also mentions that he stole cigarettes and money from his father during this period, and that he pawned a 'one dollar' note of his father's.

During high school years, James failed a subject, and he ascribes this to being 'rebellious and irresponsible at the time'. He attended a hostel, which he enjoyed because it offered him 'freedom from the house'. He says he did well at sports, especially in soccer, but he stopped playing 'to spite my stepmother' – as it is her favourite sport. James seemed to get on well with a male teacher, with whom he used to go swimming in the afternoons, but he mentions that his parents became 'suspicious about our relationship'. According to the offender, the teacher was only 'a father figure' to him. Since his incarceration, this teacher has been very supportive – he provided the offender with a computer and, on occasion, with financial support.

During Grade 11, James started smoking (cigarettes – 'if I could get hold of it and sometimes dagga') with his friends. Also, during Grade 11, the offender received a warning when he was found with pornographic material (a magazine) in his possession. Then the same year, James was expelled from school, because he and another learner 'slipped into the girls' hostel at night and fondled (sexually) the girls (who shared a room)'. They were caught and expelled from school. This, according to the offender, was not his first visit to the girls' hostel at night.

James claims that he never bullied anyone at school, and he states that he once got involved in a physical fight (during Grade 11), apparently over a girl. The fight occurred during a school break. During his matric year, 'everything went well', according to James, with no incidents or truancy.

When asked about cruelty to animals, the offender replied, 'Yes, but never in a conscious way.' He explains that when he was drunk he would kick the dogs, and that he at times enjoyed throwing darts at the dogs. He says he once strangled a dog, but was stopped by a girlfriend he was seeing at the time. This 'freaked her out, and she ended the relationship.'

Substance use and abuse

As is evident, James started using and abusing alcohol and dagga at an early age. He notes that he 'smoked' more than he drank alcohol. He says his father and stepmother knew about this, but did nothing about it, as he never smoked or drank alcohol in their presence. Apparently he quit smoking dagga when he was sentenced to prison.

Contact while in prison

Regarding visits in prison, James states that his uncle and his stepmother's parents (when they were still alive and in their 80s) visited him on a regular basis. The school teacher (mentioned above) also has contact with the offender.

Another regular visitor, and sound support structure for the offender, is a social worker. James met this social worker after being incarcerated (at the first prison – for his current sentence – he has been shifted to three other prisons since then). The social worker is more than 20 years older than James, and she was 'requested to resign' (according to the offender), because she provided him with special favours such as 'sweets, yoghurt and keratin (a supplement for muscles)' while on duty. James says the prison staff and authorities became suspicious because the social worker was 'too friendly' with him. After some questioning, the offender admitted that they 'kissed only three times in her office, but nothing else/more happened.' The social worker still supports him (for more than eight years now), and as has been mentioned, she keeps regular contact with him (through letters, telephone calls, and actual visits), provides him with money to use in prison, and paid for his studies. The social worker's 'forced resignation' was confirmed by the deputy head of the prison where this occurred.

Since his arrest, James has had no contact with his stepbrothers, even though he wrote a letter to his eldest stepbrother for his twenty-first birthday, 'apologising' for what he did. He also wrote a letter to his stepmother in 2010, but she never replied. His social worker friend made contact with his stepmother on Facebook, and James's stepmother expressed the desire not to have contact with James.

The offender mentions that he made numerous attempts to re-establish contact with his biological mother, and he contacted her from prison on numerous occasions. Apparently his mother suffers from arthritis, and, according to the offender, she remarried in 2007.

Intimate personal relationships

When asked about his feelings for his social worker friend, James said that in the beginning he was sexually attracted to her and that he really loved her. He reiterates that it is 'not like before anymore' – as in the beginning there was a lot of 'fire and passion'. He admits that it was easy to charm her. When some correctional officials (at the prison where he is now housed) were questioned, they confirmed that the offender and the social worker hold hands and kiss during visits, so much so that they cautioned them about their behaviour during visiting times.

James says his uncle used to 'worry about my connection with her, but I don't think anymore ... he realised she really loves me and that she supports me.' He mentions that there is little contact between the social worker and his uncle (and his wife) because 'they do not approve of her.'

Gang involvement

While incarcerated, the offender never joined a gang, and he was not involved in any other misconduct (besides his 'acquaintance' with the social worker at the first prison being recorded on his institutional file). The offender mentions that one man 'shielded' him from the gangs, and in return he requested the offender to perform oral sex on him. This occurred 'only three to four times'. James says while he performed oral sex on the fellow inmate, he 'thought about women – it made it easier.' According to James, this fellow inmate was in love with him, but he never felt the same way towards the man.

Education

While incarcerated, the offender completed two diplomas in theology, a ministry degree (not from an accredited institution in South Africa), and certificates in biblical counselling, addictions, and healing. James also completed N4 to N6 – electrical engineering (paid for by the social worker).

James attended the following correctional rehabilitation programmes:

- Time management
- Life skills
- Communication skills
- HIV/Aids
- Interpersonal relationships
- Anger and conflict management
- Drug addiction.

When asked what value these programmes had for him, James said they taught him about 'stress, parenting skills, assertiveness, self-respect, bullying behaviour, telephone skills, how to write a letter, the importance of work, gender and violence, healthy relationships, and taking action for change'.

Leisure and recreation

James enjoys playing soccer at the prison. He also participates in volleyball, touch rugby, cricket, softball, and chess.

Adaptation in prison

Incarceration was initially a shock to the offender – especially while he was awaiting trial. He mentions being very traumatised, and being teased and bullied during this time due to uncontrollable eye and lip twitching (which still occurred during the assessment).

Emotional well-being

The offender admits that it was very easy for him to manipulate other people (that is, correctional personnel). This is also evident with his intimate relationship with the social worker. The offender notes that, prior to the crime, and at the time of the crime, 'I had a lot of anger, rage and hatred in me' – this, he says, commenced at the age of five and escalated during his high school years. He blamed his stepmother and his father (who could not or did not protect him) for all his unhappiness. The offender states that he was very isolated in high school, did not have many friends, and hardly communicated with his parents as he 'shut them out'. Reflecting on his school years, the offender says he wanted to 'be in, to be accepted, to show off, to be part of the group ... the in-boys; ... I was lost that time, and I think I rebelled.'

James admits that during his childhood, if he 'was pushed hard and far enough' he could get very angry, violent, and aggressive. During such a rage, he once 'grabbed a friend at the throat' during an argument.

James says he fears to 'face' his stepmother again, because she 'had a hold over me as a child, but I know I need to face her some time.' It is clear that James's upbringing (or lack thereof) and his childhood exposure and experiences shaped his personality make-up and subsequent insecurities.

Risk indicators for the parole board

James attended many correctional rehabilitation programmes and therapy sessions with three correctional social workers (not including his social worker friend at the fist prison where he was incarcerated).

The following risk factors (although not exhaustive) should be highlighted to the parole board:

- an early onset of antisocial and truant behaviour (running away, stealing, lying, and smoking)
- history of violent and aggressive behaviour (cruelty to animals, involvement in physical fights, and acts of violence and aggression)
- history of substance abuse
- lack of respect for authority figures and the law
- severe manipulation skills
- unresolved childhood trauma and feelings that may lead to further criminality if not adequately addressed: feelings of distress, anxiety, helplessness and hopelessness; a need for love, attention, recognition, and acknowledgement, lacks a sense of belonging; rejection; a lack of positive non-violent role models; a lack of trust in adults; abandonment; lack of security and protection; resentment; revenge; poor parent–child bonds and attachments; inappropriate sexual stimulation; exposure to domestic violence; negative peer association; proviolent attitude and thinking patterns; susceptibility to negative influences; no parental support; and isolation
- lack of respect for self and others
- lack of personal boundaries for self and others
- poor family relationships and familial support structure
- poor and superficial intimate personal relationships
- low self-esteem
- history of poor or limited self-management strategies
- post-traumatic stress disorder (stemming from childhood through to adulthood experiences)
- emotionally removed or numbed – hence, the offender's superficial and unrealistic intimate emotional relationships
- lack of self-identity and sense of self (no self-worth) due to poor parental bonds and attachments
- limited coping mechanisms for stressful situations
- limited conflict-resolution skills or ability.

It needs to be stated that the offender displayed good insight and understanding into his own behaviour – especially the causes and triggers of his behaviour. He understands the damage and harm that he has caused out of sheer resentment, revenge, and financial greed.

According to the general strain theory (GST), there is a direct link between strain and delinquency (Francis, 2014). The GST stipulates that specific strains or stressors during childhood may result in criminal behaviour. These strains and stressors involve a variety of negative emotions – such as anger, depression, powerlessness, aggression, anxiety, and rage – which then in turn spill over in criminal behaviour (Francis, 2014). When James's involvement in crime is explained, the GST might be useful to link James's personal background, experiences, and low self-control with his criminal behaviour (Francis, 2014).

James was exposed to a childhood that can be characterised by the following:
- abuse
- rejection
- frustration
- distrust
- parental separation
- a lack of love
- a lack of protection
- a lack of personal safety and security
- difficulties at school
- parental and parent-child animosity and conflict.

James's subjection to these negative emotions (and experiences) resulted in maladaptive coping strategies and outcomes. This was evident in James's involvement in substance abuse, aggressive delinquency (fighting), and cruelty to animals – all expressions and outlets of his powerlessness, feelings of anger and rage, and low self-control. These unaddressed and unresolved negative and maladaptive emotions, coping strategies, and personality traits contributed to James's involvement in criminal behaviour (Francis, 2014).

8.8 Forensic criminology

Criminological presentence evaluation reports depict the offender as an individual to the court. Criminological foci include:
- the causes
- motives
- modi operandi
- crime influences
- socialisation processes
- meanings of events and people
- the criminal event itself
- antecedents to the crime.

The criminologist should also assess the perpetrator's:
- personality make-up
- functioning
- meaning of life
- upbringing
- schooling
- education
- intimate personal relationships
- personal achievements.

All of the aforementioned factors are then taken into account by the court for mitigating and aggravating purposes to conclude to an individualised and appropriate sentence for the offender (or the accused). Lastly, a relevant and applicable criminological explanation and relevant (and recent) research findings of the behaviour are also offered in court by the criminologist (Hesselink-Louw, 2004).

In this regard, Figure 8.1 (see section 8.2.4) can be read to explain the important role of criminological theory and research findings in preparing a presentence evaluation report. Theory and practical application play pivotal roles in a criminological presentence evaluation report or a victim impact statement. It is this very factor that distinguishes a criminological report from other behavioural scientists' (or therapists') reports. The other unique contribution of the criminologist is the assessment of the crime, criminality, and victimology in its totality, where a scientific outlay is given on the aetiology, antecedents, precursors, influences, motives, modi operandi, high-risk situations, and risks of the offenders (or the accused). The criminologist's knowledge of criminological theories and recent research findings on the behaviour in question provides a unique explanation of the crime, and underlines the dynamics and uniqueness of each case.

Until 2009, the late Dr Irma Labuschagne was the prominent criminologist utilised in South African courts. Labuschagne was one the pioneers of forensic criminology in South Africa. From the 1980s up to 2009, Labuschagne compiled over 1 000 criminological presentence evaluation reports for the legal courts in South Africa (Hesselink-Louw, 2004).

Since Labuschagne's entry into forensic criminology, various other criminologists have entered this practice; however, there is still a need for improved participation of criminologists in the courts (Bezuidenhout, 2011).

8.9 Criminological victim impact reports/statements

According to Bezuidenhout (2011), a victim impact statement includes an individualised objective view representative of the victim to the court regarding the impact of the crime on the victim. The experience and consequences of the crime for the victim, indirect victims (that is, family and friends) and the society are all included. Of importance is the victim's reaction (that is, post-traumatic stress symptoms) to the crime. A victim impact statement can also be utilised by the parole boards in South Africa to outline the circumstances of the crime and the effect thereof on the victim, indirect victims, and society – thus shedding more light on the effect of the crime on the victim during the parole consideration process and assisting parole boards to make informed decisions (Jones, 2013).

The criminologist elaborates on the following:

- emotional, physical and psychological harm, injury and/or loss experienced by the victim
- the victim–offender relationship
- the specific needs and rights of the victim
- the victim's opinion on the type of punishment for the offender.

In domestic violence cases, where the perpetrator is the only breadwinner, the victim often does not want the offender to be removed from society, but to remain in society to continue with financial support to the family. This is often considered for mitigating or aggravating purposes related to the offender's sentence.

As with correctional profiling and court work (forensic criminology), the basis of a criminological victim impact statement comprises assessment – in this instance – assessment of the victim in all facets.

CRITICAL REFLECTION

Mr D has been in the service of the South African Police Services (SAPS) for the past 27 years. He was one of the police members involved in two incidents of violent unrest and strikes where one person was killed while another person was seriously injured. Mr D has been accused of the misuse of his power, the use of excessive force, murder, and attempted murder. Imagine that, as a criminologist, you have been requested to compile a criminological report for presentence and victim impact purposes.

Your focus for the presentence report should include, although not be limited to, Mr D's:

- childhood upbringing
- personal achievements
- conflict with the law
- career path and promotions within SAPS
- SAPS institutional misconduct or infringements
- substance abuse
- history of (and/or tendency toward) violent and aggressive behaviour
- proviolent attitudes
- personality traits pertaining to violent and aggressive behaviour (and/or the lack thereof)
- SAPS training (skills, attitude and readiness to use force)
- SAPS support structure or the lack hereof within the force
- personal and familial relationships
- ability to cope in dangerous, threatening and volatile situations
- work frustrations
- personal tolerance level
- coping mechanisms (with stress, under pressure, violence or the threat of violence)
- behavioural triggers
- personal and familial support structure
- work circumstances (for example dealing with violence on an everyday basis)
- post-traumatic stress symptoms linked with being in the employ of SAPS
- the impact of the high rate of crime in South Africa on Mr D and his functionality within SAPS and in society.

The foci for the victim impact statement should include, although not limited to:

- society's frustration with and mistrust of the police
- behavioural expectations of SAPS
- SAPS's image (for example corruption, ill-discipline, and involvement in crime)
- incidents of SAPS misuse of power and brutality, and the history hereof
- the role and behaviour of the crowd (the strikers or in unrest situations)
- the role and behaviour of SAPS's members during unrest and violent strikes
- SAPS and the obligation to maintain law and order, to curb crime, and to protect society
- the loss of life
- and harm caused and the impact hereof (in terms of fear, frustration, mistrust, loss of income, loss of a loved one, and other emotional or physical consequences).

The victim impact statement in the case study below demonstrates the foci of a criminological assessment, and it illustrates important determinants to take into account when compiling a victim impact statement.

CASE STUDY: A victim impact statement

This case study is based on the following source: Ex-wife of 'Modimolle Monster' tells of torture, 2012. (The case of the so-called 'Modimolle Monster' was discussed in Chapter 2.)

Ina Bonnette

WARNING: Offensive language and harrowing testimony

Conrad Bonnette was killed within earshot of his mother. Despite pleading for mercy, he was still killed. 'This contributed to Ina Bonnette's trauma.' The State's last witness was Dr Susanna Gräbe, an expert on sexual violence. Gräbe gave her expert opinion in the field as she did not examine the victim, Ina Bonnette. She testified that between 10 and 30 per cent of rape victims did not sustain injuries to their genitals. 'In most cases rape victims have more physical injuries than genital injuries.'

The former wife of 'Modimolle monster' Johan Kotze on Tuesday told the High Court in Pretoria how Kotze tortured her while telling her he loved her. Ina Bonnette, who at times had to wipe away tears, described during cross-examination what she endured at Kotze's hands and how his three co-accused raped her.

Bonnette said she left Kotze in 2011, but twice visited his house in Modimolle to fetch her belongings. She went to his house again on January 3 after he phoned and said there was still a box with her things. After giving her a glass of water and talking to her outside, he told her to go in. When she walked into the darkened room, Kotze pulled a towel over her head and threw her onto the bed. When she saw there were three black men in the room, she tried to get up and started kicking and screaming. Kotze sat on her and shouted for two of the men to help him. They tied Bonnette's hands to ropes already fastened to the window and bed. Her mouth was taped shut so tightly she could hardly breathe.

'He kept on throwing insults. He said today you're going to feel what its like to be fucked by k****rs.' He said he had to sell his farm in Bloemfontein for a whore. 'He said I, my father and Conrad had belittled him. The more I shook my head to show that it was not true the more he assaulted me.' Sithole helped Kotze remove her pants. Kotze started hitting, punching, and pinching her. 'The three others were there the whole time and I begged them with my eyes to help me,' she said.

Bonnette described in detail how Kotze returned to a cupboard several times for objects to torture her. 'At one stage he took pliers out of his pocket and twisted my nipple. I had implants in my breasts but it was very, very bad. It was unbearable,' she said. Kotze tortured her further with pliers and a long silver object, cut off her other nipple, pushed a rifle against her head, and threatened to shoot her. Bonnette said the other three accused took turns to rape her after Kotze told them they could now feel what it was like to have sex with a white woman. 'Then he came to lie next to me and told me over and over how much he loved me and how I had ruined his life.' He pushed the firearm against my head and said when my child arrived he was going to bring him into the room and force him to have sex with me. 'If that did not work, he would shoot him.'

After Kotze told the others to leave and dressed Bonnette, she heard her son's motorbike. '... I heard him walking down the passage. Then I heard my child saying "No uncle, please don't," and then a shot. Then again "No uncle, please don't," and a shot, and another shot.' After it was quiet for a long time, someone came to free Bonnette, and she found her son dead in the next room. 'I called out

"Boeta, Boeta," but he did not react ... I saw a bullet wound on his knee and in front on his shirt ... I realised Conrad was dead and I jumped up and screamed, we have to get out of here. 'If Kotze comes back, he will kill all of us.' 'I was so confused ... I just kept on shouting we must get out.'

Bonnette afterwards spent almost eight days in hospital, had to undergo a number of operations, and was given antiretroviral medication.

Bonnette, who was in court on Wednesday, started crying as the sentence was read out. She was supported by family and friends. 'A person just has to stand strong,' she said after the sentencing.

She urged victims of abuse to report the crime and ensure they followed the right channels. 'Jesus put each of us on this earth for a purpose, and that purpose is not to abuse,' Bonnette said.

'Justice has been done. [Kotze] deserves his sentence.' She said the sentencing marked the start of a new phase of her life. 'Time will heal the humiliation, but the hurt will never go away.' She said she would go to her son's grave and have a long talk with him afterwards. 'And I can tell him: "My son, justice has prevailed".'

Women, Children and People with Disabilities Minister Lulu Xingwana welcomed the sentence. 'Justice has been done,' she said, holding Bonnette's hand. 'We hope that this sentence will bring closure and peace to [Bonnette] and her family to know that those who have violated her and murdered her son are finally behind bars,' Xingwana said. 'We hope the monster and his co-accused will rot in jail.' After the sentence was handed down, family members of Kotze's co-accused cried. One woman started wailing (Ex-wife of 'Modimolle Monster' tells of torture, 2012).[3]

A victim impact report was handed in at court. Table 8.2 highlights criminological inputs and foci for a victim impact statement.

Table 8.2 Criminological foci for a victim impact statement

Personal interpretation of partner's actions and decisions	Substance use and abuse	History of threats of violence
The victim–offender relationship	Relationship dynamics such as domestic violence, discord, and conflict	Parent–stepchild bonds
Power and control issues	Self-esteem within the relationships	Triggers and antecedents for behaviour
Mutual friends	Trust	Possible risk prediction for dangerousness while still living together
The victim's perception of the offender's motives for behaviour	Familial and relationship stress	Individual coping mechanisms, causes for behaviour (from the victim's perspective)
Victim and offender personality traits	Decisionmaking processes in the relationship	Correlating research findings and a theoretical explanation relating to the victims' feelings and experiences
	Relationship stressors	

3 Reprinted by permission of SAPA.

8.10 Criminological profiling

According to Labuschagne (2009), criminological profiling encompasses detailed criminological foci on the following:

- the causes and motives of crime
- identification of the perpetrator
- identification of the social, criminal and specific behaviours in context
- the roles of victims and bystanders
- the victim–offender relationship
- the physical and social contexts in which the crime occurred.

Labuschagne (2009) offers a much wider criminological perspective on profiling that holistically incorporates the criminal event. In this regard, Labuschagne notes that the following should be taken into consideration:

- the antecedents to the event, interactive environmental and situational
- the event (crime) itself
- interaction between the role players and how this influences the outcome of the crime
- the aftermath (reporting to the police and their response)
- the harm caused to the victim
- the correctional process
- long-term consequences (such a the public's reaction to the event)
- the amendment of law (Labuschagne, 2009).

Labuschagne cautions that profiling as a practice does not on its own provide the specific identity of the perpetrator. Rather, 'it merely suggests the type of person that might have committed the crime under investigation'; therefore, a criminologist may never generalise, because human nature is complex and multifaceted, and each person has his or her own 'personality make-up' (Labuschagne, 2009, p. 32).[4]

Devery (2010) notes that profiling has never been a scientific process, rather a process that is based on common sense intuitions and faulty theoretical assumptions. Devery declares that in practice this 'skill' consists 'of little more than educated guesses and wishful thinking' with evidence that profiling has even disrupted investigations that resulted in serious miscarriages of justice (2010, p. 393).[5] The fundamental idea of profiling is to predict characteristics of the unknown perpetrator(s) from characteristics of the offence(s) and the victims(s). In this regard, Devery (2010) conceives that profiling relates to the practice of techniques and approaches (developed over the years) to determine the probable traits of a crime's perpetrator by analysing the details of the crime itself. However, the majority of profiling practices portrayed in the media suggest that profiling is a mysterious skill, thus the process depicts an art and not a science.

Criminological profiling is based on empirical research findings and fundamental criminological theories that explain the possible criminality traits, causes, motives, modi operandi, triggers, and high-risk situations attributed to the perpetrator. A criminological profile should rather exclude than include personality traits, and focus on unique, individualised offender-specific and offence-specific characteristics (Hesselink-Louw & Joubert, 2003).

---

4 Reprinted by permission of the Editor: *South African Crime Quarterly*.

5 Copyright © 2010 by SAGE Publications. Reprinted by permission of SAGE Publications.

8.11 Academic practical-oriented endeavours

The notion to match theory to practice and engage honours students is not a new one for criminology in South Africa. The author is aware of three universities that have instigated community engagement practices with their Criminology Honours students.

The Department of Criminology at the University of the Free State (UFS) engages the Criminology Honours students in on-site community service learning that combines criminological theory with practice. Students visit the Bloemfontein Secure Care Centre – a juvenile detention centre that accommodates children between the ages of 14 and 17 years who are awaiting trial for offences such as murder, attempted murder, assault (grievous bodily harm – GBH), robbery, armed robbery, housebreaking and theft, and 'children who are awaiting placement in a reform school' (Coetzee & Phillips, 2012, pp. 16–18). The Criminology Honours students assist with the 'Take a Lead in Life' Programme that addresses problem areas in the children's lives, and the students learn to link theory with practice – a necessary skill in practice in criminology. This programme and practical engagement tie in with one of the department's Criminology Honours modules, Juvenile Delinquency, and hence equip the students with the theoretical knowledge and practical skills to practise in criminology (Coetzee & Phillips, 2012).

Since 2009, the Department of Criminology and Security Science at the University of South Africa (Unisa) has been involved with the DCS in offender assessment practices at various correctional centres in South Africa (Herbig & Hesselink, 2012). This endeavour was advocated and initiated by Hesselink, who worked as a Criminologist within the DCS and the Mangaung Private Maximum Correctional Centre (Bloemfontein). The University of Pretoria's Department of Social Work and Criminology has also been drawn into this project; Criminology Honours students are annually oriented on offender assessment practices. This community engagement offers practical exposure to correctional criminology; students voluntarily participate in offender assessments at correctional centres near their residential areas, which affords them the opportunity to link theory with practice. This practical learning project also forms part of a Criminology Honours module, Criminological Evaluation and Assessment (which focuses on forensic and correctional criminology in practice) at the Department of Criminology and Security Science at Unisa.

CRITICAL REFLECTION

It is clear from this chapter that criminology has much to offer to practice – to the courts and to corrections.

Access the internet and research the use of criminology students (whether within the criminal justice system or private sector), especially in environments and situations where they are required to apply theory to practice.

Conclusion

Criminology in South Africa has expanded from a traditionally practised discipline known for its theory development and policy applications to a contemporary science. South African criminologists are no longer mere theorists and philosophers. Vital criminological contributions are made within the criminal justice sector. Criminological assessments in court and within corrections have proved to be valuable practices to understand the offender's behaviour and to explain the crime, criminality, and victimology from a criminological scientific stance.

This chapter outlined correctional and forensic criminology as important practical fields within the science of criminology. Adjacent to these two specialisation fields, victim impact reports, criminological profiling, and practical student involvement were illustrated. This chapter contributes to the practical sphere of the criminal justice system, where the criminologists' roles, function, scope, and contributions cannot be nullified.

Critical thinking questions

1. Access websites on Johan Kotzé and Ina Bonnette, and see what factors from a criminological perspective you can include in a victim impact report.
2. What focus points are important for a criminologist pertaining to criminological profiling? Access the article published by Hesselink and Joubert (2003), as cited in the References list, which is related to these focus points.
3. What are the core functions and foci of correctional criminology and forensic criminology?
4. Do you know of any other practically oriented projects in South Africa where criminology students are involved to gain practical first-hand experience of and exposure to the field, science, and practice of criminology?

References

Andrews, D. A., Bonta, J., & Wormith, J. S. (2011). The risk-need-responsivity (RNR) model: does adding the good lives model contribute to effective crime prevention? *Criminal Justice and Behavior, 38*(7), 735–755.

Artz, L., & Moult, K. (2012). Gnawing at the edges of criminology: working outside/in. *Acta Criminologica*, CRIMSA 2011 Conference Special Edition No. 1, 2012, 1–15.

Bezuidenhout, C. (2011). *A southern African perspective on fundamental criminology*. Cape Town: Heinemann, Pearson Education South Africa.

Brezina, T., & Topalli, V. (2012). Criminal self-efficacy: exploring the correlates and consequences of a 'successful criminal' identity. *Criminal Justice and Behavior, 39*(8), 1042–1062.

Browning, S., & Erickson, P. (2009). Neighborhood disadvantage, alcohol use, and violent victimization. *Youth Violence and Juvenile Justice, 7*(4), 331–349.

Campbell, M. A., French, S., & Gendreau, P. (2009). The prediction of violence in adult offenders: a meta-analytic comparison of instruments and methods of assessment. *Criminal Justice and Behavior, 36*(6), 567–590.

Chan, H. C., Heide, K. M., & Beauregard, E. (2011). What propels sexual murderers: a proposed integrated theory of social learning and routine activities theories. *International Journal of Offender Therapy and Comparative Criminology, 55*(2), 228–250.

Coetzee, L., & Phillips, A. (2012). 'Taking a Lead in Life': the fundamentals of criminology in practice. *Acta Criminologica*, CRIMSA 2011 Conference Special Edition No. 1, 2012,16–25.

Devery, C. (2010). Criminal profiling and criminal investigation. *Journal of Contemporary Criminal Justice, 26*(4), 393–409.

Ex-wife of 'Modimolle Monster' tells of torture. (2012, November 20). *SowetanLIVE*. Retrieved July 27, 2013, from http://www.sowetanlive.co.za/news/2012/11/20/ex-wife-of-modimolle-monster-tells-of-torture but originally from SAPA.

Francis, K. A. (2014). General strain theory, gender and the conditioning influence of negative internalizing emotions on youth risk behaviors. *Youth Violence and Juvenile Justice, 12*(1), 58–76.

Hannon, L., & DeFina, R. (2012). Sowing the seeds: how adult incarceration promotes juvenile delinquency. *Crime, Law and Social Change, 57*, 475–491.

Hensley, C., Tallichet, S. E., & Dutkiewicz, E. L. (2012). The predictive value of childhood animal cruelty methods on later adult violence: examining demographic and situational correlates. *International Journal of Offender Therapy and Comparative Criminology, 56*(2), 281-295.

Herbig, F. J. W., & Hesselink, A. E. (2009). The role and function of criminologists in the criminal justice and private sector. *Journal of Psychology in Africa* (*JPA*), *19*(3):441–448.

Herbig, F. J. W., & Hesselink, A. E. (2012). Seeing the person, not just the number: needs-based rehabilitation of offenders in South African prisons. *SA Crime Quarterly, 41*, 29–37.

Hesselink, A. E., & Herbig, F. J. W. (2010). Offender rehabilitation and counselling dynamics in the South African correctional environment: systems and prospects. *Journal for Psychology in Africa* (*JPA*), *20*(1), 143–148.

Hesselink-Louw, A. E. (2004). *Criminological assessment of prison inmates: a constructive mechanism towards offender rehabilitation* (Unpublished doctoral thesis). University of South Africa (Unisa), Pretoria.

Hesselink-Louw, A. E., & Joubert, S. (2003). Profiling as a significant outcome of assessment: the criminologist's view. *Acta Criminologica, 16*(5), 99–110.

Holtzhausen, L. (2012). *Social work: a South African practice framework for professionals working with offenders and victims*. Juta: Cape Town.

Jones, V. Chairperson: Johannesburg Management Area Parole Board, Gauteng. (2013). *Overview: placement policy and procedures of the parole boards* (Unpublished report for the Department of Correctional Services).

Labuschagne, I. (2009). The nature of the beast: a critical discussion of profiling. *SA Crime Quarterly, 27*, 31–34.

Lowenkamp, C. T., Lovins, B., & Latessa, E. J. (2009). Validating the level of service inventory-revised and the level of service inventory: screening version with a sample of probationers. *The Prison Journal, 89*(2), 192–204.

MacDonald, J. M., Haviland, A., & Morral, A. R. (2009). Assessing the relationship between violent and nonviolent criminal activity among serious adolescent offenders. *Journal of Research in Crime and Delinquency, 46*(4), 553–580.

Maldonado-Molina, M. M., Reingle, J. M., & Jennings, W. G. (2011). Does alcohol use predict violent behaviors? The relationship between alcohol use and violence in a nationally representative longitudinal sample. *Youth Violence and Juvenile Justice, 9*(2), 99–111.

Mandracchia, J. T., & Morgan, R. B. (2012). Predicting offenders' criminogenic cognitions with status variables. *Criminal Justice and Behavior, 39*(1), 5–25.

Muntingh, L., & Gould, C. (2010). *Towards an understanding of repeat violent offending* (Issue paper No. 213). Institute of Security Studies (ISS). Retrieved September 15, 2013, from http://www.issafrica.org/upload/213.pdf.

Nobles, M. R., & Fox, K. A. (2013). Assessing stalking behaviours in a control balance theory framework. *Criminal Justice and Behavior, 4*(25), 1–26.

Olver, M. E., Stockdale, K. C., & Wormith, J. S. (2009). Risk assessment with young offenders: a meta-analysis of three assessment measures. *Criminal Justice and Behavior, 36*(4), 329–353.

Schwalbe, C. S., Macy, R. J., Day, S. H., & Fraser, M. W. (2008). Classifying offenders an application of latent class analysis to needs assessment in juvenile justice. *Youth Violence and Juvenile Justice, 6*(3), 279–294.

Siegel, L. J. (2010). *Criminology: theories, patterns and typologies* (10th ed.). Canada: Wadsworth Cengage Learning.

Van der Laan, A. M., Blom, M., & Kleemans, E. R. (2009). Exploring long-term and short-term risk factors for serious delinquency. *European Journal of Criminology*, *6*(5), 419–438.

Versluis, J. (2013, November 20). Vyf doodgery: bestuurder sê drank pla nie. *Beeld*, p. 4.

Ward, A. K., Day, D. M., Bevc, I., Sun, Y., & Rosenthal, J. S. (2010). Criminal trajectories and risk factors in a Canadian sample of offenders. *Criminal Justice and Behavior*, *37*(11), 1278–1300.

Wareham, J., & Boots, D. P. (2012). The link between mental health problems and youth violence in adolescence: A multilevel test of DSM-oriented problems. *Criminal Justice and Behavior*, *39*(8), 1003–1024.

Index

This is a combined author and subject index arranged in word-by-word order, for example criminal is before criminality.

Case studies, examples, illustrations and figures are shown in *Italics*. *See* and *see also* references guide the user to the access terms used. Authors' Chapter pagination is shown in **bold font**.